REPUBLICANS AND REINCARNATION

REPUBLICANS AND REINCARNATION

The Conscience of a New Age Conservative

Cris A. Pace

authorHOUSE®

AuthorHouse™
1663 Liberty Drive
Bloomington, IN 47403
www.authorhouse.com
Phone: 1-800-839-8640

© 2011 by Cris A. Pace. All rights reserved.

No part of this book may be reproduced, stored in a retrieval system, or transmitted by any means without the written permission of the author.

First published by AuthorHouse   06/30/2011

ISBN: 978-1-4567-6432-6 (sc)
ISBN: 978-1-4567-6431-9 (ebk)

Library of Congress Control Number: 2011906958

Printed in the United States of America

Any people depicted in stock imagery provided by Thinkstock are models, and such images are being used for illustrative purposes only.
Certain stock imagery © Thinkstock.

Because of the dynamic nature of the Internet, any web addresses or links contained in this book may have changed since publication and may no longer be valid. The views expressed in this work are solely those of the author and do not necessarily reflect the views of the publisher, and the publisher hereby disclaims any responsibility for them.

For Shawgi, Anna, Alicia, and Tony, who always seem willing to engage me in a rational argument.

Thanks to Meredith Walker, Melissa Hill, Shawgi Silver, my parents and my grandfather for helping me edit and review this book. I could not have done it without you.

Forward

THE CONSCIENCE OF A NEW AGE CONSERVATIVE (PREFERABLY READ WHILE IN THE BOOKSTORE)

" . . . All gods are One, and there is no religion higher than the Truth . . ."—Marion Zimmer Bradley, *Lady of Avalon*

Okay, I'm sure you're picking up this book, simply to figure out what the heck it's about. Republicans . . . wait, aren't they all radical Protestant Evangelical Christians who attend church every week, believe the book of Genesis word for word (literally) and think all gays are going to burn in hell? A Republican could never believe in reincarnation. Could they? If that thought (or ones like it) is running through your mind, I must ask you to stop watching network news and reading the New York Times (at least for the time it takes you to read the rest of this book). Go on, move away from anything that suggest thoughts like that . . .

. . . Now that you've put at least a good 10 feet between yourself and the closest Howard Zinn, Paul Krugman, or Michael Moore piece of propaganda, let us continue . . .

Republicans come in all forms, colors, genders, sexual orientations, and yes, religions. There are Christians of all denominations (although I think most Republicans would sleep just a little easier if zealots like Alan Keyes left the party and never came back), Jews, Muslims, Taoists, (I know, I've met people from all these religions, and I can only assume there are representatives of every other major religion in our ranks), and yes, followers of New Age philosophy.

I assume you're still confused. New Age? Aren't those the peace loving, yoga practicing, tarot dealing, conversing with the dead, hippies who never realized the '60's ended? Again, please put the stereotypes down and back away slowly.

Now, take just a minute to think. Odds are, if you picked up this book you either have Republican leanings or have New Age leanings. I want you to ask yourself, whichever group you belong to, did you believe any of the stereotypes about the other group I mentioned, and have you ever been seen in the eyes of your opponents as the stereotypes for your group? Just something to think about.

New Age beliefs are hard to define, mainly because followers of New Age philosophy are a kind of uber-individualist who usually wants nothing to do with organized religion. Half of them don't like the term New Age. Instead, New Age followers tend to pick and choose what they like from the world's religions and come up with a cohesive (more or less) spiritual belief system that works for them. However, there are some overarching concepts (most of which I will deal with in Chapter 2), but for now, let me briefly sum it up as best I can. New Age philosophy states: God is a force for love; every human soul has an individual relationship with God and is striving to be closer to God. New Age philosophy generally states that there is no true religion because, for better or worse, each person's spiritual beliefs are often what they need to be in order to be in contact with God at that particular point in their spiritual development.

So what does this have to do with Republicans, you ask? Well, I am both a follower of New Age beliefs and a moderately proud Republican (moderately because more than being a Republican, I'm a conservative, and while the Republican Party is supposed to be the party of conservatism, its politicians so rarely are). I read my copy of *A Course in Miracles*, I use my tarot deck often, and I surround myself with crystals and images of angels. But here's the thing, I'm also a Republican, and, unlike many in the New Age community, I see no conflict in that. I don't mean I'm a conservative apologist who holds his moderate conservative views closely to himself; I am a dyed in the wool, hard-core, supported the Iraq war as a cause for bringing liberty to the oppressed, thinks George W. Bush is far too liberal on domestic issues, abolish the IRS, the Department of Agriculture, Welfare, and Social Security, agrees with 90% of what Rush Limbaugh and Ann Coulter say, kind of conservative. I can only think of two, maybe three issues, that I can even come close to agreeing with Democrats on—and usually not for the reasons they tend to give. And, again, let me state that I see absolutely no contradiction between the tenets of this kind of conservatism and my spiritual beliefs.

However, I do see contradictions. I see them with my fellow followers of New Age philosophy who are liberal. I am in no way saying that they are bad people, for that would be just plain stupid; I have no doubt that their political beliefs and their actions come from a basis of the most sincere and best of intentions. But, as we all know, good intentions pave the road to Hell . . . that is, if I believed in Hell, which I don't. I see a philosophical error in their thought that compounds itself over and over again until finally, it becomes policy that seeks to do good, but can only result in disaster.

I may be naïve, but I feel that if I detail where these errors occur, then maybe they will occur with less frequency, hence the writing of this book.

I may go from unheard of in the New Age community, to viscerally hated, but just ask my angels (or at least the medium I use to communicate with them), and they'll tell you that over the many reincarnated lifetimes I've had, I've died more than once for an unpopular belief—I seriously doubt it will come to anything that extreme this time.

This book may never be read by anyone, just sitting on a shelf in a warehouse waiting for someone to click that button on the internet in an order that never comes, but I feel a need, a calling, to write this book.

May it have an impact. Please join me in seeing why Conservatism and the New Age need not conflict.

An Overview Of This Book

Chapter 1 deals with the idea of faith and politics in a very general sense. There is a segment of very foolish people who believe that government should be completely secular. This is patently absurd because all political beliefs derive from philosophical beliefs that must in one way or another be grounded in faith (and most likely spiritual faith).

Chapters 2 and 3 deal respectively with the basic premises of New Age Philosophy and Conservatism. I do this to 1) clarify what I mean by New Age and Conservative and 2) immediately limit the scope of what I will deal with within these philosophies. Both systems of beliefs have a wide range of variations of beliefs, practices, and degree of passion. I wish to only deal with the foundations of each philosophy . . .

Chapter 4 examines the commonalities between these two belief systems and why they both point to republican-democracy and liberty.

Chapters 5, 6 and 7 look at the economic implications of these two systems meeting.

Chapters 8 and 9 deal with the use of force in government under these philosophies through both the criminal justice system and through the military and its associated foreign policy related to it.

Chapters 10 through 12 deal with various social issues that the government has gotten its fingers into, and why both systems of belief dictate it should get out or at least mend its ways (a lot).

Chapters 13 and 14 speculate what a world ruled by the principles set out in the previous chapters would look like . . . and why we don't have it right now.

Finally, my point is not to necessarily provide examples and facts as to why one system of economics, government, foreign policy, or whatever else I discuss in this book is better than other systems. I am making arguments on the basis that reason and ethics derived from a New Age spiritual stance dictate that these things should be done. This is a book of theory (albeit theory informed by experience, study, and common sense) and not pragmatics. At the end of the book I will provide suggested reading attached to each topic that make arguments that are more based on the practical application than on a philosophical basis (it just so happens that the ethics implied by this book and practicality match up far more often than not.)

Chapter 1
YOU GOTTA HAVE FAITH.
FAITH: THE BASIS OF ALL BELIEF

"I believe that I can't legislate or transfer to another American citizen my article of faith. What is an article of faith for me is not something that I can legislate on somebody who doesn't share that article of faith".—Senator John Kerry, October 13, 2004, Third Presidential Debate against President George W. Bush

I have disagreed with Democrats, Republicans, Greens, and Libertarians. I have thought that certain members of each of those parties could be described as stupid, hypocritical, unethical, or just plain nuts. However, I can't remember a single statement so ethically outrageous and disgusting to me as the above quote from then Presidential candidate Senator John Kerry.

I have always felt that a person who really believed what they were saying, and who had half a brain, could never lead you too far off course. Now, like it or not, there are politicians who believe what they say is right, and they have faith that what they do is good in both parties. My stated bias clearly leads me to Ronald Reagan, John Boehner, and Rudy Guliani, but no rational person actually believes that they are evil men plotting to destroy the United States, keep the poor poor, and establish some kind of plutocracy of a few ultra-rich robber barons. No. You may disagree with how well their plans would work, but could you honestly tell yourself that those men do not believe in their hearts that their plans would make the world a better place? On the flip side, there are Democrats whom I believe are fully committed to making America a better place without reservation; Joseph Lieberman, for example, is the kind of Democratic I believe would use reason and common sense. I just don't think their plans would work. But I think I could trust Lieberman to not lead the country too far astray.

Nevertheless, what makes me trust these men[1] is that they have faith that what they are doing is right. Now, back to John Kerry's quote. It was in reference to abortion. He says that it's an article of faith for him that life begins at conception. However, he wasn't going to take that article of faith and legislate on it—he was going to keep abortion legal. Abortion is one of the few things

---

[1] A side note: there is a 7,000 year precedent in Indo-European languages that masculine nouns and pronouns should be used when referring to groups consisting of both males and females. I am not about to scrap 7,000 years of grammar standards just because some politically correct whiner is going to have their feelings hurt. If I say men, I probably mean men and women, it depends on the context; If I say mankind I mean every human being (male and female). If you have a problem with these basic facts of grammar and syntax, please grow up.

I'm liberal on (see Chapter 12 for the spiritual grounding for this), but this is the most repulsive thing I had ever heard. To have an article of faith means that you believe this to be True, capital "T." For a Catholic, like Kerry, an article of faith means the following: *God has in some way, shape, or form, declared this to be TRUE!* It's faith because you can't prove it via logic; no proof, no scientific study, no grand theorem or breakthrough in quantum mechanics is going to shed light on this subject—but if you have faith, you know it's true, even when there is no logical proof for it.

So to say it is an article of faith that life begins at conception, you must logically infer that to abort a fetus that is alive is murder. The entire pro-choice movement is founded on the idea that life begins at birth, because the pro-choice movement knows that this is probably the only way to make abortion anything other than murder. So logically, Kerry's faith dictates that abortion is murder. But he's not going to legislate on that. He's not going to make murder illegal because he says that he won't impose his faith on another person.

Thus, if you have faith that God doesn't want people to kill each other, you, as someone who wants to do what is right, would probably do everything in your power to ensure that such a rule was carried out not just by you, but by everyone. If you happen to be President of the United States that means you would take your faith that life begins at conception and put it with your faith that ending life prematurely is wrong, and logically, with the power of the office, do everything in your power to end the murder. Or that's what a faithful Catholic should do.

However, Kerry does not want to act on this. This can mean only one of two things. Either he does not have true faith in his Catholic beliefs, paying no more than lip service to something he doesn't believe in his heart; this would make him nothing more than your typical lying politician who will say what he needs to say to get elected. On the other hand, there is the far worse option: he believes but he will not act on his belief.

"Idealism without realism is impotent. Realism without idealism is immoral."—Richard Nixon

Let me paraphrase the above quote while keeping the general meaning the same. Faith without action is impotent. Action without faith is immoral. (Ironically, the man who said the original quote falls into the latter category.) The contradiction from Kerry's belief is one of these two. Is it meaningless faith that can never go anywhere because no action will be taken to enforce it, or is it action with no compass of morality to guide it? I have my suspicions, and they're not very nice, but either way, this says something about men like John Kerry (on both sides of the aisle, and there are a lot of them). They cannot be trusted.

It's irrelevant whether you happen to agree or disagree with Kerry, or someone like him, on the issue. The important part is his supposed faith, his spiritual beliefs—what should be the basis for all of his morality—are meaningless to him, and his actions as such are not guided by them. What they are guided by is up for debate; but it isn't the faith he professes to believe in, and that disgusts me.

"Faith is knowledge within the heart, beyond the reach of proof"—Kahlil Gibran, Spiritual Sayings

Before I go any further, I want to define faith—what it is, isn't, and what its limitations are.

Webster's defines faith as a "firm belief in something for which there is no proof." Now, this isn't completely true, for many people's faith is based on proof: miracles, coincidences that cannot be coincidences, a feeling. What might be a better way of saying it is that faith is a belief for which there is no verifiable, scientific proof. My anecdotal experience may inform, influence, and guide my faith, but I can't legitimately use that as proof for why another person should believe me.

Faith, at least in the way I'll be using it, is something that deals with a person's spiritual beliefs. Now a scientist may have faith that the object they are observing is a quasar and not a black hole, despite the lack of evidence either way, but that's not the kind of faith we'll be dealing with. We're only going to be dealing with the spiritual and philosophical forms of faith.

Many consider faith to be the archenemy of reason. That faith and reason are completely incapable of coexisting. Author Ayn Rand stated that "to rest one's case on faith means to concede that reason is on the side of one's enemies—that one has no rational arguments to offer." [2] This kind of view is completely wrong, but it has a valid basis for existing. The reason is that some people

---

[2] Ayn Rand, *Capitalism the Unknown Ideal.* Signet: New York, NY, P. 139

Republicans and Reincarnation

Epistemology is the philosophy that deals with how we know and learn. Is it possible to know what is true? How do we discover truth? Can we know truth?

Both Epistemology and Metaphysics, unlike other branches of philosophy, involve faith because at some early point in the reasoning of the philosophy, an assumption must be made. And this assumption must be held with complete faith that it is true beyond all doubt, despite the lack of any proof one way or another.

What is an example of the fact that an assumption is at the very base of philosophy: The world exists[3]. You're thinking that that statement is pretty obvious, but try and prove it. The fact that you can touch the book you're reading, the chair you're sitting in, feel the breeze against your face, even hear your heart pumping in your ears is irrelevant. It could be a dream, a very realistic dream, but a dream nonetheless. I know I've had dreams that seemed as real as reality. Now, this may be a valid point against your proof, but it doesn't prove this is a dream. The fact that you agree with someone else about the way the world appears is also irrelevant, because they could just be part of your dream. No matter what proof you can come up with, you have nothing in the way of concrete proof that the world exists. But I'm sure you do believe the world exists (to some degree or another). You just know that you're real, that your parents are real, even, sadly, your annoying younger siblings are real (as much as you might not want that to be true). You can't logically prove it, but you accept it as truth. You made

---

[3] For my purposes here I will be using the word "exist" to mean that which is independent of anyone perceiving it, or as science fiction writer Philip K. Dick put it, "Reality is what refuses to go away when I stop believing in it."

a metaphysical assumption—one that had to be made before you could move on any further, before you could move onto anything in metaphysics, let alone, ethics, religion, science or just about any other field.

Another assumption that actually has to be made to progress, possibly the most important assumption in philosophy, is the Law of Identity, otherwise known as the Law of Noncontradiction. As the old statement goes, which can be seen in any high school algebra book, A=A. The facts are the facts, things are what they are and no amount of thought or perception will change something from what it truly is. What is true today, is true tomorrow, was true yesterday, was always and will always be true for you, me, Uncle Bob, your neighbor down the block, and your worst enemy in the world. Truth is the same at all places, at all times, for all people. No exception. If there were an exception, it wouldn't be the truth and thus calling it the truth is in violation of the basic Law of Identity. Now, you may think something is true, but that doesn't make it true. Some people think it's true that there is some massive Jewish conspiracy to rule the world. They believe it is true, but they are clearly idiots, and no amount of belief is going to change that. Truth, like existence, doesn't have anything to do with your mind; it exists independent of your mind.

Because truth is always the same, contradictions cannot exist. 2+2 cannot equal 4 ***and*** equal 5. Something cannot be true for some people and not for others (some people can believe something is true and others believe something else is true, but either one side is right and the other is wrong, or given the fallibility of humans, they've probably both got it wrong). Now there are weird things out there like quantum mechanics that

Republicans and Reincarnation

say light is both a particle and a wave of energy. This sounds like a contradiction where there is no single truth to be found, but really this is not the case. There is a truth out there of how such things operate, we just don't understand them fully yet. This doesn't mean there is an actual contradiction, it means only that our language and understanding only exists in such a way that it can only present it in the form of a paradox. Philosophy and religion are riddled with contradictions, because trying to unravel them is often more work than people want to partake in and so the contradictions persist. Case in point—the god of the Old Testament is a "jealous" god and can hardly go an entire book without making somebody's life miserable (sometimes they deserve it, sometimes they don't); meanwhile, the same god is a god of love and forgiveness and not of wrath in the New Testament (until you hit the book of Revelations, at least, at which point the god of the Old Testament looks like a cuddly fuzzy bunny by comparison). So either God is given to manic-depressive mood swings, or we've found a contradiction. Now, to admit such a contradiction might mean having to admit that maybe not everything should be taken literally or that the Testaments have a little more human editing and a little less divine inspiration than most devout Christians would like to admit. Some may state such contradictions are merely trying to represent something as inconceivable as God with anthropomorphized human characteristics, but this argument assumes human and not divine intervention when it came to writing such things, because, I don't know, I just truly feel that if God himself were actually writing directly I would think he would be a much better writer. But since this contradiction has been allowed to

Cris A. Pace

stand, the Bible, to this day, can probably be used to support any position on any subject you can conceive of.

Now, I'll admit I can't prove the Law of Noncontradiction, because any reasoned argument requires you to already accept the Law of Noncontradiction, but I think we all accept it to be a fact.

These assumptions, these acts of faith, once made, allow for a full metaphysical and epistemological system to be created. After you know what the world is and how to know it, you move onto to how to live in it. Metaphysical truths tell us what is and is not, and what the nature of things are; what the nature of something is tells us its needs and its purpose, and fulfilling those needs and purposes tells us what we ought to do. Ethics is the branch of philosophy that deals with what we ought to do, how we should act as individuals to ourselves and to others. It's all about how to lead a good life and what a good life brings. If you are either a classical realist like me (or Aristotle) or a follower of New Age philosophy, again like me, you probably believe the point to life is to reach happiness. Ethics states that only by leading an "ethical" and virtuous life do we achieve happiness.

A key assumption of all workable systems of ethics is the concept of free will. (And I need to talk about this for a minute because it is a corner stone for all future discussions in this book.) Faith in free will is necessary because if we don't have free will then how do we actually choose between right and wrong? Now modern psychologists prefer to talk about nature and nurture and keep free will out of the discussion, because they don't like talking about something as unscientific as the soul (ironic when you consider psychology literally means "study of the soul"). Still, scientific or not, common sense and experience tells us that we are more than complicated computers operating off genes and environment (not that these aren't relevant factors, they are very relevant, but they clearly are not the complete story).

Now I'm sure you're thinking that making this point about free will is a bit unnecessary because nearly everyone believes in free will ... don't they? Experience has regrettably taught me that while people may say the words that they believe in free will, their deeper convictions and actions betray that they don't. For instance, I once had a former student take me to task over the fact that they believed I only respected students who, like the student who was complaining, achieved academically (this isn't the case, but I'll get to that in a minute). They said they couldn't really respect me because how dare I preach tolerance and then discriminate between students based only on the fact that some come from family backgrounds that encourage academic achievement and those that don't. This betrayed to me that this student believed not in free will, but that everyone was merely a product of their environment and nothing more. That students from good backgrounds achieved academically without question and those from bad backgrounds failed without question. This former student failed to recognize the many students I have had who, despite their rather abysmal family background, choose to achieve academically. This student failed to realize that there are those with what we call a strong will who refuse to necessarily be defined by their environment, but rather choose to examine which parts of their environment are rationally worth keeping and which parts aren't (when coupled with any amount of common sense this leads a person to realize that academic achievement is a worthwhile goal, and it is this proper use of the will that I greatly respect.) Now a strong willed person can also choose to disregard the parts of their environment that are rationally beneficial and ethical (even the best families can have the slacker loser who wastes all the opportunities offered them). Then there is the portion of humanity that is rather weak willed and allows themselves be defined by their environment rather than by their own will and reason. The student who complained to me, to my great disappointment, falls, I fear, into this latter category since they were so willing to chalk up all of their own achievements to environment and to leave no credit to themselves. If anything, this student was afraid of the concept that they themselves had the ability to do what they did on their own. This lack of belief in free will, I fear is not limited to a random student, but is rather a pervasive misconception of modern society. And it is one of the most important beliefs, because until people believe they have control of their own destinies, they cannot steer their lives in a direction of truly ethical behavior, for even though their actions may seem ethical to an outside observer, if it was done out of what they believed their environment dictated and not willed because it was the right thing to do, it is not an action that will lead to growth and spiritual development. What this student failed to realize was that I respected students of strong will, who then used their will to choose academic achievement; and to judge someone on the basis of their choices is not intolerance, rather it is common sense.

Finally, once we have ascertained how to lead an ethical life, most philosophies will state quite clearly that happiness is impossible to achieve alone. Man, by his very nature, is a social creature; we interact with others not necessarily because we choose to, but because we have to because we are human. We need other people. The philosophy of politics takes the philosophy of ethics and extends it from making a good individual life, to figuring out what society must do as a whole. What laws create the best society and help people lead the most ethical lives, and how best to create a society that can advance, are the purview of the philosophy of politics. It is not so much an assumption at this point, as it can be proven from previous statements, but what is still basic to effective politics, is how the concept of free will plays into politics. Because of this prior assumption, good government must necessarily recognize free will in its citizens and accept it. This theoretical good government cannot, therefore, attempt to legislate belief of any kind. Anything that falls short of this is not good government and should be replaced . . . and we'll get into the minutia of what a government should and shouldn't legislate soon enough.

Metaphysics and epistemology are theoretical branches, which are heavily influenced by certain assumptions that can only be held by faith. The only practical use of these two branches is that the conclusions of these branches are the foundation for ethics and politics. Ethics and politics are however not theoretical, they are practical—they demand to be acted upon and followed through deed and word. However, you can't have these practical branches of philosophy without making assumptions based on faith at some point.

Before I digress too far, let me come back to faith. I see that there are two kinds of faith: Faith that requires nothing more than belief, and faith that affects your philosophical beliefs (specifically your ethical and political beliefs), the faith that demands action. Someone can believe that God is both one being and three as Christianity states, it's purely faith, but it doesn't necessitate any kind of direct action ethically or politically. However, if I believe that God has said, "Thou shalt not kill," [4] then logically I would be ethically bound to not kill anyone for any reason. Politically, since we are trying to create the best possible society, this article of faith would manifest itself not only in laws against murder, but also in laws against the death penalty. So here, one's faith dictates that you do everything in your power to (ethically, mind you) see that not only you follow the rule, but that all of society

---

[4] Yes I know, the proper translation of Exodus 20:13 is actually "Thou shalt not murder" which makes it a far more complicated issue when it comes to such issues as capital punishment. The word "kill," however, is an absolute, which allows for none of the subtleties and exceptions that "murder" implies and requires. I choose the incorrect translation for the sake of simplicity at this point in the book. We will return to the "No kill" rule and its implications often in this book, so please forgive this minor error this one time.

Republicans and Reincarnation

is made to follow the rule. Why? Because you believe the rule was given not to you but to everyone, thus you believe the rule must be followed by everyone to achieve a better society.

Certain articles of faith must be acted on not only in one's personal life, but in the political life, too. Still, I'm sure this brings up the question of religious tolerance . . .

You know I'm all for religious tolerance, but just because some radical fundamentalist sect says it's okay to beat your wife bloody because she was seen by another man without her shroud on doesn't make it right. I really don't care if it's an article of faith for them. My faith dictates that it is wrong to do that kind of harm to another human being (a conclusion which can also be easily reached through pure reason), and if I'm in the position to, I'm going to make sure that that kind of behavior is illegal. I would do it in a heartbeat. You can well believe I would impose harsh punishment. When you are confronted with an article of faith that you are not only opposed to, but are convinced is gravely wrong, you have an obligation to see that it not become the norm. I will go as far to say that you need to resort to any means necessary so long as those means are not in contradiction with any other article of faith and/or reasonable conclusion you hold (and since both reason and most faiths dictate peace whenever possible, I'm not advocating violence against someone you disagree with).

Tolerance must be extended to the first kind of faith without question. Faith that merely defines the world we live in is what we have religious tolerance about. I believe that God is a greater consciousness of which each and every human soul is a part of—my best friend, Chris, believes that God is a being separate from himself and made up of three parts: the Father, the Son, and the Holy Spirit. Now I think his belief is wrong in the sense that I think his view of God is narrow and limited, and I'm sure he thinks I'm wrong in my opinion of God in the sense that he thinks I'm going to burn in Hell. Each of our faiths is held like a rock, and I doubt we'll ever see eye to eye on this (at least in this lifetime), but we're still friends. Thomas Jefferson said, "It does me no injury for my neighbor to say there are twenty gods, or no god. It neither picks my pocket nor breaks my leg." Jefferson seems to have an understanding that not all faith dictates action, and the kind that does not dictate action must always be tolerated. Even if my next door neighbor worships Satan, if he doesn't cause me or anyone else harm, I must be tolerant of his beliefs; I don't have to like them, in fact, I will avoid all contact with my Satan worshiping neighbor, but I do have to tolerate them. Sadly, there are those who don't recognize that these two kinds of faith exist and believe that they must legislate belief as well as action. I can only at this point say that these people clearly choose not to recognize things that the good lord gave them like free will, reason, and brains. Further, I can only hope that democratic principles keep their power limited—very limited.

On the other side of the coin is faith that dictates action. Here tolerance does not always have to be in action. Disagreeing with ideas is where tolerance is to be extended to, but actions are a completely different realm. Faith that dictates action must be judged according to your own faith/philosophy as being right or wrong, good or evil. We all saw nineteen men convinced by their faith that it was God's will to hijack planes and kill thousands of innocents. Neither I, nor any rational human should

Republicans and Reincarnation

have tolerance for this kind of faith. It is a kind of faith that leads to destruction and chaos, and must be opposed and eradicated, at every turn. (I will get into the subtleties of when and where violence is called for later on.)

But not every difference in beliefs is so radical. Let's take, for instance, gay marriage (again, I'm going to grossly simplify this for the argument's sake). Certainly not a life or death issue here, but strongly held beliefs nonetheless. One side believes that gay marriage would be an affront to God, the other that all humans must have the same rights since we are all equal. Both are non-hypocritical views based on reasons derived from their respective faiths and assumptions. I would again argue that either side, if in power, has an ethical responsibility to act on their beliefs, irrespective of the opposition. Is this tolerance? Yes, because tolerance means you allow the opposition to exist and think the way they want, even if you don't act on it. Think about the word tolerance for a second . . . think about people you "tolerate." Does "tolerate" suggest you like them, agree with them, follow them or do what they want? No. If you tolerate someone you would rather they not be near you, but there is nothing you can do about it right now, and so you tolerate them. If there is no persecution of the opposition solely for their beliefs, then you are tolerant. Moreover, it is the ethical responsibility of the group not in power to try to convince people to come to their side because they have the better argument, not to demonize or attack the party in power, but to reason with them.

I'm sure you're thinking this whole chapter is advocating for the separation of church and state. But if you go back to the Founding Fathers, the separation they spoke of was one based on free will. They did not want the government to say this or that religion was sanctioned, but that all would be accepted. Not that people would not use their faith in making decisions, but that they would not force beliefs on others.

"Doubt is uncomfortable, certainty is ridiculous."—Voltaire

One final caveat on faith. Any reasonable person will admit they are probably not in complete contact with the mind of God. No one who hasn't reached enlightenment can say with absolute certainty that they know what God wants, no matter how strong their faith. And because of that, even the most strongly held faith, when held by a reasonable person, must admit that while their God may be right, they, as a human being, may not have perfect knowledge of that divine wisdom. As such, even the strongest believer, when dealing with others, should always have a reasonable basis for their actions. One must at least question if not continually ponder when their reason dictates one thing and their faith dictates another, for a reasonable person would agree that truth would be where reason and faith meet, not where they diverge. As such, any reasonable person requires of themselves to constantly put their faith to the test of reason. Sometimes, especially in the more spiritual questions, reason will offer no answer sufficient to the question, but that's why we have faith. But if there is doubt, there should not be blind action based on faith alone.

Faith dictates how we see the world. How we see the world dictates how we act in it. Certain kinds of faith are to just be held and others are to be acted upon. To do anything less than act upon one's faith is hypocrisy, which is justifiably one of the few sins you find critiqued in all the world's religions.

So if faith dictates our ethical and political beliefs . . . what is the faith held by New Age Philosophy?

Chapter 2
LIBRAS, TAROTS, AND ANGELS... OH MY
THE BASICS OF NEW AGE PHILOSOPHY

"When a foolish man hears of the Tao, he laughs out loud."—Lao Tzu, Tao Te Ching

The flippant chapter titles of this book aside, New Age philosophy is a very serious and rational philosophy. It just sounds really weird if you try to tell another person about it; like the quote that begins this chapter, New Age philosophy is, at first glance, somewhat contradictory to common sense. But then again imagine telling someone from another world about this guy who lots of people worship, he is three separate beings but at the same time only one being, he was born to a virgin, he and his own father are the same being, and he rose from the grave, and as a sign of faith people still routinely drink his blood and eat his flesh. Sounds pretty crazy doesn't it? But then again, a lot of deep metaphorical concepts were simplified and a lot of it is simply an issue of faith bringing understanding. It may sound insane if you don't believe in it, but it makes perfect sense to the follower.

First off, before I begin, let me make perfectly clear that I am not in tune with any kind of higher knowledge that the rest of you haven't reached yet. I don't speak with angels (well I speak to them, but I don't ever get a verbal response back), I don't have visions; I've seen what I would call a miracle or two in my time but I wouldn't go so far as to say I was the direct cause of them. I am taking my description of New Age philosophy from a lot of different sources. If you want to read more about it, and in greater detail there is a suggested reading list at the back of the book. Second, I will fully admit that this is a good deal of my own take on New Age philosophy, and as a practitioner, I think that gives at least some weight. I am only trying to identify the broad principles of these spiritual beliefs that apply to the practice on a whole, but there undoubtedly will be New Age people who don't agree with my description. Still I think what I will say can be applied to the mass of people who accept New Age beliefs.

Okay, now that's out of the way . . . as the title suggests New Age philosophy is often associated with Astrology, the use of Tarot cards, and a belief in Angels and Ascended Masters who help us in our journey through life. Also associated with New Age beliefs are the use of crystals for health, yoga practices, chakra centers, psychic powers, beliefs in lost civilizations, and the like. Some practitioners of New Age philosophy believe in all this, others only parts. Quite frankly, almost all of this is irrelevant to this book.

So what is relevant?

GOD

"In the faces of men and women I see God and in my own face in the glass,
I see letters from God dropped in the street, and every one is signed by God's name."—Walt Whitman, To See God

The first point about New Age spirituality, and the one from which all others derive from, is our belief of God. Most western religions see God as a person, a really, really wise and powerful person, but one that has been given qualities of people. He is loving, he is wise, and he can get really angry come the Judgment Day. But no matter how you spin it, most religions generally give God personal qualities.[5]

New Age philosophy here is very different. The vision of the God of New Age beliefs is a God of love, yes, but not in the way that, say, the God of the New Testament is a God of love. The New Age vision of God is one of love . . . period. God is love . . . period. Aristotle once defined his vision of the gods as being thought contemplating thought[6]. The New Age vision of God might best be described as "Love contemplating

---

[5] These are often seen as a metaphor but it's still an anthropomorphized vision.

[6] The actual wording is closer to "though which has itself for its object" (Metaphysics 1075a9) but that's a little too technical to understand.

Republicans and Reincarnation

and giving Love." God is love, he[7] knows only of love without limit.

I could go on, but it would seem even more repetitive. This is a God that doesn't seek vengeance, punishment, or even judgment. Beyond just being absolute love God does one other thing—create. Creation is a natural extension of love, because the nature of love is to spread itself. Being an infinite being of perfect love, his creations are by nature perfect. Wait, you say, we aren't perfect, nor is this world . . . and I will get to that in a few moments if you'll bear with me. God tends to (that I know of at least) create other beings, most notably angel and human souls.

Now angels, while a fascinating subject, are not particularly relevant to the discussion of this book. Suffice to say, angels are spiritual beings, beings of pure love like God, who act as middlemen[8] between God and people. The most common type of angel is the guardian angel. Everyone has one (I've read in some places that everyone has two) these angel are there with other spiritual guides to help whatever individual they are placed with make it

---

[7] I use the pronoun, "he" instead of the more accurate "it" because we generally don't think of things we apply "it" to as A) being alive or B) something worthy of love, and rotating between he and she would just be annoying. I will also not be capitalizing all the pronouns in reference to God, despite tradition and usual grammatical rules. This capitalization suggests a separation in degree between he and you that only exists in your mind and I refuse to help reinforce that foolish belief by capitalizing all the "he"'s and "him"'s.

[8] Although angels have no gender to speak of, they can take on a dominantly masculine or feminine aspect as their duties require.

through life. There are many New Age resources on how to listen, speak, and feel the presence of these angels.

However, angels do not generally concern themselves with the world of men in the sense of daily concerns. Their goal is more one of spiritual growth. So let us turn to something a little more near and dear to all of us.

Souls, Minds, Bodies

"Spirit is the Thought of God which He created like Himself.[. . .] The term 'soul' [. . .] would, however, be equivalent of 'spirit,' with the understanding that, being of God, it is eternal and was never born."—A Course in Miracles: Manual For Teachers-Mind-Spirit
The Birth of the Soul

The human soul. The part of you that is . . . well . . . you. The part that is actually alive and thinks. The soul is, like its creator, eternal, and is impervious to death. The soul was originally created perfect. Beings of perfect love with perfect intellect and perfect free will—just like their creator, and one with God in existence, sharing this perfect state of being, of love. Equal to God, inferior only in that he created us.

Then a problem arose.

(Don't ask me what the problem was. If I knew, I'd likely be on a higher plane, possibly enlightenment, helping others through more effective means than just writing a book.)

Whatever the problem was, for some reason, we became introduced to a new concept: fear.

The Soul and Fear
"Fear is the mind killer, it is the small death that leads to total oblivion."—Frank Herbert, Dune

Fear, not hate, is the true antithesis of love. Behind all hatred is a fear of what is hated. Think of it this way, hate like love is an action that causes you to become emotionally tied to the subject of your love or hate, but fear, on the other hand, fear causes you to pull away from the object of your fear. Hate is what happens when love is corrupted by fear, thus it cannot be the opposite of love. According to most New Age thought, if you strip all fear away, layer after layer, you will find a single fear at the heart of it, the fear that God does not love us because we are not worthy of that love. This is the original fear, the only fear, and the one that we are all trying to overcome.

But if it's a fear so pervasive that every soul on Earth shares it, how can we overcome it—easier than you would think. It's really easy in one sense. Why? Because it's a stupid fear. It's almost laughable to conceive that a being such as God, who is nothing but love, could not or would not love us, his creation. Sadly, we have yet to laugh at the insanity of this joke, to the point where at some level we actually believe it. And worse yet, we have subconsciously placed upon ourselves limitations that further this delusion that we are not worthy of love.

So now, here we were—a gaggle of souls separated from our creator, not by his will, but by our own fears. These fears blocked us from hearing his voice, telling us that he loves us, and these fears weren't just going to die on their own. Something had to be done. Something had to bridge the gap between us and our creator over the chasm of fear. Enter Reality.

> *The World as We Know It*
> *"Nothing real can be harmed. Nothing unreal exists. Herein lies the peace of God."—A Course in Miracles—Introduction*

Again, I'm not going to claim I know the perfect history of the world, or whose nutty idea it was to come up with it, but the generally held New Age belief is that the world was created after the introduction of fear to our collective consciousness. The world is a reflection of our fear in many ways, but more accurately, it is a reflection of our thoughts. Matching up with many Eastern traditions, New Age belief states that the world is really a reflection of thought. In other words, it's an illusion. It's not real. Welcome to the Matrix.

This world is not real in the sense that it exists outside of our thoughts. It doesn't. It is here as a place to learn. What do we have to learn? Lots of things, but mainly it is also that we learn that fear is not real. Moreover, if fear is not real, then all that exists is us and God and the love between us. All of which is eternal. Life is the classroom where we learn this. When we do that, then this world will melt away and all we will see again the light of God.

Free Will

> *God: And you can't mess with free will.*
> *Bruce: Uh huh. Can I ask why?*
> *God: (excited) Yes you can. That's the beauty in it.*
> *—Bruce Almighty*

Republicans and Reincarnation

Now, I've heard a common objection to that idea of the world. If God's perfect and his creations are perfect (which they are, don't forget that) then how could perfect creations make such a blundering mistake as creating fear in our collective minds?

The answer is free will. A being without free will is nothing but a machine. A creation that only does what it is told, when it is told, in the way it is told. The perfect slave, but rather boring. Perfection requires free thought and since our souls are perfect, they have to think for themselves. Slight problem with perfection, and this may sound like it doesn't make sense, but think about it for a minute: To be perfect we have to be capable of making mistakes. Like I said, run that over a few times, it will make more sense the more you think about it. Perfection is eternal, mistakes are not as they can be corrected, thus for all intents and purposes a mistake doesn't even exist in the vastness of eternity . . . they can just be really annoying when you're in the middle of them.

So, we collectively made a mistake and separated ourselves from God. The separation was a mistake that needed to be corrected, but God couldn't very well do it for two reasons. 1) We weren't listening to him; if we were, we would never have made the mistake we did. 2) God sees only our perfection, and for a being that exists outside of time, a temporary imperfection, like the one we have gotten ourselves into, really doesn't exist, so he doesn't exactly recognize that there is a problem (in the grand scheme of things he's in the right here, it's just our time-limited minds that see a problem). At most he sees us as a parent sees their child when the child is having a nightmare—he knows something is wrong, not exactly what, but he is holding us, telling us he loves us and waiting for us to wake up.

Nevertheless, we did need to learn that our mistake was just that, so, for one reason or another, the world was created. A place where our little delusions could play out, and hopefully we could see that our delusions are insane and we need to let them go. The world is a giant classroom from which we are to learn many lessons, all leading to the ultimate lesson that God loves us unconditionally, always did, always will.

"But why can't I just go to that lesson right now?" you ask. It seems so simple. It is. And to someone who knows what they're doing, differential calculus equations are easy. I can probably describe them in a way that sounds just as easy as "God loves you" but essentially it just sounds easy. Think about this: to you, making breakfast is easy, describing what you do is easy, maybe even giving instructions to another person is easy, but that's because you already know how to do it. If a four year old who doesn't know what they are doing tries to make breakfast, sure they know it looks easy, and sounds easy, and they've seen you do it with ease, but when they try to do it, well, you wake up to a kitchen with every pot and pan you own dirty, flour and eggs all over the place, and something you can only assume was supposed to be a pancake but may require a HAZ-MAT team to dispose of. When it comes to God loves you, you're the four year old. I'm not trying to be insulting here—it's just that it may seem easy, but really, you have to understand all the other prerequisite lessons before you can move onto the advanced stuff.

And thus, we are placed in this world. It serves its purpose for a time to show us the nature of our mistakes and once we all have realized these mistakes, this world will disappear from our consciousness since we'll be with God again we'll have no use for this limited dimension. And that blessed day when all return to God, this limited world will cease to be.

The Afterlife, Reincarnation, Karma

"Reincarnation is not an exclusively Hindu or Buddhist concept, but it is part of the history of human origin. It is proof of the mindstream's capacity to retain knowledge of physical and mental activities. It is related to the theory of interdependent origination and to the law of cause and effect."
—***The Dalai Lama*** *(from the Preface to "The Case for Reincarnation")*

Now obviously, you're not expected to learn everything in one mere lifetime. How anyone could think a loving God would give you just one shot is just short of insane. Such an idea is possibly the cruelest aspect of the traditional Western conception of God. No loving God could just haphazardly let some people be born infected with AIDS in the middle of third world Africa and others be born in upper class America with every opportunity open to them. That would just be sick and demented, not to mention evil. No, New Age belief has the wonderfully useful concepts of reincarnation and karma.

Reincarnation: the idea that you live, you die, you spend sometime in the afterlife, you get reborn. It is wonderfully simple. Further, if you look at the development of many cultures they tend to have an evolving look at the afterlife. The most primitive of cultures have no afterlife or simply believe that everyone just mills about without much purpose (Don't believe me? Go read *The Odyssey*). The more developed cultures tend have some kind of Heaven and Hell (again using Greece as the example—but this can be seen in multiple cultures—the later myths deal with Tartarus and the Elysian Fields). Finally comes a belief in reincarnation (in Greece you just have to look at the philosophy of Plato, especially *Phadeo* and *The Republic*). In fact, until the advent of Christianity that caused a backslide in philosophy in this respect, almost no civilized society believed in anything but reincarnation is some form[9].

Why do almost all societies believe in reincarnation? Probably because when you really think about it, it's really the only logical explanation. All the terrible or great things that happen to someone aren't the result of fate or luck or chance or, worst of all, a capricious God. No. For the most part, they are learning opportunities as we evolve.

In greater detail, here is how it works (or as close as I can piece together):

You live your life. Hopefully you use your life to learn something . . . or not (free will again). You accrue what is generally called karma.

You die. Sorry to tell you this, but it will happen. However, you, that part that is really you, your soul, doesn't die. It goes on. Why, because, remember, God made it perfect, and what is perfect obviously can't be harmed and is completely and totally eternal.

---

[9] I include in this Judaism, of which the Pharisee sect is believed to have accepted reincarnation, and possibly sections of early Christianity before early Church attempts standardized the dogma into the basic tenants of modern Christianity.

Now that you're dead, one of several things can happen. First, and least likely you can choose not to move on. We tend to call souls that don't move on ghosts. Still, they are rare. If you should choose to accept the fact that you died and it's time to give up the ghost, you'll move onto what I will just generally refer to as the afterlife.

The afterlife is not really a single place[10]. But it is not heaven and hell . . . per se. What the afterlife is really depends on the person who has just died. If you believe that there is nothing after death, your soul will simply sit in darkness, a big black box of its own making, until it either realizes on its own that it still exists or realizes this with the help of other spirits and angels trying to help it get out of its self-created prison. The next most common afterlife would be a, for lack of a better term, purgatory. Many people die thinking they have lived terrible lives, that they are not worthy of God's love, and that they deserve punishment. They try to send themselves to Hell. Not because God thinks they should go there, remember God loves you UNCONDITIONALLY, but because they think they deserve it. The problem with trying to send yourself to Hell is that there is no Hell. While I'm not sure of the exact nature of the "punishment," from the various sources I have read most souls more or less ooze about what appears to be a dark, cold, fog filled, wasteland, having no contact with anyone and being tortured by their own conscience. It doesn't sound that bad, but from what I've read about it, Dante's *Inferno* is a day spa in comparison. Again, spirit guides and

---

[10] There are of course some intricate and technical points that I'm going to gloss over, this is only a generalized view, not a definitive study.

angels are trying to get these people to move beyond this self-imposed hell.

Now I can already hear the question: What about those people who are so evil they don't have a conscience? Hitler, Saddam, any host of serial killers all the way down to unscrupulous lobbyists, personal injury and defense lawyers, and IRS employees. Well there are two reasons why their consciences will try to punish them too. The first is that many of the people we think of as being evil, and let's be honest here, probably have some bad wiring in their brain in a literal sense. It may be that a fully competent soul has been given a lemon of a brain (for one reason or another) that just doesn't function properly. That's why courts first determine if you're mentally competent to stand trial. The other reason is that many of these evil men are evil not because they have no souls but because they have chosen to listen to their fears so much that it is overpowering; they have a conscience, but they don't listen to it. Proof of this can be seen by the fact that one of the witnesses to Saddam Hussein's execution described the madman's last moments with the words "I saw fear, he was afraid[.]"[11] "Clearly if even a butcher like Hussein is afraid of death, and likely the punishments that await him, then even the people we call evil are not completely bereft of conscience. Dying however tends to give that once overpowered conscience a megaphone to shout with. And it will shout at them until it feels they've paid their time. Now does this mean that Hitler will one day get out of this hell . . . well . . . according to New Age

---

[11] MSNBC. "I saw he was afraid" by Michael Hastings http://www.msnbc.msn.com/id/16401644/site/newsweek/

Republicans and Reincarnation

philosophy, yes . . . but that will be a very, very, very, very, very, *very* long time before his conscience[12] lets him out.

On a side note, sadly some of the most common people to end up in this purgatory are suicides. Why? Because they, more than most people, believe that no one, not even God, loves them, and they are worthy of nothing more than this kind of punishment. So don't assume that just because someone is receiving this kind of existence that they are necessarily an evil person. They just made the mistake of giving into their fears.

So let's say you don't hate yourself completely, or you've suffered enough that your conscience is willing to let you get out of purgatory, where do you go now? Heaven? Again, not in the traditional sense. Yes, you get to go to a place of light and love and beauty and peace. But it lacks two main points of what true Heaven would be. The first being that you're still not completely with God because, while you may not hate yourself, you probably haven't completely put all fear behind you; you can see the light more clearly from this level but you are still not one with the light. The second reason this isn't true Heaven is that it's not eternal. Not to say you can't stay there for a very long time and enjoy the peace, but you still can't stay forever, because you can't learn everything over there.

---

[12] Now I don't mean that people deserve punishment nor that the part of you that knows right from wrong wants you to suffer. Rather fear knows what it is, and the part of you that is afraid knows that when you dispel fear it will cease to exists since it has ceased to be relevant and like all things of this world it has survival instincts and by punishing you, by punishing itself, it keeps you believing in a cycle of karma, of reward and punishment that it thinks is required.

This Heaven is actually more like a different kind of school. There are lessons to be learned on Earth and there are lessons to be learned in this temporary Heaven. In this temporary Heaven, you just have a more direct line with teachers such as Ascended Masters (e.g. Jesus, Buddha, Saints, et cetera) and angels. Here you can put your lessons to work in one of two ways.

The first is by being what is called a spirit guide. These are souls that either try to help souls out of purgatory or go to Earth and try to help the living here. They're somewhere between a guardian angel and a personal psychologist. They whisper in the ears of everyone what they should do, that we should calm down, pointing us to the next book that may contain the next lesson we are to learn, turning our heads just at the right time to see for the first time the person we are going to marry one day, and of course screaming at us when we should hit the brakes so as to avoid killing ourselves on the freeway. Like our fears, our conscience, and that spark of God himself in us, we can listen to our spirit guides or we can ignore them. Life just tends to be easier when we try to listen. Spirit guides are usually, but not always, the souls of people you know either from your current life or from past ones. When grandma said on her deathbed that she would always be with you, looking out for you and helping you from the other side, she may not have been kidding.

However, let's say you've had enough of helping others try to learn their lessons, and want to learn a few of your own, and then we finally come to reincarnation. On some metaphysical level, you will sit down with your guardian angels and spirit guides and you will plan out you life. Where you will be born, when (and from that level time doesn't necessarily flow in a linear fashion—you can die in 1990 in one life and for your next life be reborn in 1890), with what family, what lessons you will be learning, and what challenges will be placed upon you, and the when, where, and means of your death. Not to say you don't have free will. You do. What you plan out is, when I'm 24 years old I'm going to lose my job and have no opportunity to find another job in the area. That's a challenge you give yourself. How you deal with it, now that's up to you. Will you learn from it and move onto the next lesson, or will you have to go to the next challenge, or as is all too often the case, the next life, until you learn that one lesson. You can come back and choose to learn absolutely nothing this life, that's your right with free will—but why would you want to?

And where is God in this heaven? Where he's always been showing he loves you and inside your own soul giving love. It's not his fault you weren't looking and listening to his declarations of love.

Now sometimes, just because you didn't wind up in purgatory doesn't mean you don't feel guilty about the things you've done in your past lives. Let's say you were a bloody general for several lifetimes. Maybe the times called for it, maybe by your bloodthirsty habits you actually saved more people in the long run. But still you feel guilty about all the blood on your hands. Now you may decide to come back and place yourself in a position to become a doctor and redeem yourself through helping others. Or you could decide to come back with a debilitating disease and suffer through it as your penance. Alternatively, you could decide to be born into a war torn area and experience the kind of suffering you caused from the other end. This is called karma . . . making up for your past problems.

But does that mean every child born with AIDS in Africa must have done something like being an SS officer in a past life and is doing it to make up for their past deeds? NO! Often many of the more advanced souls, those Ascended Masters I spoke of, will come back into lives with great hardships not because they need to suffer, but to bring out the humanity in others. Think of it this way, the Holocaust while an unspeakable evil that we would all love to see never repeated, did bring out numerous acts of absolute goodness from those who helped the Jews. The fact that more than 20,000 are honored as Righteous Among the Nations for helping Jews during the Holocaust by the Yad Vashem in Jerusalem does show that the adage that the light of humanity burns brightest when things are darkest, is true. Sometimes, perhaps too often, the suffering of another is often the very thing needed to teach us something about the power of love and hope. The point being that just because someone seems to be suffering from the bitch that is karma, don't necessarily assume that they deserve it and move on—they may be an opportunity for you to help and learn.

So what is all the point of this constant rebirth? Ironically, it's to learn that the cycle of rebirth is not necessary. It's to learn that karma is our creation, not God's. We don't need to do penance to seek forgiveness from God. He would forgive us our trespasses if he acknowledged them, which he doesn't, because to him we are perfect, mainly because we, in the sense of our souls, are perfect. And when we drop all those fears that cause us to act in not so perfect ways, we shall see ourselves as perfect once again. The point of all the suffering and misery of this world is to prove to ourselves that the suffering and misery isn't necessary.

So really, to a New Ager, the idea of death is a little silly. Your soul is not only eternal, but it's coming back to Earth at some point so you never really die. Granted there are a few who never come back to Earth, but they've reached oneness with God, and I'd hardly call that death either.

The New Age

"The empires of the future are the empires of the mind."—Winston Churchill

One of the facets of New Age beliefs is the belief in a New Age (who would have thought that the name actually had some meaning). A corner stone belief for most New Agers is that society as a whole is on the cusp of a major change. At some point in the not too distant future, there will be more people on the planet who are closer to God than ever before in history. And I'm not talking just the numbers of people who can be counted as being at a higher level, with six and a half billion people it was inevitable that there would be more enlightened people around—I'm talking about a higher percentage of the world being more enlightened. At this point this will make the path back to God clearer for everyone. The amount of spiritual growth that has occurred over the last five thousands years will be doubled or tripled in only a century or two.

Yes, I know that sounds more like a stoned hippie in the middle of the '60's. Actually it kind of is. The reason for this is that not only do you plan out your life, but there is a bit of a master plan for this world on how to get people out of the cycle of birth, learning, death, and rebirth and get all of us back with God (or at least a general sketch since with free will any full-out plan is impossible). That plan called for a good deal of souls of higher than average enlightenment to hit the Earth about 1950 (the baby boom generation). Not the entire generation—a small portion at most. This portion was of a slightly higher spiritual level than the average person. Their supposed job was to start changing the systems of the world to better foster spiritual growth. They got half of the way there. They began asking a lot of the right questions about the inefficiency and hypocrisy of the systems of the world. They sensed they were closer to God than the majority of humanity and wanted to be even closer. Here is where the problem came up. They discovered drugs and generally they stopped growing up. Right ends of wanting to get back to God, just really bad means. And, along with a lot of other incorrect means, the 60's culture spread. Moreover, most of the generation lost its impact because the answers they came up with were either worthless or worse than the systems they were questioning. Yeah, that free will thing doesn't always work out perfectly in the short term.

Then the next generation came in around the mid '70's. They weren't much better, not as naturally screwed up as their hippie parents, and some being plagued with obvious hippie names like Starchild and Windsong, but given the fact that they were being raised by a generation that is perpetually stuck in their teens, they came out remarkably well. The general New Age term for these people is Indigo Children (a reference to the fact that if you could see the color of peoples' auras, theirs would be a bright Indigo color). General figures put the 1970-1990 births generally at anywhere from one in five to one in thirty of this generation being Indigos. According to New Age belief, these Indigos are here to completely break down the systems and social problems that are keeping people from opportunities of spiritual growth. Once they have accomplished this task of tearing down all those problems, the next generation, called Crystal children, born about 1990 and after, are supposed to rebuild everything the Indigos tore down.

What exactly these changes are, are, as typical of any religion, annoyingly vague. I've heard utopian visions of peace and harmony to the more realistic idea of greater peace on Earth than we presently have and more people more quickly moving toward enlightenment. Realist that I am, I don't see humanity reinventing itself overnight, but I am more than willing to believe that it can easily increase it's current speed of spiritual evolution. Even if the "New Age" is only a slight acceleration, it is long overdue and greatly welcomed.

Faith

"There are more things in heaven and earth, Horatio, Than are dreamt of in your philosophy."
—*William Shakespeare, Hamlet, Act 1 scene 5*

So that's the broad strokes of the metaphysics of New Age philosophy. Now onto the epistemology. How do we know all this stuff? How do we find the truth? Well no shock here, New Age belief is basically a religion minus the organization, so we mainly find truth through faith. It's a pretty standard epistemology for every religion on Earth.

However, I wouldn't say we go completely off faith alone. Science backs us up on some of this. Quantum Mechanics certainly justifies the idea that this world is an illusion, not to mention the idea of God[13]. It further suggests that the possibility for the ability for thought to directly affect the physical world (New Agers would see these as psychic powers). Modern studies have been investigating the power of faith and prayer, which seem to have more than a mere placebo effect. Further, other studies have given great credence to the idea of the afterlife. I could quote these studies directly, but why bother? I'll be the first to admit they are not definitive proof with the same kind of scientific certainty of Newton's third law of motion (for every action there is an opposite reaction). As of yet I don't know of any scientific study that has disproved any of the ideas I set forth earlier either, and quite frankly only a complete fool would believe that only what they can prove exists. As the saying goes: for those who believe, no further proof is necessary, for those who don't believe, no proof is possible. And since this book isn't intended to convert anyone, I'm not going to bother trying.

Most New Agers also have a healthy amount of anecdotal information. In anecdotal information I'm including books written by such psychics as Doreen Virtue and James Van Praagh and the like. There are also many mediums who don't write books but whom

[13] Again, I could go over all the reasons I say this, or you could reference the books at end, they make these points very well, and I would just be restating what they say.

Republicans and Reincarnation

people get in touch with to contact lost loved ones or talk to their spirit guides and guardian angels. These people claim to have the ability to listen or see and speak to the other side or higher power or whatever you want to call it, and I, along with most New Agers, believe them. Goes back to that faith thing. Not to say that there aren't charlatans out there. There are. A lot of them. And New Age philosophy, like every religion and spiritual belief on the planet, has its fair share of very naïve fools who are ready to have their money taken from them. Still, just as with your Christian televangelist asking for all your money or your Islamic fanatical Imam asking for your life to kill the infidel, there are many fake psychics out there. I won't deny it. New Age philosophy has them, but please be kind enough to realize that this is not a problem that only New Agers have. (Further, if you aren't open to any of the ideas and going to take me to task over using them as a basis for belief, honestly, why are you reading this book?)

Additionally New Agers look to messengers from God. Jesus, Buddha, Krishna, Moses and a whole lot of others. The difference here from most religions is we believe most religious prophets are what they say they are, messengers of God's word . . . We just don't think anyone of them is preaching the whole and complete truth (and more often than not that their followers may have not copied everything down exactly as they meant it).

Many New Age beliefs are rested upon strings of coincidence that lead people to a book or a documentary or an idea that leads to more and more ideas. But in the end, it all comes down to a matter of faith.

How a New Age believer *should* act

"Teacher, which is the great commandment in the Law?" And Jesus said to him, "'You shall love the Lord your God with all your heart, and with all your soul, and with all your mind.' This is the great and foremost commandment. The second is like it: 'You shall love your neighbor as yourself.' On these two commandments depend the whole Law and the Prophets." Matthew 22:36-40

Believe it or not, God wants you to be happy. Unbelievably, deliriously happy. And I'm not talking about the moment you get that promotion, your first kiss, when she says yes to marrying you, or when you hold your newborn child in your arms for the first time kind of happy. I'm talking about real happiness, not this here one minute, gone the next stuff. Happiness, the kind that lasts for your entire life and afterlife. Why? Because you deserve it. And you should do whatever it takes to get that happiness.

Now, obviously you can't just do whatever you want. New Age philosophy takes it as an assumption, as basic as the sun rises in the East, that you can't be happy unless you're virtuous and kind. Remember we're trying to get back to God, who is nothing but love, so love would be the major guiding point here.

When you really think about it, almost every major religion on Earth has basically the same moral code. Honesty, tolerance, patience, generosity, friendliness, kindness are in every religion. The don't kill, don't steal, don't lie, don't cheat, and don't betray rules are pretty common too. When you stop to think about it, the major difference between most religions on how to act comes down to more the minutia of details and specifics, mainly ones about how to worship god (on what day, with what words, and what rituals). New Age philosophy is no different. Be kind to those around you, treat them fairly, do what makes you happy (just don't hurt anybody intentionally while you're out making yourself happy).

The only main difference between New Age beliefs and some other religions is the attitude to learning and fear. Many religions (and I'm going to be nice here and not name names) don't exactly encourage learning. They have their dogma, their book, their religious leaders and you are not to question them. Here's the problem with that: everyone is at a different place in their journey back to God, and the beliefs of one system may not be what you need to learn in this life. Many religious systems may work for many people during their current life, but not for everyone, and it's only by questioning those beliefs and listening to your own heart (where God is supposed to be after all) that you find the truth that you are supposed to in this lifetime.

The other difference is that many religions (again, I'm not naming anyone) have a very bizarre attitude to fear. They use it. They actually brow beat their followers into believing they should be afraid of God, 'cause he will crush you like a bug if you don't do exactly what he says! That you should all be God-*fearing* followers or face fire and brimstone. God is not something to be feared, and sadly as long as that belief continues about a being that should not be feared, because love should never be feared, most people are not going to get very far in their journey because fear will never bring you to happiness. So here we go with a quick rundown of New Age ethics:

1. Love God. Don't fear him; love him, because he loves you.
2. Love yourself. I realize many people have a problem with this, but if God loves you, maybe you should too. Be happy.
3. Love all of mankind. God loves them too. Try not to do harm to them and help them just like you like to help yourself.
4. Don't be afraid. Fear is the problem, not the solution.

Other than these basics, it's kind of hard to detail specifics about how to live your life. As you move up the karmic ladder, the rules kind of change. Initially that may sound odd, shouldn't everyone be living by the same rules? But think about it, do we hold children to the same rules as adults . . . no, of course not, that's why they can say the most inappropriate things at the most inopportune time and they get away with it. A toddler steals something we scold them, we don't lock them away for ten to fifteen. Think about the fact that half of playground activity would register as assault if adults tried it. Further, do you have to live by the same rules a saint does? That would be a 'no' again. Depending on what level you're on, the rules that you live by change. I can say the higher you are the more charitable, loving, creative, and teacher-like you get. However, everyone takes a different path through each of these levels so hard and fast rules are a little pointless. All I can say is that reason, common sense and your heart are usually good indicators . . . but then again, watching the evening news tells me how lacking common sense and the heart are in people's decisions.

I can, however, give a brief view of the levels themselves and point out some general levels that do appear often in New Age discussion. From the Eastern basis of New Age belief comes the idea of levels of consciousness, which correspond to the body's seven chakras, or energy centers. Parallels can further be drawn between these two systems and various Eastern and mystical beliefs on the afterlife, and higher consciousness, Edgar Cayce's description of heaven, and most recently in Deepak Chopra's eloquent and thoughtful book *How to Know God,* in which Chopra posits seven ways to see God as either a Protector, a Law Giver, a Being of Peace, a Redeemer, a Creator, a God of Miracles, or finally in line with the ultimate New Age view, a God that just IS. Further, many in the New Age community have tried to draw parallels between these seven levels and the seven original planets of classical astrology and with the levels of the Tree of Life in the Cabbala, which is the latest New Age fad at the time of this writing. However, the levels of consciousness and chakras will serve to make my point.

Eastern belief holds that as the soul progresses it goes through several progressive levels of consciousness on its journey to Enlightenment. Some call these levels "bodies" and the idea is you shed each body as you shed your old beliefs until you have shed all your incorrect beliefs and are left as nothing but the pure you that is an energy one with God. Not surprisingly, there is a correspondence to the bodies in the Eastern concept of the chakra. Chakras are probably most familiar to yoga practitioners as the energy centers of the body. Each chakra is associated with certain types of energies of our life: Power, Love, and Creativity. As one goes up the main chakras, the energy becomes "purer" in its closeness to God. One can easily draw from this is not only an energy system in yoga and other Eastern medical practices, but that these are a metaphor for the progression of the soul.

	Level of Consciousness	You are aware of	Chakra	Energy Deals With
1	Physical	The Physical world, you exist because you can feel it	Muladhara or Root Chakra	Safety, Security, the Physical
2	Emotional	Your Body and your Soul	Svadisthana or Sacral Chakra	Desires, Emotion
3	Mental	Of the fact that your soul is part of something greater	Manipura or Solar Plexus Chakra	Control, Willpower, freedom
4	Astral	That you are a part of the whole universe and have a purpose in it	Anahata or Heart Chakra	Love, Compassion
5	Etheric	That you are an interconnected part of the whole that one might call God	Visuddha or Throat Chakra	Expression, Creativity, Communication
6	Cosmic	That you are, in a sense, God	Ajna or Third Eye	Intuition, Psychic powers, insight
7	Enlightenment	The title says it all	Sahasrara or Crown Chakra	Oneness with God

The chart above is a gross simplification but obvious parallels can be drawn. Let me go over the seven levels again in greater detail.

Level 1: Let's call this the Physical level. Not to be condescending here, but I unhappily believe that this is where the mass majority of people in the world are at. This is a view of the world that sees the world as just the world. There is little belief in a larger universe outside of this physical world, and if there is, it is of a very scary God of wrath that is capricious and will likely damn you to hell in a heartbeat if you do anything to offend him.

At this level of existence, people are concerned only with the present. Their immediate physical needs. And, sadly, there is a certain logic to it. If you're starving, most people don't have time to think about God. Further, it's also true if you're too worried about making the house payment or holding onto the wealth it's taken you years to amass. People at this level may be very ethical people, or they may be complete criminals. There is nothing wrong or right about the outlook of this level in the way someone behaves; their actions may be viewed as right or wrong, but it is not the outlook that creates right or wrong. The problem is that one can never be truly happy at this level. Food, comfort, shelter, money, sex are all base pleasures at this level with no additional meaning. And people at this level stand the greatest chance of winding up in those self-made hells I talked about in the afterlife.

Level 2: If I'm wrong and most of humanity isn't stuck at level one . . . then I would bet anything that 90% of the 6.5 billion people on the planet haven't passed level two. Here things don't just exist in the present but the past and the future. This is called the emotional level. Pleasures begin to have emotional context and life now becomes the life of a human being instead of just an evolved animal. People have stopped viewing themselves in a random universe or an existence controlled by a capricious God. Now there is justice and a just God, the good are rewarded and the evil punished . . . of course with reincarnation and karma, everyone gets punished for something at some point, thus guilt comes into play (as any Catholic will tell you). Western culture (especially America, thanks to our Puritan roots) is mired in this attitude. Success and achievement is placed central because that's a sign that you are good.

I would say that this is probably the hardest level to get past. The reason why is because it works for the most part. You're born, you live, you die, and you're rewarded or punished. The idea reincarnation is abhorrent to people at this level because while life may be good or not good, they see it as a struggle to achieve, and what they want is rest, which to them is not found in this life. The idea of a cycle of eternal rebirth comes off to them as their worst idea of all the possible hells. They want peace, but the thing that could bring them peace also comes with the idea that they have to work even harder for lifetimes for it. But a one shot, a simple do my time and I'm done, theory of this universe is so much simpler. Then they get all the joys they loved about this life and none of the pain. They get to leave the pain behind. They don't have to face it, because the Heaven of level two is just there. Seventy-Five years of work and then eternal bliss . . . awww isn't that nice. This is why I believe it to be the major stumbling block, many people are not in a place to realize that the journey is not a one shot deal and then you're done whether you have forced yourself to learn anything or not. Since you don't have to learn anything of the deeper meaning, you risk backsliding into level one (yes you can backslide . . . keep in mind we were all at level seven at one point) and from there backslide into your own personal afterlife Hell. It's a vicious circle.

Level 3: Here one sees life as a little more than just this lifetime. I'm not saying that everyone at this lifetime believes in reincarnation, but they see more meaning to life than just living. That life is the instrument through which we learn, not merely something we have to do. In level one life is the point; level two one begins to realize that there is a point to life; in level three life is not a race to which we are trying to reach an end as with level one, but a journey with things to be learned along the way. The focus of people begins to center on the journey not the end. Cliché as that may sound, it's survived as a cliché for a reason—there is truth in it.

This level is called the Mental level because it is where we begin to live in our mind and not our bodies. This level is often associated with meditation. That's not a far jump because to begin to see your life as a series of lessons rather than just one big test you have to take the time to actually analyze it thoughtfully, i.e. meditation. One tends to find the peace one was looking for in level two, sadly though that's just not enough. We find that although we have control of our lives on the physical world we begin to realize that that part of our existence is an illusion.

Level 4: The Astral stage is just that—we just begin to leave our bodies. We begin to see only our mind and our spirit and are fully into the process of giving up the illusion that is "reality" in the physical world. High levels of meditation and thoughtfulness are in this level. We also finally see that we are interconnected with others and with God. As such, our lives become one of far more love and compassion than at the previous levels. Not because we're all that altruistic, rather we simply see that everyone is interconnected and what hurts you hurts me in the long run.

In level four, we see a higher level of meditative state indicative of being closer to true Enlightenment. However, there is a gap here from level five much like the gap between levels two and three—not quite as great but there is still a gap here. Mainly because as levels one and two were levels of the physical world, and three and four are of the mental world, there is a gap between your mind and your soul that only a leap of faith can overcome.

Level 5: The Etheric stage is completely leaving your mind behind and living in your soul. Deep meditation can touch upon this. As can any action where you open yourself to yourself completely and tune out the world and your mind, most often this is through some sort of artistic expression, but by no means is that the only aspect of this level. As I said there is a major void between this level and the previous one; however, I don't think it is as hard to bridge as the gap between levels two and three. My personal feelings are that after you have made it past level three there is a steady acceleration toward the end goal that I would compare to an avalanche. It may be hard to start an avalanche (comparable to the first three levels) but once one starts, it is near impossible to stop (these latter levels). At level five you begin to not only hear God through your meditations, but you act as one with him in your life. You realize you are a part of God and that in effect you are an instrument of God.

Level 6: Once securely in level five I believe that one quickly (by quickly I mean no more than a single lifetime) progresses to the sixth level. People at this level are very easy to spot. We generally call them saints. These are people generally so close to God that miracles and signs of their connection to God are as easy to them as breathing. The fact that it is linked to the Third Eye Chakra, which is a symbol of psychic powers, is no coincidence, because the powers spring from a closeness to God. Now I'm not saying everyone with psychic powers has reached this level, far from it, but souls which have reached this level do command a great deal of control over such powers when they want to.

Level 7: Enlightenment, the only place to go after being a saint is to be one with God. You know the people who have reached this level by name: Buddha, Christ, Lao-Tzu, Krishna and a whole host of other Ascended Masters and deities from religions all over the world.

Right now they don't come often. Hopefully that will change.

Now if I'm right about these levels (and don't get hung up on the number, for all I know there are only 3 levels or 1000, depending on how you want to view it) then it would be impossible to come up with a single ethical code for New Age beliefs. The proper ethics of each level must be designed to teach you what you need to know to reach the next level.

Now a saint may live by a code of giving constantly and thanklessly, and they may find infinite joy in that for it brings them closer to God. But shove the same code on a person at the physical level 1 and all they will feel is resentment; at level two pride for being viewed as good by others; at the third level obligated by some code they are beginning to understand, but not fulfilled or happy. And if it does not lead to happiness and joy, then it does not lead to a closer relationship with God, and thus these morals of a saint could actually drive a person away from God rather bring them closer.

Further there are so many subtle variations within each level that a bold, simple rule of ethical behavior might not work for everyone. It is rather a personal journey for everyone. To reach the height of each level, realize that it is not enough, and move onto the next—that's life according to the New Age.

One last point I wish to make is that no one religion fits into just a few of these levels. Depending on how you want to interpret their teachings, any religion can likely fit any one of these levels. The Dalai Llama is likely on level six or seven but there are probably Buddhists at only the first level; I know many in the New Age movement have a great contempt for Christianity and see it as a religion of those stuck at the first levels (an incorrect view) but when you consider the sheer number of documented miracles attributed to Christian saints it is impossible to believe that Christianity does not lead people to the highest levels of the scales. All roads eventually lead to God. It's not the belief, it's how you believe and how you act on it.

Then the question becomes how does this fit into politics? Should we just let everyone do their own thing? That's an easy one: NO! But if we can't have rules that fit everyone how can we have a government? Well, the short answer is a conservative government.

However, before I elaborate on that, let me take some time to define what I mean by conservative.

Chapter 3
WE'RE RIGHT IN MORE WAYS THAN ONE
CONSERVATISM 101

"If you analyze it I believe the very heart and soul of conservatism is libertarianism. I think conservatism is really a misnomer just as liberalism is a misnomer for the liberals—if we were back in the days of the Revolution, so-called conservatives today would be the Liberals and the liberals would be the Tories. The basis of conservatism is a desire for less government interference or less centralized authority or more individual freedom and this is a pretty general description also of what libertarianism is. Now, I can't say that I will agree with all the things that the present group who call themselves Libertarians in the sense of a party say, because I think that like in any political movement there are shades, and there are libertarians who are almost over at the point of wanting no government at all or anarchy."
—*Ronald Reagan*

What is a conservative? Is it some evil person who wants to make the rich richer and the poor poorer, rape the forests and engage in nonstop oil drilling, kill everyone who isn't of a certain religion or ethnic group, keep women barefoot and pregnant, is dumb, uneducated, yet somehow unbelievably rich . . . and whatever else the latest trashy commercial from the Democratic National

Committee says? One can easily answer this: NO! No, no, no, no, no. Remember what I said in the introduction about stepping away from the stereotypes, I meant it.

Well if it isn't what the bleeding hearts say it is, then what is it? Well the problem is that conservative is a term that doesn't have a hard and fast definition. Part of this comes from the problem that what is considered conservative changes from era to era. A politics joke goes as follows: "if you believe that all races are equal and deserve complete equality under the law, in the 30's you'd be a radical, in the 50's you'd be a liberal, in the 70's you'd be a conservative, and in the 90's you'd be a racist." While ideas may not change, nor any one person's view on a particular idea, society's acceptance of an idea does. And with that, change comes what is perceived as a conservative in any given era.

Another problem is that the words Republican and Conservative are almost interchangeable in the public's mind. Even I've done it a lot in this book. However, the fact is that so many people who call themselves Republicans actually have no understanding of conservative policies or ideals (presidents who are usually identified by their middle initial come to mind). From this point on in this book, please do not confuse Republicans (who can be real idiots) with the philosophy of Conservatives.

The other problem is that political ideas don't just sit on an either/or kind of deal. Mainly because we are not talking about one issue we're talking about literally hundreds of issues each in which there are probably three or four possible takes, if not more. The traditional ways of representing politics is on the Right/Left continuum. You have a line and where you are on that line is where you are politically. On the far right, you have Fascism, and moving from right to left, you get Populists, Neoconservatives, Conservative Republicans, Liberal Republicans, Centrists, Conservative Democrats, Liberal Democrats, Socialists, and finally Communism (which ironically usually looks just like a Fascist state, but with a different spin from the PR department). The problem is that this doesn't always work. Libertarians are nowhere to be found; neither are Anarchists, or a whole host of other factions and groups.

The next most common way, and the way you'll likely see if you take an internet test to see what your politics are is the two-axis scale. The Up/Down axis generally deals with economic freedom, and the Right/Left axis generally deals with Social Freedom.

Now Economic Freedom deals with how much you want the government to control the economy. Higher or lower taxes? Should the rich pay more taxes than the poor or get to keep the money they earned? Should welfare and social security programs be set up or should people take care of themselves and rely on private charity if anything? Should the government regulate safety, health, and employment at your business or should you be allowed to conduct any kind of business you want so long as it doesn't hurt anyone or should the government keep you from controlling a market? Should environmental protection exist or should you be allowed to pollute, or more importantly how much power should the government be given to control pollution? The first part of each question would generally mean further down on the scale, bottoming out at communism . . . if you chose the second part of each question more often then you're likely higher on the scale and closer to good old-fashioned capitalism.

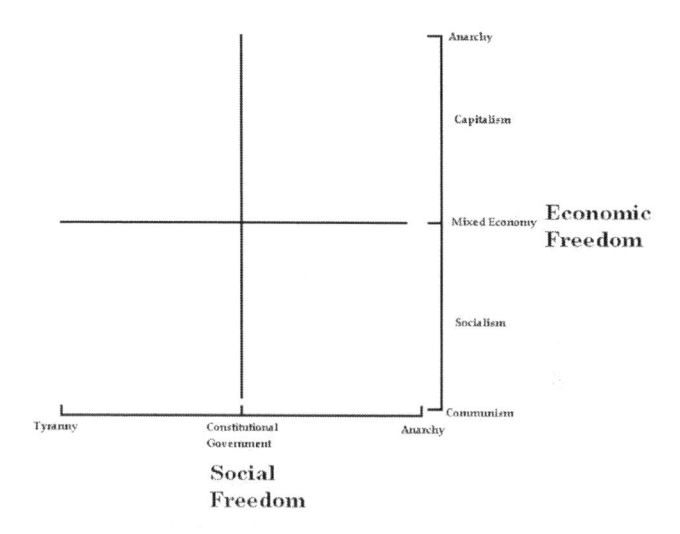

Republicans and Reincarnation

```
                              |— Anarchy
                              |
                              |
                              |— Capitalism
                              |
                              |
                              |                    Economic
      ────────────────────────┼— Mixed Economy     Freedom
                              |
                              |
                              |— Socialism
                              |
                              |
                              |— Communism
   └──────────────────────────┴──────────┘
  Tyranny    Constitutional          Anarchy
             Government
           Social
          Freedom
```

On the question of Social Freedom . . . . Should you be allowed to do anything in the privacy of your home or should the government keep a close eye on you? Is your privacy sacred or can the government invade your privacy for public safety reasons? Should you be allowed to marry anyone you want or can the government tell who you can and cannot marry? Should we reform criminals or should we punish criminals? Should everyone have a say in government or only a portion of the population? Should the government or the private sector fund the arts? Should abortion be legal or illegal? Is everyone entitled to a college education through public funding or only through private funding? Should smoking marijuana be legalized or be illegal? If you agreed with the first options in these questions you're more to the right on scale shown above and considered socially liberal, if you found yourself agreeing with the second part you're probably more to

Cris A. Pace

left on the scale and believe in a strict constitutional government (I didn't put anything with tyrannical overtones because it's so far out there in modern 1st world society, it's hardly worth mentioning).

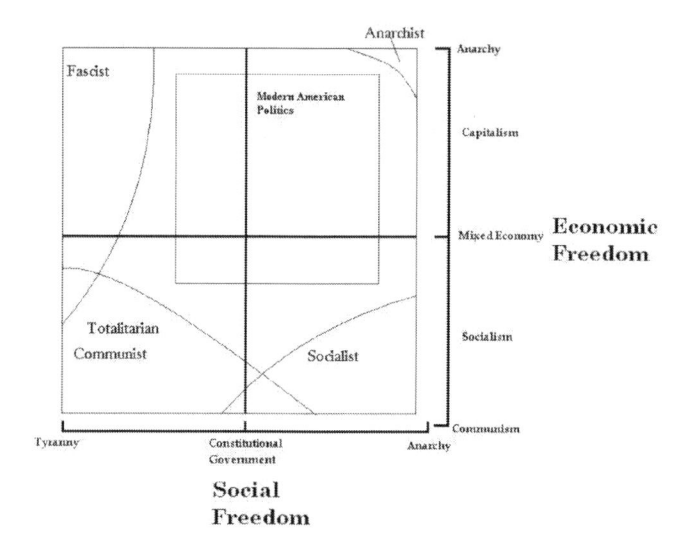

[Figure: A two-dimensional political chart with "Economic Freedom" as the vertical axis (ranging from Anarchy, Capitalism, Mixed Economy, Socialism, Communism) and "Social Freedom" as the horizontal axis (ranging from Tyranny, Constitutional Government, Anarchy). Quadrants are labeled: Fascist (upper left), Anarchist (upper right), Totalitarian Communist (lower left), Socialist (lower middle-right), with "Modern American Politics" boxed in the center.]

So if you're low on both freedom on the economy and socially you probably would be happy under the rule of Joseph Stalin. In the bottom left hand corner you have many of your modern dictators as well. They control every aspect of your life.

In the lower right hand corner you would like lots of government control over the economy but few over you social freedoms. I can think of few governments in reality that look like this. The best example in reality might be a 1960's hippie commune style of living (but the Obama administration does seem to be pushing in that direction).

Continuing counter clockwise we reach the upper left hand corner where you have your more libertarian governments that control little of both. At the far upper right hand corner you have pure anarchy and a complete lack of government. In the middle of the grid or so (actually just above the center with much more area in the capitalism sector), you have more of the government of the United States in its early days or a philosophy usually called classical liberalism, which depending on the definition can cover a rather wide ground.

And finally in the upper right hand corner we have fascist government like the World War II Axis power or your standard Islamic totalitarian regime today (I'd name the countries . . . but we'd be here all day).

Modern American politics can be put into a smaller part of the whole scale. It's centered around a little up and to the right of the usual center of the whole. The chart to the left more or less identifies where different political groups are. The big whole in the center is usually identified as people who are centrists even though the reality is that most people who identify themselves as centrists really mean they have no opinion on any political topic.

Cris A. Pace

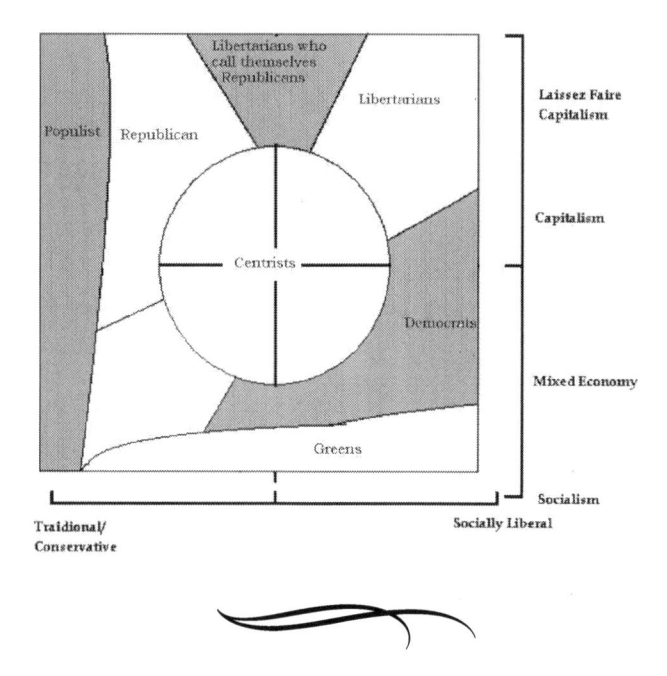

[Diagram: A political spectrum chart with a circle labeled "Centrists" in the middle. Surrounding regions are labeled: "Libertarians who call themselves Republicans", "Libertarians", "Populist", "Republican", "Democrats", "Greens". Right-side vertical axis labels: "Laissez Faire Capitalism", "Capitalism", "Mixed Economy", "Socialism". Bottom horizontal axis labels: "Traidional/Conservative" (left), "Socially Liberal" (right).]

"No man is an island, entire of itself every man is a piece of the continent, a part of the main[.]"
—John Donne

However, while this scale works for most governments they fail to grasp a revolutionary change in politics that occurred in the 20th and continues in the 21st century. That is the idea of Isolationism versus Globalization. Now your economic liberal may not believe in trade barriers at all, but you have in that same group people who believe that we should help turn the world into capitalist countries, and merely those who don't care. Your standard Republican/conservative may believe in strong defense, but the War on Terror has clearly revealed a large difference between those who would merely keep our borders safe and those who would change the whole world for the better.

The Isolationist side believes that what happens in their country should happen in their country and what happens in other countries should be that other country's business: That government, philosophy, culture, and economics of each country or area should be left alone. Politically and socially, this leads to the attitude that what happens in one country isn't our problem. This is a policy that the worst genocidal butchers of the 20th and 21st centuries have reveled in, because no one interferes with them. Economically this has led to numerous people attempting to stall or impede the growth of the capitalist system to the world, under some deluded, infantile belief that people would rather live in the humble simplicity of a third world nation.

The Globalization side believes in the idea that liberal democracy is not just a neat idea that works for parts of Europe and America, but a natural right for every human. They believe that despite the short-term shortcomings of economic globalization, there is a benefit bringing a capitalist culture to the world because it brings more freedom and a higher standard of living. The further you are into this area the more you would believe it is the duty of any free nation to do anything in its power to ensure that liberty is spread throughout the globe, even if that requires military means in some situations.

Okay, so now that we have some basic criteria of politics, what do conservatives believe? And the answer is going to sound really strange at first because conservatives, in the modern sense, are liberals. However, to make that last sentence make sense we have to go back over two thousand years to the beginnings of political philosophy

> *"For even if the end is the same for a single man and for a state, that of the state seems at all events something greater and more complete whether to attain or to preserve; though it is worth while to attain the end merely for one man, it is finer and more godlike to attain it for a nation or for city-states. These, then, are the ends at which our inquiry aims."*—Aristotle

The "end" Aristotle is talking about in that quote is happiness. To the Ancient Greek philosophers Plato and Aristotle the end, the point, of human life was to be happy, or in the Greek, eudaimonia. Now they didn't mean by this word, I just had a wonderful meal, or just got a promotion, or in the middle of your honeymoon, or the birth of your first child kind of happy. What they meant by the word of eudaimonia is a happiness that at the end of your life, you can look back at the entirety of it and be happy, absolutely, completely, without hesitation or regrets, Frank Sinatra singing "My Way" kind of happy. Yeah there will be low points, but as the whole is always greater than the sum of its parts, the whole of your life is a perfectly happy one. To them there is but one way to achieve this happiness, and that is the virtuous life. The traditional four cardinal virtues: Courage, Temperance, Moderation, Justice, along with a whole host of other virtues (friendliness, charity, wit, good temper, ambition, numerous intellectual virtues, etc . . . just to name a few) are what you need in life to live the best life possible, the life of happiness. And for Plato and Aristotle, who effectively started the true debate of political philosophy, the state had the end of providing this life of happiness to its citizens. Fundamentally, this idea of the purpose of government has not changed much in the last two and a half millennia.

However, the governments that Plato and Aristotle proposed as being the ideal governments were far from perfect. For one thing, both philosophers had trouble seeing any government larger than the city-states of Ancient Greece. Plato, in *The Republic,* created a utopia that was elitist, communistic, and bears a great deal of similarity to the world of *1984.* Aristotle, not only flawed in the fact that he did not see past his culture's racist and sexist attitudes, was, at least in the writings that have survived, a little vague as to the ideal sort of government. Aristotle believed that the best forms of government were monarchy, aristocracy (rule by the best), and what he called polity as opposed to the worst three tyranny, oligarchy (rule by the rich), and democracy (for Aristotle the term democracy meant a form of government ruled by the lower class, people uneducated with few material means who would use their power to steal what the upper and middle classes had . . . history seems to have borne that out—further keep in mind most Western governments are republics, which is more in line with Aristotle's description of a polity, not true democracies in the technical sense). The first three listed, despite the differences in form, worked for the good of the whole trying to make all citizens capable of leading the life of virtue and happiness; the latter three forms worked only for the good of those in power. Aristotle, while producing numerous suggestions on the ideal state, was vague to the exact form as he viewed each city-state needed to tailor their government to their own needs and temperaments. While he did lean in bias toward polity (think of a republic ruled by a very large middle class), his only real standard for a good government was that it provided the means for its citizens to lead virtuous lives.[14]

Regrettably, however, history was slow to pick up the entire idea of government being for the good of the people, and the Hellenistic and Roman Empires barreled over the west, to be O so unjoyously followed by the Dark and Middle ages with feudal systems that had most people worth less than dirt, and since the Church was in power, the upper classes were sinners too and in the grand scheme of things not much better. So the ideas of Plato and Aristotle were little considered outside of scholastic monasteries. Luckily, following this abysmal period in Western history followed the Renaissance, the Reformation, and an Age of Enlightenment. With the era, starting around the mid-1600's and hitting its stride in the mid to late 1700's, the Age of Enlightenment provided again an ideal of government for the betterment of the people in a practical sense. But more than just that, it developed the ideas of what is now known as the "Social Contract" and natural rights. Natural rights are those rights that we have at birth by virtue of being human. Every American has heard of three of them: Life, Liberty, and the Pursuit of Happiness. Added to

[14] I fully realize that I have just grossly simplified the political philosophy of the two greatest philosophers in history to a single paragraph, and in no means wish to imply that their philosophies have no relevance beyond what I have stated here. Quite the contrary. And while I could wax poetic for volumes on their political wisdom and insight, it will not give any deeper insight into our question of what is a conservative.

the traditional list of natural rights, is the right to own property. The social contract is the idea that governments are created through the consent of the people that the government rules over in order to protect the majority of their natural rights by sacrificing some of those rights to the government (sacrifice our complete right to property by allowing some of property to be taken as taxes, sacrifice our complete right to freedom and agree to obey laws which will in the end protect us). While the theory is most completely laid out in the works of the philosopher John Locke, they are nowhere more eloquently stated than in the second paragraph of the Declaration of Independence:

> *We hold these truths to be self-evident, that all men are created equal, that they are endowed by their Creator with certain unalienable Rights, that among these are Life, Liberty and the pursuit of Happiness.—That to secure these rights, Governments are instituted among Men, deriving their just powers from the consent of the governed,—That whenever any Form of Government becomes destructive of these ends, it is the Right of the People to alter or to abolish it, and to institute new Government, laying its foundation on such principles and organizing its powers in such form, as to them shall seem most likely to effect their Safety and Happiness. Prudence, indeed, will dictate that Governments long established should not be changed for light and transient causes; and accordingly all experience hath shewn, that mankind are more disposed to suffer, while evils are sufferable, than to right themselves by abolishing the forms to which they are accustomed. But when a long train of abuses and usurpations, pursuing invariably the same Object*

> *evinces a design to reduce them under absolute Despotism, it is their right, it is their duty, to throw off such Government, and to provide new Guards for their future security.*

The most important change the idea of the social contract made from the original philosophies of Plato and Aristotle is the nature of government. Plato saw government as good. Aristotle saw that there were good governments and bad governments. The theory of the social contract realized that the only perfect government would be no government, because only then could people be allowed to utilize their god-given right to freedom, thus all government becomes a bad government. The reason we need government is that while freedom is our right, all of us aren't ready for it. Or at least all of us aren't ready for complete freedom. And before you take offense to that line just consider some people are greedy, stupid, and violent—we need a police force, court system and military to keep them in check. Hence, the statement by Founding Father James Madison, "If men were angels, no government would be necessary." Men are not angels, and thus we need the necessary evil that is government to protect us from those who are not always listening to the voice of the divine within them.

This movement of the belief in the idea that governments are created to protect the rights of the people is called *Classical Liberalism*[15]. The term Liberalism here does not mean what the common person today means when they say "liberal." The word Liberalism comes

---

[15] For the sake of helping understanding I am going to use Liberalism with a capital "L" to designate Classical Liberalism, and liberalism with a lower case "l" when I mean liberal in the modern sense as an opposite to conservative politics.

from the Latin word *liberalis*, which means "free," and is the same word from which we derive the word "liberty." Classical Liberalism takes its cues from the sense that government is meant to protect our liberty, our freedom, and our natural rights. And realizing that the only system that would allow perfect freedom isn't perfect because not everyone is ready for perfect freedom, governments are tolerated by Liberals, but only as a necessary evil. Let me say that again—NECESSARY EVIL. The problem is that if the general public isn't ready for perfect freedom, then there is no chance that those in power are ready for the power to limit that freedom. It is simply that of the two options, giving up a few rights is the better of two unenviable choices. The traditional thought of the Classical Liberal, as Jefferson put it is, "The government which governs best, governs least."

"The point is, ladies and gentlemen, that greed—for lack of a better word—is good. Greed is right. Greed works. Greed clarifies, cuts through, and captures the essence of the evolutionary spirit. Greed, in all its forms—greed for life, for money, for love, knowledge—has marked the upward surge of mankind."—Michael Douglas as Gordon Gekko, Wall Street

Classical Liberalism comes with several main features in its philosophy: Economic Liberalism, constitutional and limited governments, representative governments, individualism, and individual rights.

The first of these is Economic Liberalism, known by such other terms as free market economies, laissez-faire, or plain old Capitalism. Of the natural rights government is supposed to protect, property is one of the most basic. As Classical Liberalism states, you have the right to the product of your work. Wait you say, does that mean I have the right to all those burgers I made at McDonalds when I was a teenager? No, and here's why. First off, you didn't own the materials that you made the hamburger with, the McDonalds Corporation did, and since they didn't sell them to you, it's their property that you just can't take (that would be theft). Second and more importantly, I did say you have the right to the product of your work, and McDonald's completely agrees with me on that, but instead of giving you nothing but finished hamburgers, McDonald's paid you money in return for you work. Granted it probably wasn't much money, but then again you were only qualified to flip burgers at the time and you agreed to the job, if you didn't think you were getting paid enough you would have not taken the job.

The laissez-faire capitalism belief is that given the chance, human self-interest, tempered by rational thought, will lead to the overall betterment of humanity. Now some of you might be skeptical about this, but there is no reason to be. Man is a naturally benevolent and charitable creature; yes we're greedy, what sane person doesn't want more of something or the other. It's natural—it's right. At the end of every act of selfishness is a desire to be happy. And shouldn't we want more happiness in our life? If your answer to that question is no, then see a psychiatric professional immediately! Now you're saying, but money doesn't buy happiness. True. But as a good friend of mine would always point out "While money doesn't buy happiness, it sure makes a good down payment, meanwhile poverty never bought anything." Now while my friend has typically displayed an unusually high amount of cynicism, he has a point that some money is required to be happy. If you can't pay for food, rent, or the kid's new braces I doubt you would call yourself happy. Now, happy people tend to see money as a tool, a means to help them reach happiness, not an end in itself. However, I would have to say that I would be very surprised to find anyone who is truly happy, in the Aristotelian sense of a life that is complete and lacking nothing, who does not live, at least, a middle class lifestyle. Further, you should want that, you should want everything it takes to make your life happy. Hence, greed, or at least self-interest, in the sense of wanting stuff that will lead to a happy life, is good. Possibly even more importantly, greed is ethical. Perhaps thinking back to that high school economics class you might recall a book called *The Wealth of Nations* by a man named Adam Smith published in 1776. In *Wealth of Nations* Smith laid down the basic principles of the capitalism as it was beginning to emerge in Europe at the beginning of the Industrial Revolution. Most people think of Smith's work as describing the practicality of capitalism, which it does; however, what most fail to realize is one of the main thrusts of *Wealth of Nations* is not that capitalism is practical, but rather that it is ethical, and that almost any interference of government into the economy is not only foolish in a pragmatic sense, but unethical and immoral.

Not only is government interference in the economy immoral, and impractical, but, as modern Nobel Prize winning economist Milton Friedman would be happy to point out, that the more interference in the economy a government gets into, the less liberty in all areas for the citizens of that country. The government's job in all of this is to ensure the system works. Classical Liberalism holds that the government's only interference into the economy should be only as much taxation as the government needs to run, no more, a system of laws to protect from theft and fraud, and a police and court system to enforce those laws. Here ends the government of classical liberalism's foray into the economy.

There are many other valid justifications for capitalism, but I will get to them later on in the book when we're directly discussing economic policy.

"That government is best which governs the least, because its people discipline themselves."—Henry David Thoreau

Now after economic freedom, the next central tenet of Classical Liberalism is the concept of constitutional and limited government. Classical Liberalism set down that government should not have absolute power. As with the tenants of capitalism that the more government gets involved the worse things get, the idea of a limited government says that this idea is pretty true for most areas of life. The full words of the James Madison quote I gave a little earlier run thus: "If men were angels, no government would be necessary. If angels were to govern men, neither external nor internal controls on government would be necessary. In framing a government that is to be administered by men over men, the great difficulty lies in this: you must first enable the government to control the governed; *and in the next place oblige it to control itself.* [Italics added] A dependence on the people is, no doubt, the primary control on the government; but experience has taught mankind the necessity of auxiliary precautions." Yes, we need government to do certain things that no one else can be trusted to do. However, as human beings are the ones in power, and human beings are not always rational or good, we need some way to make sure that they don't get out of hand when we put them in positions of power.

Every American is familiar, I hope, with the concept of checks and balances[16]. Of the three branches of government, each of the three is dependant on the other two branches to get anything done. No one branch of government can go off on its own and do whatever it pleases. For example, if the Congress passes a bill, the President can veto it or the Supreme Court can declare the law unconstitutional. Most of these checks and balances are stated in the Constitution. Further, the Constitution lays down a long list of things that the government cannot do and rights the government cannot infringe upon. The original list was kind of short: no nobility, you can't be arrested without reason unless public safety absolutely demands it, no taxes on income (yeah, that was originally in there, but the 16th Amendment changed that, may every politician who voted for that amendment burn in hell for all eternity, mores the pity however there is no hell) to name a few. The list was augmented by further amendments to the constitution: free speech, free press, right to bear arms, no slaves . . . you know the list. To one degree or another, this is the concept of a limited government.

Now originally a Classical Liberal believed that government should do only those things that the private

---

[16] If you're not, you need to go back to your high school and slap your old government teacher for being an idiot.

Cris A. Pace

sector or individuals could not do. At the time, the 1700's, this was a military, a court system, and a police force. Nations like Great Britain came fairly close to this ideal. And keep in mind that a 2 cent tax on two-thousand pounds of a breakfast beverage was seen as a valid reason to shoot some tax collectors and start a revolution at the time, because, that was the government going way too far (ah, the good ol' days).

Great Britain also brings up another point of constitutional and limited government. Great Britain to this day does not have a written constitution. They have several written documents, and lots of traditions and habits, but no single document like most countries do. However, Great Britain is certainly a limited government for the most part. Meanwhile countries like China, North Korea, and the former Soviet Union all have written constitutions. Lot of good that does for protection of rights. Now given a choice, I'll take the U.K. over any of those hellholes any day. So while we may call the idea constitutional government, just having the document doesn't mean anything, it's following the premise of limiting government's power that is important to classical Liberalism.

"No taxation without representation"—Unknown person who didn't realize that with representation it's just as bad.[17]

This leads us to that great idea of representative government. Not to be confused with that insane idea

---

[17] Okay, so it was really from a sermon by Reverend Jonathan Mayhew, but I needed to make a point.

called democracy. Representative government, also called republicanism (not to be confused with the Republican Party) believes in what is called a republic, a government where the laws are created and administered by representatives of the country. Classical Liberals believed in this form of government as opposed to both monarchy where power was in the hand of one man, and democracy, where the power was in the hands of far too many. "Wait, wait, wait," you're shouting at me, "we're a democracy!" Nope. Your 5th grade teacher lied to you. The idea that we're a democracy ranks right up there with Washington chopping down the cherry tree and Lincoln freeing the slaves—complete and total lie. The Founding Fathers, Classical Liberals through and through, often spoke of the "tyranny of democracy." The unfortunate thing about democracy, that even Plato and Aristotle recognized thousands of years ago, is that a complete democracy is bent only on the whim of the majority. Now I could name off the times that the majority has been wrong and fill a whole book (maybe two) with those examples, but rather than that let me demonstrate a few times when the popular sentiment was wrong and the work of smaller groups acting against the will of the majority proved to be right:

- The American Revolution was supported by about only a third of the colonists in the thirteen colonies. Popular opinion would have likely kept us a British colony.
- The Civil War was probably the most unpopular war in history. Had Lincoln not stood against public sentiment for the majority of the war the South would have gone its own way.

- World Wars I and II were hardly popular with the American public until we were attacked; yet many Americans went over to the Europe and Asia to fight because they caught onto the concept of good and evil far before their compatriots.
- The resistance movement in Nazi Germany.

And let us not forget those times when the public has been, all too easily, swayed into doing something stupid:

- Nazi Germany
- The Russian Revolution
- The Chinese Red Army
- The Reign of Terror after the French Revolution
- The fact that this country actually elected a socialist like FDR not once, but four (!!!!) times.

All in all, the general public of any country doesn't have the best track record for overall intelligence. The Caesars long ago realized that give them food and entertainment and you can get away with a hell of a lot. The Democrat Party has realized the same thing, promise them everything, to hell if your plans actually work or if you can ever pay for it, and you can get elected. The masses are fickle, ignorant, and short sighted. Individual people can be good, honest, decent, logical, and compassionate, but seldom if ever does that describe a large group of people. While we want to limit the power of government, we also want to limit who is in control.

Hence, we have a representative government that does not allow the public to go all helter-skelter in their policies. A group of people, hopefully of greater merit than the general public, is chosen to control the power of the government (if you're rolling your eyes at that, I am too). Now they can be chosen through various means: Rome was based mainly on money for getting into the Senate, here in America we chose a democratic means of picking our representatives (thus we are a democratic republic, not a pure democracy), in supposedly representative China it's who can suck up and repeat the party line the best. The idea being that, at least theoretically, when you have a limited government it stops the government from going too far, and with the representative government it stops the public from going too far.

This is an idea that the modern American may have trouble with. Primarily because we have been straying further and further from a democratic *republic* with the power vested in the representatives to do what is best for the people, to a *democratic* republic where the representatives seem only capable of reading poll numbers and following the latest caprice of the mob. This is partly because of an incredibly horrific education system that for nearly two centuries has idiotically been calling America a democracy and thus spawned the mob mentality that pushed the country closer and closer to a democracy. In the beginning, many of the ideas of the mob never got very far. However, nowadays no problems get solved, because most problems require long-term solutions, and the mob, like a petulant child, needs immediate gratification for all its needs. Social security, welfare and healthcare were all created to appease the public, not because they particularly made any logical sense, and solving them will require hard and drastic steps, none of which any representative in the House, Senate, or White House will ever really do because they all want to get reelected.

However, back to representative government. When used in the fashion the Classical Liberal imagined it, it does offer another check on the use of government power.

"We hold these truths to be self-evident, that all men are created equal, that they are endowed by their Creator with certain unalienable Rights"—Thomas Jefferson, Declaration of Independence
"Liberty is not the power of doing what we like, but the right of being able to do what we ought."—Lord Acton

One of the final tenets of Classical Liberalism is the belief and protection of individual rights. I've already covered most of these with the ideas of economic liberty and the need to prevent the government from getting out of hand both with limited and representative government. But the reason for these is the belief that the individual human being has rights that supercede all man made law.

The ideas of Classical Liberalism are based in very religious thought. The idea is that man is a creation of God, and the rights that God has given man, first and foremost being free will, can never be trumped by the laws of man. Life, liberty, property, pursuit of happiness, all that fun stuff. Government is there to protect these rights from the infringement of other people or organizations. Thus, we have a military to stop outside governments from coming in and enslaving the country under some pathetic communist/fascist/Islamic government. In addition, we have police and court systems to protect

Republicans and Reincarnation

from internal threats of criminals. However, Classical Liberalism stops here, when it comes to the government. To a pure Classical Liberal the government does not go beyond this point—the government will make sure that no one impedes your right to pursue happiness by killing or robbing you, but the government doesn't care if you're a miserable wretch all on your own. You have the right to pursue happiness; you have no right to actually have happiness regardless of whether or not you've earned it. Now if you earn it or achieve it, bully for you. But it's not the government's fault (if you have a truly Classical Liberal government) or point to care about your unhappiness. Remember, because of free will it's also your right to be a miserable, unhappy, lonely, worthless, lazy excuse for a human being if you choose to be, just so long as you don't get in anyone else's way to choose between happiness and misery for themselves.

If you do get in someone else's way, if you violate their basic rights, according to Classical Liberalism, guess what happens . . . you lose yours. You violate someone else's right to property and the government has the right to take away your rights to property, liberty, and theoretically your life (although, with the possible exception of IRS agents, I don't think you should be executed for theft). This is why when you commit a crime, which again theoretically, has violated the rights of someone else, you can be fined, imprisoned or even put to death and it's all very legal and good.[18] The government's job in this is to set the rule, laws, and administer the system, police, courts, and prisons.

---

[18] In case you're wondering, later I'm going to argue why the death penalty should be suspended, except in the case of IRS agents.

Now there is no full list of rights that a person has. As the quote of Lord Acton above suggests we have the right to do whatever is right and good and true. Now keep in mind that this means that rights, natural rights, are only means. No one has the right to an end, unless you have worked and earned that end. We have the right to pursue happiness, because pursuit is an action, we have no right to happiness itself because happiness itself is an end to which we all strive. To a Classical Liberal such things as the right to leisure (which, believe it or not, is in the U.N. Charter of Human Rights) are ridiculous—you earn leisure, because it's an end; you have the right to earn to seek and pursue a career that will give you the opportunity to have leisure.

Essentially, what is right and virtuous, the means to a happy life, are your rights. What exactly those are, depends greatly on your code of ethics and faith. Classical Liberalism never really set down a full list that everyone could agree with. And, frankly, that's what the rest of this book is about.

With the late 1700's Classical Liberal principles were put into practice, or at least, people attempted to put them into practice. As with any attempt to put theory into practice, multiple ways of interpretation and implementation arose. There were two main schools that came out of Classical Liberalism. Those two are liberals (lower case "l" or as I call them lunatics) and conservatives (and you thought I'd never get here). And now we come to it. The word that we have been trying to get to for two and half chapters. Conservative. What is a conservative?

Republicans and Reincarnation

In his book *The Conservative Mind* author Russell Kirk laid out six principles of conservative ideology. To quickly summarize them, they are as follows:

1. Conservatives believe in "a transcendent order, or body of natural law, which rules society."
2. Conservatives have an "affection for the proliferating variety and mystery of human existence[.]"
3. Conservatives have a "conviction that civilized society requires orders and classes."
4. Conservatives believe "freedom and property are closely linked[.]"
5. Conservatives have "faith in prescription and distrust of 'sophisters, calculators, and economists' who would reconstruct society upon abstract designs."
6. Conservatives believe that "Society must alter, for prudent change is the means of social preservations; but a statesman must take Providence into his calculations, and a statesman's chief virtue [. .] is prudence."[19]

Now, I can just see you rereading those six points trying to figure out what some of them mean. So here that list goes in non-pompous-elitist-speak:

1. Conservatives believe that there are very hard and fast rules to life. Natural right usually being one of them. Right and wrong is also one of those rules, that there is actually such a concept, and it has nothing to do with what you think. Right is right no matter where you live, when you live, who you are. It's a

---

[19] Kirk, Russell. *The Conservative Mind*. Regnery: Washington, DC, p. 8-9

truth, not an opinion. For instance, slavery. Slavery is wrong, no matter who you are and when and where you live. Now, it may be a more forgivable sin for a sixth century BCE Athenian to have owned a slave than for someone in nineteenth century America, because of the different cultures, the development of philosophy, the arguable economic necessity to have a slave class in ancient civilizations, but it was still wrong. Justice, Virtue, Liberty, all these concepts have an aspect of truth to them and as such are part of the natural order of the universe. We should govern a society as best we can according to these rules.

This is opposed to the liberal tendency to try things that are not only contradictory to common sense, but human nature in general. For instance, that wacky liberal idea that says we can have a better world, just so long as you give up your property rights (taxes, taxes, and some more taxes). Not only is this idea repugnant on principle, but I haven't noticed it working. Probably because as that conservative belief in rules goes, ethics and pragmatics aren't completely separated in the real world.

2. Conservatives believe that life is worth living. Obviously, we believe it should be lived according to those natural rules of order, but believe it or not, between what is absolutely always good for everyone and what is unquestionably wrong for everyone is a lot of gray. First off, sadly, we're only human and we can't be expected just yet to know all the rules. More importantly, even if we had all the rules, there are still a million different ways to live each life according to those rules. Life is a giant smorgasbord of choices and

Republicans and Reincarnation

opportunities and beliefs and chances. The rules will point you in a general direction, how you get there is up to you, and to a traditional conservative (this will unfortunately change with the advent of "social conservatism") this means looking to society and its traditions and norms. However, even a conservative will admit that these traditions are not set in stone and when they come blatantly in contrast with reason and common sense, they should not be held to.

The liberal counterpart to this is liberal tendency of telling people how to live their lives (and yes, I admit people who call themselves conservatives nowadays are guilty of this sin too, I'll get to that later). The extreme form of this is the nature of socialist countries putting you on an education track from an early age and basically deciding what your job, class, and income level will be for the rest of your life from how you do on a 4th grade test (and it's even worse in communist countries).

3. Let me repeat #3 for a minute because this is a trickier one: Conservatives have a "conviction that civilized society requires orders and classes." What! I hear you shouting, are you saying we keep people in classes, castes, making the poor poor and the rich rich, and never the twain shall meet! As usual, as I hope you figured out by now that when I anticipate your shock at something I've just said, the answer is . . . No. But there are rich people and there are poor people. There are smart and dumb, nice and mean ones, driven and lazy ones, talented and rather dull ones (believe me, my day job is as a high school teacher, I've seen the whole spectrum). And the fact of the matter is

there is nothing wrong with having rich people and poor people, as long as they're rich, poor, or middle class based on their merits. Contrary to what your average liberal believes, if I'm smart, driven, talented, and amiable enough to make connections then, yes, I do deserve more than that lazy, stupid, untalented jerk who thinks the government should subsidize his journey through being a couch potato. It's the great thing about democratic representative government and capitalism—people get what they deserve for the most part. Yeah there are problems, but look at the societies that try to get rid of classes: France immediately after the French Revolution (the first liberals to try to put their ideas into practice) . . . watch your head, it might come off . . . or we could try Soviet Russia where everyone is in the same class, a class called miserable and wishing for death to end the pain. While classes are a natural thing, what does need to be improved and monitored is the assurance that opportunities of promotion through life are kept on a purely meritocracy based system, and all forms of overt racism, sexism, and the like are kept down by the government and openly if not radically opposed by individuals.

4. Now really do I need to explain this one? Just for the sake of reiteration, but not to insult your intelligence, I will. The more a government regulates the economy, no matter how good the intentions, the less freedom you have. I'm not talking about freedom in the sense of you can do whatever you want; I'm talking about freedom in sense of doing what's right. Laws are a necessary tool in modern society, but the more laws we have to deal with, the more time we have to spend

making sure we do not run afoul of these rather arbitrary laws. The more time we take to worry about arbitrary laws, the less time we have to make our lives happy. More importantly, while money doesn't buy happiness, it is necessary for happiness and the more money the government has the less you have . . . and the more things the government can do with that money to screw up your life.

5. I can quote "faith in prescription and distrust of 'sophisters, calculators, and economists' who would reconstruct society upon abstract designs" but what does that really mean? It means we don't like intellectuals who sit in their ivory towers telling us how the world runs. Yes, experts have their use, many uses, but they seldom have any use in telling people how things should be done. Academics have really weird ideas on how the world should work, and very little common sense on how the world does work. Case in point, academics in colleges across the country are far more often socialists and communists than the general public, and because they have more education than the general public they like to think that they know better. Unfortunately, for them, real life tells us that socialism and communism never works well. Further, if my education taught me anything, it was to not trust people with education just because they have an education. In the modern world a B.A. is more a sign that someone has the drive to complete something difficult than it is a sign that they actually know something . . . to most people, and in many but not all cases rightfully so, a M.A. or Ph.D. is more a sign of a person who is a little too disconnected from the real world and too obsessed

with their books and studies (not to say that applies to all people with advanced degrees, but certainly a good portion). Why we should listen to these people when they have no practical evidence on their side more than our own common sense is beyond the ken of any conservative.[20]

6. Finally, no conservative resists change, as some liberals would have you believe, but a conservative does resist change that is not calculated, deliberate, well reasoned, and slow enough that its effects can be observed and its course readjusted should it need such a change. Society never reacts too well to sudden change. Thus, change should be slow. And change should never be attempted on a grand scale that has no basis other than pure abstraction. There should be some basis in history or having been tried on a smaller scale and worked successfully. Conservatives are an ethical and principled bunch, but we are also pragmatic. The system that is based on the best principles and still doesn't work . . . still doesn't work. If a system works partially and adheres to our principles, we'll take it if it is an improvement on the old system, and like the old system try to tinker with it slowly to improve it . . . but if no ethical option is open, we'll take the lesser of two evils that works.

So, conservatives believe in small government, capitalism, meritocracy, tradition, and slow change. Great, you say, so what's the problem . . . why don't I see that when I look at conservatives on the TV? Why is it that

---

[20] However, I think no conservative would disagree with the point that far too much of the general public is ignorant, lazy, or just plain stupid.

all "conservatives" on the political shows seem to want to only talk about keeping abortion and gay marriage illegal? There are three answers to this question. 1. Many people like to call themselves conservatives with having no idea what the word means (there are idiots in every political party, live with it). 2. A good portion of the media is liberal, and they like to pull out only the really wacky 'conservatives' to trot out for the public (not to mention the fact, whether you're liberal or conservative, you don't stand the best of chances of getting near a microphone unless you're a few cards short of a full deck). And 3. Well that's going to take another brief history lesson (sorry, I'll try to make this as painless as possible).

"Bad laws are the worst sort of tyranny."—Edmund Burke

Traditionally, any history of conservatism begins with a British statesman named Edmund Burke. Were there conservatives alive before Burke? Of course, he didn't just pull his idea out of thin air; however, Burke is the first man to fully articulate the cornerstones of conservative Liberal thought as an opposition to liberal Liberal thought. Burke held to the Liberal idea of liberty and limited government, and was a champion against tyranny, and one of America's most vocal supporters in the British Parliament before and during the Revolutionary War. However, unlike many modern liberals, Burke did not believe in liberty to the point of insanity, and while a supporter of the American Revolution, was possibly one of the strongest critics of the French Revolution for it's desire to turn society upside down instantaneously and for (as Burke predicted) falling quite easily into tyranny and bloodshed. Burke saw government as a social contract as his Classical Liberal predecessors had, but he did not just see it as a contract between the government and the people. For Burke the contract was between not only the government and people but also with all future generations.

> "*Society is indeed a contract.* Subordinate contracts for objects of mere occasional interest may be dissolved at pleasure—but the state ought not to be considered as nothing better than a partnership agreement in a trade of pepper and coffee, calico or tobacco, or some other such low concern, to be taken up for a little temporary interest, and to be dissolved by the fancy of the parties. It is to be looked on with other reverence; because it is not a partnership in things subservient only to the gross animal existence of a temporary and perishable nature. It is a partnership in all science; a partnership in all art; a partnership in every virtue, and in all perfection. *As the ends of such a partnership cannot be obtained in many generations, it becomes a partnership not only between those who are living, but between those who are to be born. Each contract of each particular state is but a clause in the great primaeval contract of eternal society, linking the lower with the higher natures, connecting the visible and the invisible world, according to a fixed compact sanctioned by the inviolable oath which holds all physical and all moral natures, each in their appointed place.*" [Italics added][21]

---

[21] Burke, Reflections on the Revolution in France.

Republicans and Reincarnation

For Burke the past also had its reserved place, as that which we gain all knowledge, and to ignore it would be a most grievous mistake.

Burke championed the standard for the Classical Liberal and conservative belief that representative government was just that, representative. Elected officials were not to be just mouthpieces for public opinion but were elected to exercise their reason and judgment, not parrot their constituents.

One of Burke's chief complaints about what we would now call liberals is their desire to completely change the world. The American Revolution, which Burke supported, originally sought nothing but that the rights of the colonists as British citizens be continued. They wanted the status quo, and only when they were deprived of it did they say goodbye to merry old England. The French Revolution had no such sanity. The French Revolution didn't even seek to instill the ideas of Classical Liberalism. The butchers behind the French Revolution sought to turn society upside down, and do it immediately. While predating Marx, the French Revolution in principal at different points attempted to create a communist utopia (a plan that has always historically failed, usually ending in genocide). And while the French Revolution failed, the liberal desire to remake society overnight has not, and it is this insane feature of liberalism that Burke, and his philosophical descendants, detested and fought against.

I could go into great detail of all of the developments in conservative thought after Burke. Names such as Washington, Adams, Monroe, Calhoun, Churchill, and a list of writers you probably haven't heard of since high school English would probably come up. But conservatism is an ever changing philosophy, its foundations and principles hardly ever change, but the specifics of individual philosophies do adapt to the times and places they exist in—and quite frankly most of the history lesson would be just showing the same principles over and over again, in situations that don't have a direct application to the modern world.

So we turn to modern conservatism, and modern conservatism begins officially with an Arizona Senator named Barry Goldwater. While there are many writers, politicians, and philosophers who had expressed the ideals of conservatism and the problems that face the world of the last hundred years or so, Goldwater's presidential election campaign in 1964, was the first opportunity for conservatives to have control over how the government is run (even though it was an opportunity we lost). It was still a symbolic restart of conservative values in American policy, which had been near dead for many decades.

Barry Goldwater was a rather blunt, shoot from the hip, US Senator from what was at the time the rather unimportant state of Arizona. Overcoming, to the shock of some, his more established, and more liberal, east coast Republican rivals he became the Republican nominee for the 1964 presidential nomination. And while he lost in a bitter campaign to Lyndon B. Johnson, he redirected the course of the Republican Party from a party slightly less liberal than the Democrats, to a party of conservatives with such ideals as the following from his acceptance speech at the 1964 Republican convention:

> "We Republicans see in our constitutional form of government the great framework which assures the orderly but dynamic fulfillment of the whole man, and we see the whole man as the great

reason for instituting orderly government in the first place."

And:

> We see—We see in private property and in economy based upon and fostering private property, the one way to make government a durable ally of the whole man, rather than his determined enemy. We see in the sanctity of private property the only durable foundation for constitutional government in a free society. And—And beyond that, we see, in cherished diversity of ways, diversity of thoughts, of motives and accomplishments. We don't seek to lead anyone's life for him. We only seek—only seek to secure his rights, guarantee him opportunity—guarantee him opportunity to strive, with government performing only those needed and constitutionally sanctioned tasks which cannot otherwise be performed."

And of course:

> "I would remind you that extremism in the defense of liberty is no vice. And let me remind you also that moderation in the pursuit of justice is no virtue."

Goldwater provided a philosophical base for the modern conservative era. Less Government. Strict Constitutional application of governmental power. Free Market. Strong Defense. States Rights. The Individual above all.

One of the major points to come out of Goldwater's run for president was turning a mediocre actor and former head of the Screen Actor's Guild into a major political force. That's right we are now going to skip the 60's (because the behavior of that decade has almost nothing to do with conservatism) and 70's (because wouldn't we all like to forget the 70's ever happened) and skip straight to conservatism actually becoming more than a neat idea bantered around the dinner table or by the minority in congress, but as the major force in the country. And the man that this centers around is none other than Ronald Reagan.

Reagan's philosophy of conservatism can best be first pointed to in his Goldwater campaign speech "A Time for Choosing" which includes such statements as:

> And this idea that government is beholden to the people, that it has no other source of power except the sovereign people, is still the newest and the most unique idea in all the long history of man's relation to man.

> This is the issue of this election: Whether we believe in our capacity for self-government or whether we abandon the American revolution and confess that a little intellectual elite in a far-distant capitol can plan our lives for us better than we can plan them ourselves . . .

> . . . Yet anytime you and I question the schemes of the do-gooders, we're denounced as being against their humanitarian goals. They say we're always "against" things—we're never "for" anything.

Republicans and Reincarnation

Well, the trouble with our liberal friends is not that they're ignorant; it's just that they know so much that isn't so . . .

. . . No government ever voluntarily reduces itself in size. So, governments' programs, once launched, never disappear.

Actually, a government bureau is the nearest thing to eternal life we'll ever see on this earth . . . .

. . . Those who would trade our freedom for the soup kitchen of the welfare state have told us they have a utopian solution of peace without victory. They call their policy "accommodation." And they say if we'll only avoid any direct confrontation with the enemy, he'll forget his evil ways and learn to love us. All who oppose them are indicted as warmongers. They say we offer simple answers to complex problems. Well, perhaps there is a simple answer—not an easy answer—but simple: If you and I have the courage to tell our elected officials that we want our national policy based on what we know in our hearts is morally right.

We cannot buy our security, our freedom from the threat of the bomb by committing an immorality so great as saying to a billion human beings now enslaved behind the Iron Curtain, 'Give up your dreams of freedom because to save our own skins, we're willing to make a deal with your slave masters.' Alexander Hamilton said, 'A nation which can prefer disgrace to danger is prepared for a master,

> and deserves one.' Now let's set the record straight. There's no argument over the choice between peace and war, but there's only one guaranteed way you can have peace—and you can have it in the next second—surrender.
>
> Admittedly, there's a risk in any course we follow other than this, but every lesson of history tells us that the greater risk lies in appeasement, and this is the specter our well-meaning liberal friends refuse to face—that their policy of accommodation is appeasement, and it gives no choice between peace and war, only between fight or surrender . . .

Throughout Reagan's governorship of California, and later his presidency, he kept to these and a few other central concepts. The most important of these was a belief in capitalism and the defense of America. He was not perfect, nor did he never make a mistake,[22] but he always acted on what he believed to be in the best interest of the country he unquestionably loved.

However, out of Reagan's presidency came the four main strands of modern conservatism: Economic, Social, and Neoconservatism, and shortly after Reagan the bastardization called Compassionate Conservatism reared its ugly and mentally handicapped head. We'll deal with each of these separately (and as briefly as possible). While all of these claim the title of conservative, they are not all in line with the principles of conservative thought and are really only conservative in name.

---

[22] Just look at the weak-willed buffoon he picked as his V.P.

Economic Conservatism

"History suggests only that capitalism is a necessary condition for political freedom. Clearly it is not a sufficient condition."—Milton Friedman, Capitalism and Freedom

Modern economic conservatism is, believe it or not, what I have previously referred to as economic Liberalism. Although your average American may be a little more familiar with its other name: Reaganomics. While Reagan certainly didn't invent these principles, he certainly tried to adhere to them as best he could (that is the best anyone could with a spend happy Democratic Congress holding key defense bills at ransom). These are of course the ideas that the less government we have the better. That fewer departments of the government, less regulation, heavier enforcement of the regulations that do exist (this is the one that the government often forgets to do), no tariffs, free trade, and lower taxes create far more prosperous economies.

One of the key features of modern conservative economic thought, in addition to adherence to the previous points I've made, is that lower taxes are better for any society. This is predicated on a theory called the supply side economics, which, among other things, states that if a government lowers taxes then more money will be available to the general public. The general public from the bottom of the barrel poor to the richest of the rich will all then have more money to one degree or another. What will they do with that money? What do you do when you have money? You spend it or invest it. Very few people still put money under the mattress so that money is put into use in one form or another into the economy. One way or another, this will translate to profit for companies (some of you are having some kind of revulsion to the word profit. If this is the case, slap yourself, profit is good and I'm about to show you why). These companies will do one of two things with their profits: either give to their shareholders or invest it. If shareholders get it, they'll invest it in all likelihood, so, in one way or another, the majority of the money is being invested. What do companies do with invested money? Well they give raises, they hire more people, and they build new divisions that also require the hiring of new people. One way or another people are going to have more money from either getting a raise or getting a new job. More money for everyone starts this whole cycle over again to a lesser degree, but still it revolves through creating even more growth. Moreover, what the supply side economics theory says is that since everyone has more money then there is more money to tax, and although less of a percentage is being taken, since it's a bigger pie being taken from, the government actually comes out with the exact same amount of money. And believe it or not, history and the numbers have borne this theory out to be correct. Just consider that the 2007 receipts for the IRS were the largest recorded in history (look up number in millions) and consider that is after Bush's much hated tax cuts and in light of such economic bad news as 9/11, skyrocketing oil prices, Katrina, and Iraq. I would be an idiot to say that the tax cuts were the only reason for the windfall at the IRS—economics is far too complex a function of society to have only one cause for any single event—but it would also be patently foolish to believe they were not a factor. Further, one must keep in mind that these effects are not instantaneous, nor should one assume that even after the time delay effect the government will be taking in the exact same real amount of dollars—it won't—but only a fool would believe higher taxes are better for the economy.

Now theoretically you could lower taxes too low (we aren't there yet) or not regulate certain industries enough (which we have seen) to actually be capitalistic. Capitalism means a bare minimum government influence, not a complete lack government involvement.

But aside from just making more money, conservatives hold true to capitalism with minimal government interference because it is absolutely necessary for liberty. The more money you have the more freedom in choices you have, this is an obvious fact of life, and that includes the freedom to make mistakes or do nothing. More than that, the more economic freedom a country has is often one of the most reliable indicators of how free politically that country is. A government that allows people to use their money in whatever way they choose is a government that is founded on the belief that people should be free.

NeoConservatism

"The world must be made safe for democracy. Its peace must be planted upon the tested foundations of political liberty. We have no selfish ends to serve. We desire no conquest, no dominion. We seek no indemnities for ourselves, no material compensation for the sacrifices we shall freely make. We are

Cris A. Pace

> *but one of the champions of the rights of mankind. We shall be satisfied when those rights have been made as secure as the faith and the freedom of nations can make them."*
> —*President Woodrow Wilson*[23]

Neoconservatism is actually a broad theory resting on three principals: (1) economic freedom which I've already discussed, (2) social conservatism which I'll get to later with much disdain, and (3) international interventionist tendencies which is what I want to deal with right now as it is what is most often associated with the term neoconservative. Now a more nuanced discussion of policy would reveal that not everyone who agreed with the foreign policy I'm about to set forth is a neoconservative, but I'm getting the feeling that you're about to track me down and beat me with the nearest blunt object if I don't just get to the point, so once again we're just going to simplify things for the sake of hitting the major points.

Now what is this neocon belief about foreign policy? Well, if you listen to some on the left it is the idea that neocons like war for the sake of war or war for the sake of helping out their business partners. Then again, I get the feeling some on the left are convinced that Republicans like to drink the blood of infants . . . so let's leave the opinions of the left out of this.

The foreign policy aspects of the Neoconservatism began in the 1970's with a strong desire to see an end to Communist expansion in the world. It was a policy

---

[23] Yes, I realize Wilson is not a conservative by any stretch of the imagination. But the sentiment of this quote is a good one. And as someone who cherishes reason I can find truth even in the words of my opponents.

originally stated by Barry Goldwater and quite expertly continued by Ronald Reagan. Early neocons sought not just to ensure containment of Communism in the sense that no more countries would fall to it they set out on a long term goal of seeing an absolute end to the conflict and the destruction of communism. Luckily, for everyone involved Communism contains the seeds of its own destruction in its insane and inept beliefs about human nature. Thus no major war was required to destroy the Soviet Union which collapsed under the weight of its own failing communist economy; Communist China, in an attempt to not repeat Russia's mistakes has already begun capitalist reform that will likely lead to either democratic reform or a revolution that will likely give us a democratic country within two or three generations. However, with the fall of Communist power in the world, the Neoconservative belief evolved into the idea that humanity is on an upward climb toward liberty, thus America must export liberty through economics, diplomacy, and if necessary war wherever possible.

This is actually a very dividing idea in the conservative movement. Many conservatives point out, quite rightly, that conservatism is a philosophy that despises war and wishes to avoid its evils at all costs, not only for the cost in terms of economics and loss of life, but also for the very reason that war almost always leaves a government with more power than it had before the war began. Others would point out, again rightly so, that in modern day with such problems as Islamofascism as a major threat, we are at war whether we admit it or not, and only by admitting this problem will we be able to reach a state of peace which conservatives want.

The neoconservative strain of foreign policy does share with the origins of conservatism, and with Liberalism, the innate belief that all beings are "endowed with certain, inalienable rights." Further those who adhere to this interventionist foreign policy, whether they would identify themselves as neocons or not, tend to believe that as it is government's responsibility to protect liberty, just because its not your own country one cannot just sit idly by as others have their liberties torn asunder (that policy worked so well in the 1930's if you'll recall). That to ignore abuses elsewhere in the world is what allows evil to exist and in the end puts the blood on our hands for our non-intervention. When one considers the 6 million victims of the Holocaust, plus I am frightened to calculate the number of dead from the century's other acts of genocide, due to America not wanting to get involved, that's a lot of blood to wash off our hands. And make no mistake, our indifference has made us guilty. Hence the desire of most interventionists to stop as many of these genocides as possible.

Social Conservatism

"The good Lord raised this mighty Republic to be a home for the brave and to flourish as the land of the free—not to stagnate in the swampland of collectivism"—Barry Goldwater, Acceptance of Republican Nomination Speech 1964

Why this is called conservatism is an idea that constantly baffles me to no end. Social conservatism became a main issue in modern day politics under what

Republicans and Reincarnation

is known as the Reagan Revolution. Reagan's campaign team was able to join true conservatives, moderates (known as Reagan Democrats), and religious groups (most notably Jerry Falwell's "Moral Majority") to get Reagan elected to the White House. It is this religious group that has created modern social conservatism.

Now, as I said before conservatives like tradition. Burke considered society a contract between not only those who are living, but also between those who are living, those who are dead, and those who are to be born. As part of this contract, we take those traditions from the past, and as a good conservative, try to keep them as long as they serve their purpose (but no longer). Now social conservatives take this many steps further and believe it is the government's job to not just adhere to tradition but to enforce tradition—and not just enforce traditions as long as they serve their purpose, but rather to ensure stagnation. And I'm not just talking about traditions of government, but traditions of society. Of the major issues that social conservative busybodies like to concern themselves with are abortion, the institution of marriage, pornography, homosexuality, and what is taught in classrooms (on a good day . . . on a bad day I have to hear drivel about the crap that Hollywood puts out).

Nonetheless, social conservatives forgot one major tradition of Liberal government, and that was Liberal governments don't get involved in the social lives of its citizens. Social traditions are, traditionally, the purview of parents, church, to a very small degree education, and the social community that a person lives in—but most importantly they are the purview of the individual. It used to not be the tradition of government to get involved in these things—government was originally for protecting you from other people's violent natures and from other governments. Morality had nothing to do with government; we had society itself to fulfill that function.

Social conservatives are actually everything a conservative hates. They are people who to extend the powers of the government to include such things as what kind of sexual practices consenting adults should engage in. What *consenting adults*[24] want to do with each other in privacy, as long as their not plotting criminal acts that will harm other people, it's not my concern—and it shouldn't be the government's either. I really couldn't care less if sodomy is going on in someone's house between consenting adults, because, guess what, it has absolutely no bearing on my life in any way shape or form, never will, never could. Yet up until 2003 there were laws against it in this country . . . ? . . . Who in their right mind thought that such a thing needed to be made a crime? Did they have nothing better to do that day than to pass a law like that?

The main reason this group of extremist tends to exist and isn't laughed out of politics is that the liberal fronts of America have extremists of their own with the exact opposite agenda. Normal thinking Americans are forced to tolerate battles between church wackos that

---

[24] I just want to emphasize the term "consenting adults" here. Two very important words. For instance outlawing, jailing, and (I, who am generally against the death penalty, still wouldn't really voice an objection to) executing NAMBLA and all its members for endorsing the rape of children isn't social conservatism, it's common sense and basic morality and certainly within the purview of any just government in protecting people from the violence of others.

want to put the Ten Commandments on every public building and ACLU crazies who want to ban every cross in America or any sign that anyone in this country believes in a god. Without one set of lunatics to counter balance the other we would likely be in a Puritan colony or a communist commune, as neither is a particularly pleasant idea, both sides must either be tolerated . . . or we could do the smart thing and tell both sides to keep their screwball ideas to themselves.

If you'll remember that list of the foundations of conservatism, I would point you back to the second point, that conservatives have an "affection for the proliferating variety and mystery of human existence[.]" Conservatives, true conservatives, believe that life is a mystery, and no matter how much we would like to think we understand what God intends for our life, we are reasonable beings that cannot have absolute certainty of God's intentions . . . and if you have absolute certainty I better see some major miracles before I'm going to believe you actually know. And since we cannot have absolute certainty, even those things which we may find morally repugnant, if they do not harm us or anyone else, a true conservative will be disgusted, and may choose many a method to stop these practices, but none of those methods would be the government.

Still, don't for a second think that social conservatism has anything to do with the philosophy of conservatism. It doesn't.

Compassionate Conservatism

Cris A. Pace

> *"Government is never more dangerous than when our desire to have it help us blinds it to its great power to harm us."—Ronald Reagan, Acceptance Speech Republican Convention 1980*

Here's another term that gets thrown around these days, but really has nothing to do with the philosophy of conservatism. Like social conservatives wanting to use the government to control what you do with you genitals, compassionate conservatives also don't understand what the words "limited government" mean.

Compassionate conservatives are really a bunch of apologists for the philosophy of conservatism. They believe that in the face of liberal desire to create a welfare state, they will compromise and give liberals half of what they want and only create a partial welfare state. These are predominantly politicians more afraid of what pundits will say and of losing some votes than actually holding to their supposedly conservative beliefs.

This has led to "conservatives" like George W. Bush who is far too willing to spend money on welfare projects, and creating a Medicare reform, not to mention $700 billion giveaways that will in the end just further drive this country in ruin. As such while a true conservative would like to at least halt the expansion of government powers, if not give them a heavy cutting, compassionate conservatives seek to create new powers and new programs.

Anyone who says that they are a compassionate conservative really isn't compassionate. Is the parent who says they want to be their child's friend compassionate? No, that makes them a friend and nothing else. Parents like that are permissive and poor role models; more often than not, they raise brats who know nothing of responsibility and only of immediate gratification. No parent like that could be called compassionate. Just the same, most politicians who look for this label are seeking to avoid being called mean or cold, and for the opinion of the public are willing to put the future of this country in jeopardy.

Compassionate conservatives are neither.

If you're a little confused at this point, I wouldn't be surprised. How on earth could New Age beliefs that this world isn't real, and conservative beliefs in logic and reason and tradition, in other words in a very real world, ever coexist? How can these disparate philosophies, each with numerous subdivisions, ever see eye to eye. Well actually they do.

Chapter 4
LET FREEDOM RING! SHARING THE SAME CORNERSTONE OF BELIEF

"Knowledge of Three things are necessary for the salvation of man: to know what he ought to believe; to know what he ought to desire; and to know what he ought to do."—St. Thomas Aquinas, Two Precepts of Charity.

And we come to that really annoying piece of seemingly contradictory logic. If this world is an illusion, a product of soul's imagining, one big dream . . . why should we care about how it works and more importantly why should we care about living in it? Shouldn't we only care about waking up right now, getting out of this dream, and nightmare for some of us, and leave it all behind. Yeah, that would be great, kinda wish I could write that one sentence that would make us all immediately go to enlightenment . . . but regrettably, I don't know what the words to do that are. And if history is any indicator neither do the enlightened beings who cross our paths from time to time.

A friend of mine once told me "The problem, as I see it, is that Democrats want to change the world for the better, but have no clue about how the world works, and the Republicans understand completely how the world works, but have little desire to change it." (On a further down note, with the advent of social conservatism and compassionate conservatism it can no longer be said that Republicans understand how the world works.) I bring this line up because it in some way illustrates the two philosophies of New Agers and conservatives. A conservative philosophy, probably better than any other philosophy, understands how this world works and how to operate in it. A New Ager understands, or so I believe, the nature of existence (in the sense that this world is only an illusion) better than most. Both understand the world, but they understand different worlds. While a New Ager may want to change this world to model the true nature of existence most don't really know how to enact that kind of change.

However, before we can get conservatives to recognize the true nature of the universe or get New Agers to deal in this world if only for a time, we have to see the points where and why these two philosophies work together. The first, and possibly most important, of these is freedom.

Free Will & Liberty

"Give me liberty or give me death."—Patrick Henry
"He [God] tells you but your will; He speaks for you. In his Divinity is but your own. And all He knows is but your knowledge, saved for you that you may do your will through Him. God asks you do your will."—A Course in Miracles, Chapter 30:II Freedom of Will

Here is the point that most religions don't get, because they don't fully believe in free will: Religions don't save people; prophets and saints don't save people; books of holy scripture don't save people; other people don't save people—individuals can only save themselves. Many religions believe that you can't find your own salvation;

it has to be granted to you, because even if you have perfect free will, it's what got you into trouble. Hence such sayings as "Not my will, but thine [God's] be done." So many religions believe you have to subvert your will to God's, because your free will is bad, and his isn't. Thus your own will, except through the choice of subverting your will, can't save you.

Now New Age philosophy does not say this is wrong. But they do say it isn't completely correct. Just as Newton was correct about gravity, but Einstein was more correct, such is the traditional western view of free will and the New Age view. Man does not choose between his will and God's, because his will and God's are one in the same. Man chooses between following that part of his soul that wills love and that part that wills fear. If that seems like extreme hair-splitting, I'll admit it is, but it's an import hair to split[25]. The typical New Age view sees the human mind/soul split into two parts one is the true part of the real universe, which is in contact with God; the other part is the part that was created when we made some mistake eons ago that separated us from God[26]. This second part is based in fear and conflict and separation. Our consciousness is somewhere in between and it's not so much as choosing between these two sides as realizing that one of these sides doesn't exist. A good analogy might be that children do not will themselves or

[25] Nor is it a revolutionary hair to split. Plato and Aristotle were splitting the human soul into a battle of reason and passion long ago.

[26] Typically the New Age term for this side is called the Ego, and the side connected to God is called the soul. However, this has almost nothing to do with ego in sense of arrogance or in the Freudian Ego/Id/Superego sense.

choose to not be afraid of the monsters under their bed; they just eventually realize they don't exist.

Still free will is a very important concept in New Age belief, because if we focus on fear, then it interferes with our true will, which happens to be God's will too. Thus, New Age beliefs really dislike things that try to get in the way of free will. Guilt and fear imposed by culture, society, and religion (guilt and fear are big with traditional religions). But also, more immediate impediments to free will. Getting shot in the head, for instance, is a major problem in exercising one's free will, even for a New Ager who believes in reincarnation it is at least a major problem in the short term. Debilitating diseases, extreme poverty, fear of nuclear holocaust, living under tyranny, all major hindrances in carrying out free will. This will if nothing else, delay the return of the soul to God by that much longer.

Therefore, in many ways many parts of this world, religion (or at least religion when poorly used), in particular, is an obstacle to free will. Which explains many New Ager's distaste for organized religion, we tend to forget that it has its good parts too, lots of beautiful and wonderful parts.

And the corresponding point to the idea that salvation is not given by religion in politics is that liberty is not given by governments, it is actually according to conservatives an obstacle to liberty in most cases. The more laws, the less liberty. The less liberty, the less of a chance a person has to pursue happiness. Liberty is achieved by individuals in how they live their lives and government only offering protection from outside interference, without getting in the way itself.

So what is the point of religions and government? Well to a New Ager or a Conservative the answer is the same: while religion and/or government cannot give salvation and/or liberty, they can remove the obstacles in your way. Guilt is an obstacle to enlightenment; religion (at its best) can help you relieve your guilt. Tyranny is an obstacle to liberty; the proper government can prevent tyranny. And this is the cornerstone that both these philosophies share. Free will and liberty are almost (though not perfectly) interchangeable concepts, and while they may not be exactly the same thing neither can come to its fullest fruition without the other. Life without the full use of free will and liberty will not lead to happiness in this life, nor enlightenment in the next.

Now an intelligent person would likely point out that you still have free will even if you have a gun to your head or if you're being tortured on the rack, a state that completely lacks any liberty. And an intelligent New Ager might even go as far as to point out that due to karma and the nature of the cycle of rebirth, you choose to put yourself in that situation, thus the torture is in itself an act of free will because there is the possibility of learning something from that experience. These would be excellent objections, except for the fact, as Aristotle pointed out it is not enough to have something unless you're going to use it to it's fullest. You have a life if you're breathing, but you're not really living if all you can do is breathe, because life is more than a biological function, it's mental and spiritual function as well. So it is with free will, just because you still have a choice of whether to take being on the rack as something to despair over or to face stoically does not mean you have free will in the fullest sense of what free will was intended to be. So to live the full life and to use free will in the full sense requires liberty.

Quality versus Quantity of Life

"Death is more universal than life; everyone dies but not everyone lives."—A. Sachs

Now a second cornerstone belief shared by both philosophies, and hinted at in the last section, is distinguishing between the quality and the quantity of life. Whereas our liberal adversaries or Christians may show great concern over the quantity of life, conservatives and New Agers have more concern over the quality of life.

What I mean by quantity of life is the idea of the biological function. The years on earth, the state of health, to a degree the amount of money and stuff you have (although these do play some role in the quality of your life as well). What I mean by quality is the spiritual and mental functions of life being used to the fullest extent. Having full use of your free will, having education to know how to use your free will, being happy. For instance, I would say that a woman who lived only into her 30's, dying of a degenerative disease, but who had close friends, created moving works of art, and touched those in her life has a life of great quality. Compare that with a woman who lives into her 80's in the upper middle class, bitter, never having done anything with her life other than being a housewife (and hating every minute of it) and who has distant and cold relations of mutual disdain with her children, dying alone. Certainly the second woman had more stuff, longer life, better health, but you wouldn't call that a better life, in fact the example I give sounds more like a complete waste of a life in which nothing was learned, and no positive effect on the world was made. These are extreme examples, I'll admit, but it illustrates what I mean by quality versus quantity.

For the New Agers this is easy to understand—if you have a possibly infinite number of reincarnated lives to learn from, how long you live your life becomes an exceedingly irrelevant matter. What a New Ager cares about is how much is learned in the time that you have, not how long or how much you have in that life. Now it's very understandable why someone who believes they only get one shot before they are judged for all time, that they would want as much time as possible before the end[27].

But this dichotomy is more obvious in the difference between liberals and conservatives. Liberals are more than willing to ruin the quality of life for not only the rich but also the middle class if they believe it will help the masses. Don't believe me, just look at FDR's socialistic plans of the New Deal, or LBJ's nearly communistic Great Society, which nearly gutted the middle class to create a welfare state. (And that's not even to mention that the fact that these plans don't really help the masses that they were intended to aid). When you try to aid the most number of people without thinking about what you're doing to the quality of living of other people, you're not only trying idiotically to please all the people all the time, but also ignoring the basic logic of reality.

---

[27] Now I am not saying that all Christians have a quantity over quality mentality, far from it. But any honest look would reveal it is a very prevalent belief.

Republicans and Reincarnation

To take this extreme let's look at the philosophy of communist ideology (wasn't the phrase "Better Red than Dead" a liberal expression? A perfect example of valuing the quantity of life over the quality). The belief in the quality of life comes from a belief in the individual human soul. Ignoring for the moment that communism rejects the idea of a soul; it more disturbingly rejects the idea of the individual. Thus, only the plans that aid the whole, or at least the most, are considered valuable. This is preposterous if not insane. How the whole could have value, while the individual does not. I realize that the whole is greater than the sum of its parts, but even that statement assumes the parts have some value. So if the whole is to have any value the parts must have some value too (you can't add a bunch of zeroes together and say it adds to more than zero). So if an individual has value, even if it is infinitesimal in comparison to the whole, then one cannot justify the acts against the quality of that individual's life by saying how many people will be helped.

What do I mean by this? Well, for instance, let's take the case of the joke that is the national education system.[28] Now, the typical liberal answer to the education system would be more money, more teachers, and more schools. A fairly quantitative solution. The slight problem is that the liberal belief that throwing money at a situation can solve it (welfare, healthcare, the environment, world aid) never seems to work. There is a simple reason for this, more schools or teachers, and to a great degree more money for teachers won't solve the problem. Why? Because let's say you double the amount of schools in the country and get teachers to staff them. You haven't solved

---

[28] And before you ask, Bush and his No Child Left Behind Act, don't even come close to being conservative or qualitative.

the most inherent problem in our current education system—most teachers are morons! And they're protected by even bigger morons in the teacher's unions! What did you think would happen when you have a concept like tenure, which says that no matter how inept you are at your job, your employer can't fire you without cause (cause for a school would constitute enough to fire a hundred people in any normal job). And then when they fire the moron, the teacher's union will sue the school. Get rid of the teacher's unions, start firing the incompetent, and hold everyone—staff, faculty and students—to professional and rigorous standards and you'll probably have a lower rate of burnout among competent teachers and won't even have to raise their salaries to get good teachers. (Although if the quality of teaching went up in the country, I wouldn't complain if the country chose to reward them with a raise, further to start attracting the more qualified we may have to put the cart before the horse and up salaries first, but I'll get to that later). But notice most reforms you hear about focus on money and occasionally test scores (quantitative) and not standards and professionalism (qualitative). This is because more schools and more money and more teachers can be easily observed and thus if you can see it must be helping.

Aside from this particular pragmatic example, this attitude has the effect of caring about the number of people helped, not how well or even if they really are being helped, leads to a mentality of where the government is seen as higher than the individual citizen. Because the government can help more people than the individual, so what if it's a little less money, or a little less freedom, or a little less choice . . . we're helping more people . . . . But not really because government can never do anything better than the private sector (a whole lot of individuals), and also government never tends to stop with a little money or a little encroachment on freedom. It always has to take the next step. (There are many more aspects of education reform that need to be addressed, and will be in Chapter 11)

However, before you think I'm completely heartless, I am not suggesting the other extreme to this—I'm not. Yes, quality of life is important, it's very important. But quantity of life is also import. If it's the choice between one person living a really good life or a million living an okay life . . . oh, tough call . . . go with the million. The problem is that life is seldom that cut and dried. But I'm sure some of you are thinking of the old maxim that the needs of the many outweigh the needs of the few. Basic logical principal. But this is only if you are faced with helping this group or helping that group. Life seldom presents such easy choices. The government more often sacrifices the rights, property, or liberties, or opportunities of one group to help another. And ethically it is wrong, if not evil, to sacrifice any group or individual for any group no matter how large unless that sacrifice is voluntary. And since government can never do anything without sacrificing someone or something, quantity should and can never be a deciding factor.

Long Term Planning

"Think ahead. Don't let day-to-day operations drive out planning."—Donald Rumsfeld

Tied in heavily to the quality vs. quantity issue, is that when people are after quantitative solutions they often only go after immediate gratification. Those after changes in quality are usually the kind of people (hopefully) who understand that quality takes time, usually a lot of time. Thus, both conservatives and New Agers are long-term thinkers and planners. For conservatives this is quite an obvious observation. After all conservatives are notorious for their slow deliberative stances, not to mention such far thinking passages as the already quoted Edmund Burke that society has a contract "not only between those who are living, but between those who are living, those who are dead, and those who are to be born." The "those who are to be born" suggests that long standing conservative belief that they want to create policies and reforms that are not just temporary patches or duct tape and bailing wire fixes to problem, but substantive changes that will last as society grows. Solutions that don't need a new fix every new election, but real changes.

However, with New Agers, the long term planning seems counter intuitive doesn't it. Isn't one of the main themes of New Age belief a heavy emphasis on the live for today, live in the moment, [pick the hippie slogan of your choice] kind of thinking? Yeah, actually. New Age thinking is bound to the idea that there is only the 'now' that you only have the present to live for. Actually if you delve into New Age metaphysics, time is an illusion just like the physical world, so there is only the 'now' to live in. However, much like almost every other religion on Earth, we do see a long-term plan of things to come. With a belief in reincarnation, long term planning is even more in vogue among us than in other forms of beliefs. "Buy now, pay forever" is in some ways how karma works, so New Age beliefs does have some effect not only on a personal level (is this going to come back and bite me in the next life?) but also for the whole of humanity (the point is to not only get to Enlightenment, but to get EVERYONE to Enlightenment).

Two Worlds, Two Worldviews, One Way to Navigate

"Politics are the divine science, after all."—John Adams

So those are three of the main philosophical cornerstones that New Age philosophy and conservative philosophy agree on, and there is one more, happiness; but I am going to put that off for a minute. But what about those cornerstones of conservative thought laid out in chapter three. Sure New Age belief agrees with the first two points that the world is based on transcendent rules and that life is an open road with infinite variety. But what about the conservative beliefs in social order and freedom and property . . . that at first glance seems somewhat contradictory to New Age belief. And what about the last two points about disliking abstract theory and overnight change in favor of slow deliberate change? That's not the New Age movement? Right? Or what about all that stuff about reincarnation, the afterlife, and levels of Enlightenment . . . how does that have any relevance to conservative thought, let alone politics?

Well first off, these differences stem from a dichotomy that philosophers have recognized effectively since the dawn of philosophy. This world and the next. The physical world and the spiritual world. Or, for you philosophy majors out there, the world of substance and the world of the forms. New Age belief recognizes both of these worlds. If anything it tends to the spiritual world.

Conservative thought tends to be more focused on the physical world. How can these two ever work together? For a New Ager it's quite easy. Let me explain.

First since there are two worlds let's go back and reiterate what both worlds are for a New Ager. The spiritual world is the real world. No space, no time, only us and God and perfection. For some reason we blew it, and were filled with the fear that we didn't deserve it. And to help us learn that fear is useless and the rules of the next world as they should be (fear free) this physical world was created. This world, the cycle of karma and reincarnation, life in general is a giant classroom. As the New Age text *A Course in Miracles* states, "It is a required course. Only the time you take it is voluntary. Free will does not mean that you can establish the curriculum. It means only that you can elect what you want to take at a given time.[. . .] It does aim, however, at removing the blocks to the awareness of love's presence[.]" *A Course in Miracles* and numerous other New Age texts, not to mention every religion, tries to re-teach you those spiritual laws of the spiritual world which, once internalized, will take us all back to the spiritual world and we can leave this physical world behind.

Sounds great doesn't it. But a quick problem comes up for every New Ager, and every follower of every religion actually, how do I survive in this world until then? This world is a classroom and is designed, if used properly, to teach us everything we need. And that's all well and good, but most us are stuck at level one and two of those stages of enlightenment I listed earlier. Even if we're at level three or four, we still probably have a lifetime or two before we can reach enlightenment. And those lifetimes come with annoying human things like jobs, and bills, and bosses, and endless streams of crap on the evening news to deal with. And there's the good stuff too, friends, family, lovers, pets, kids, careers (yes it can and should be fun), vacations to Italy. Do I have to give that up?

The laws of the spiritual world are true, and the laws of this one are an illusion. But an annoyingly persistent illusion. And the fact of the matter is that like it or hate it, we have to live in this world. Now, New Age belief, like every religion does provide some suggestions, guidelines, and ethics for individual ethics in dealing with others. But, like most religions, it's kind of shaky when it comes to government.

So what would the ideal form of government set up by a New Ager look like? First, any New Ager would understand that they cannot now or ever force anyone to a higher level of enlightenment. Free will is the most basic and true law of the spiritual world, and even though we aren't in the spiritual world, it only makes logical sense that you can't break a spiritual law to teach someone the spiritual laws you're hoping everyone is going to get. So ideally, the perfect New Age government would be anarchy. No laws, free will galore. But there's a slight problem we all know that's not going to work. Don't we?

Actually we don't. If one looks at writing typically endorsed by New Agers, the writing of say Doreen Virtue or Deepak Chopra (just to name two, the list could go on much longer, and I by no means wish to say that these writers are wrong, I just think they need to look at it a different way) are predominantly dealing with how individuals should live their lives. When they veer into talking about political policy they make this really weird assumption . . . actually they make two. First, they assume that the mass majority of people will have already made the personal changes that are endorsed by the writing of the New Age. I am constantly amazed at this assumption. Mainly because the policies they endorse require a near universal acceptance of the ideals that they are advocating. Sorry, but if we could just expect people to act like better people just because we have a government that says we should all share and love each other, then Russia, China, and North Korea would have been the Communist Utopias Marx so insanely envisioned. Yet if I remember my history and what I see in the news these were or are some of the worst hellholes in the history of the Earth this side of Auschwitz. The second assumption they make is that by making the policy changes they are endorsing, that the people who are not at the higher spiritual levels will somehow change to adjust to the new more enlightened society and become more enlightened themselves. I have no doubt if we were to try this that a lot of people would climb to a higher level. But I also think that it will only take a portion of the people to a higher level. And the peace loving policies of many in the New Age community, while certainly well intentioned, have the disturbing tendency of leaving the world open to more attempts from tyrants and terrorists to get away with their acts of violence.

So what? Didn't I already say I believed in reincarnation? So what if I am blown up. Good point, but it fails to acknowledge one little point. Did you ever hear of someone reaching enlightenment while being tortured? Raped? Shot in the head? Blown up? No, I don't seem to remember those stories either. Most stories of people I know of reaching enlightenment or sainthood occur when they have time to contemplate and meditate and hear the voice of God without distraction. Sure, they almost always suffer after that revelation, but not during it (and the point of that suffering, a lesson to show us that pain is transitory, if often missed). So letting this kind of evil remain doesn't exactly help anyone. If anything, it could hurt a lot. The kind of suffering that could result from not stopping evil is possibly, if not likely, to cause some people who have a tenuous grasp on the ideals of levels two or three to backslide to levels one and two . . . or worse.

So if nothing else we have to have some government. Not a lot but enough to get rid of the obstacles that can hinder people in their growth. This is completely in line with the conservative belief in limited government. Governments exist for a New Ager to get rid of the obstacles, but not to encourage spiritual growth, because to do so would be to try to subvert free will. Government for a conservative exists to protect basic rights, to ensure the liberty of means are open to its citizens, but not to be concerned with the ends because those must be earned by the individual.

The Ends and Means of Government

"Upon this point all speculative politicians will agree, that the happiness of society is the end of government."—John Adams

Thus, New Age and conservative philosophy both would prefer next to no government, but being logical, realistic, and sane, both philosophies must accept the necessary evil of government (at least until everyone—and I do mean everyone, a couple level one people with no government to hold them back could ruin it for everyone—reaches level four or five, then we probably won't need it). So we need a limited government. That much is clear. Now what should this government do? Well this comes back to the old philosophical question of ends and means. What are the specific obstacles we want the government to get rid of, what are the ends of government that we wish to achieve? And once that is established we have to figure out how we are going to achieve these ends, otherwise called the means.

Now in reference to the ends of government, the Founding Fathers offered us some really great lines:

"We hold these truths to be self-evident, that all men are created equal, that they are endowed by their Creator with certain unalienable Rights, that among these are Life, Liberty and the pursuit of Happiness.—That to secure these rights, Governments are instituted among Men[.]"

And, of course:

"We the people of the United States, in order to form a more perfect union, establish justice, insure domestic tranquility, provide for the common defense, promote the general welfare, and secure the blessings of liberty to ourselves and our posterity, do ordain and establish this Constitution for the United States of America."

Fairly clear on the face of it. Justice, peace both internal and external, general welfare (just so we're clear, they meant trying to keep the standard of living going up, not welfare in the sense of an egregious quasi-communistic program that doles money to the least worthy in society), liberty. Nice little list of things for the government to do. (Notice that liberty is in both the listing of the Declaration and the Constitution.) Also, pay attention that the founders chose the word "promote" not "ensure," "secure," "establish," or any other host of words that would suggest an active role, in describing the general welfare. They were to promote it, push gently in a general direction, make sure as many of the obstacles as could be put out of the way were out of the way. The founders understanding basic classical Liberalism knew that they could not create a higher standard of living, they could merely create an environment where it could flourish and hope it would. Given the driven nature of American mentality for the past two hundred years, it did.

However, as nice as those two passages are in ideals or simply the beauty of the language, they're kind of vague. They should be vague. A document that's meant to last for generations can't be too specific because if it is, it will become outdated as the society changes. But this book isn't for the ages, it's for the here and now. So we need something a bit more specific in what the current ends of government need to be. For a New Ager those ends should be involved in removing the obstacles for spiritual growth. And what are the obstacles to spiritual growth? You probably are already a step ahead of me when I say that that depends on what level of spiritual growth you are at. Luckily, we also have a little help from modern psychology in this respect.

Cris A. Pace

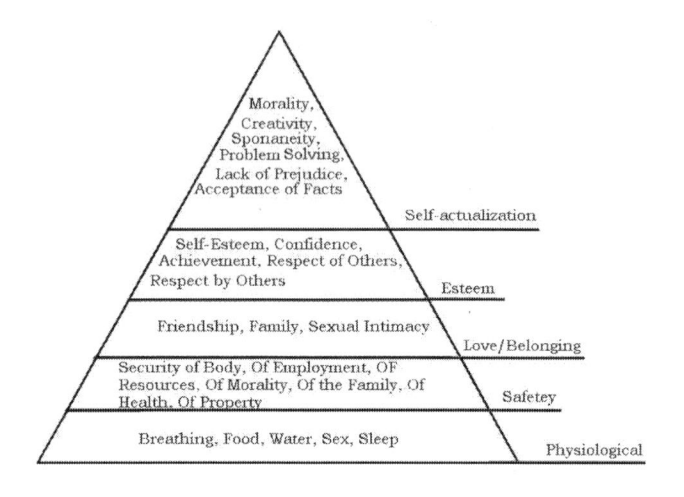

```
                    /\
                   /  \
                  /Morality,\
                 / Creativity,\
                / Spontaneity,  \
               /Problem Solving, \
              / Lack of Prejudice,\
             /Acceptance of Facts  \
            /_____\  Self-actualization
           /  Self-Esteem, Confidence,   \
          / Achievement, Respect of Others,\
         / Respect by Others                \
        /_____\  Esteem
       /    Friendship, Family, Sexual Intimacy \
      /_____\  Love/Belonging
     / Security of Body, Of Employment, OF         \
    / Resources, Of Morality, Of the Family, Of     \  Safetey
   / Health, Of Property                             \
  /_____\
 /     Breathing, Food, Water, Sex, Sleep              \  Physiological
/_____\
```

The seven levels of spiritual development I laid out earlier do not just have parallels throughout the world's many systems of religion and mysticism, but also in teaching of an American psychologist named Abraham Maslow. In Maslow's most well known theory, he postulated that every human being obviously has certain needs, but that for all people (or at least all sane people) these needs progress in essentially the same order. That first physiological needs—needs related directly to the body—need to be met (food, air, water, sex). After the body has been taken care of the next necessary form of needs are safety needs. These safety needs, safety of the body, safety of family, safety of your employment are primarily concerned with keeping all those things that you got in the first level are going to be there tomorrow, the next day, next year and probably for the rest of your life. Basically, what most of us do during our 20's in trying to establish a secure life and future. Once you feel secure that you not only have food today but also will have it for the rest of your life, thus satisfying your safety needs, according to Maslow, come love or belonging needs. These are needs to have friends, family, a significant other, and possibly children in our lives. Wait, you say, isn't this what teenagers spend so much time on friends, torrid (though short lived) loves, and the like, how could they do this if they don't have their safety needs met (after all most of them will be booted out of the house when they turn 18). True, but this is how a person views their own life subjectively, not an objective view of their life, and let's be honest here, every teenager is so secure in their safety needs they think nothing can stop them. After love comes esteem needs, the need to feel that you've done something with your life (often achieved by raising children or not viewing your job as a paycheck but as a career or calling to excel in). And finally comes self-actualization, a term Maslow created to describe those rare individuals who feel they have all their needs met and who treat their actions not as means to ends but as ends in themselves—we might also substitute the word happiness here.

Notice any parallels between this and the seven spiritual levels

Spiritual Level	Maslow's Hierarchy
1. Physical	1. Physiological
2. Emotional	2. Safety
3. Mental	3. Love
4. Astral	4. Esteem
5. Etheric	5. Self-Actualization
6. Cosmic	
7. Enlightenment	

Now one could probably point out that one of these systems is designed to describe growth over one life and one is describing growth over multiple lives as a flaw in comparing the two. But I would counter that, first, the parallel from the physical to the mental and then the spiritual is undeniable, and second, that I contend that this world is a classroom to teach us the rules of the spiritual world, thus shouldn't the path to growth in a single life be a reflection of the larger growth of the soul over the course of lives. Thus if these parallels exist, then even if you're stuck at the physical level, spiritually you could move through Maslow's hierarchy in a single life and it is likely that at the apex you would learn that it is not the physical realm and its world view that brings you happiness. It is at that point that you must confront the fears that hold you back to that level in order to move onto the next level. For instance let us say that someone is spiritually at the physical level, their world view, their fears, correspond to the needs of the physiological level of Maslow's hierarchy, i.e. the fear of not having enough food, or water, or stuff. A person at the physical level believes that this life is the only life. If they have any belief in God, it is a relationship of fear, that God is unpredictable and fickle, and may destroy them at any moment, a world just as chaotic and devoid of meaning as if there were no God. Thus all that matters is what they eat, what they can own, what they experience pleasure wise.

How does one move past this? Well it certainly isn't by living in North Korea. If you live your life constantly in fear of death from a government decree or not paying off the right official just enough, or wondering where the next crust of bread is going to come from then it's unlikely

Republicans and Reincarnation

one can progress spiritually. While living in this kind of life, or even say a lower class life in an industrialized nation, one can delude themselves that "if I had money," "if I had that car," "If I got her into bed," "If I was the richest man in the world," they will be happy. Thus, one of the most helpful tools to move past the physical realm is money, believe it or not. Now granted not everyone requires money to move past this level. Most do. Most need to experience the fullest range of experience in this realm and come to the conclusion that their belief that the physical world is happiness is not the case. They need to reach the point where they can realize that there must be more to it all. And that in turn will force them to strip off one of the first layers of fear, the fear that the physical is all there is. Now granted a person could theoretically move past this stage of enlightenment living in abject poverty, and progress to the next level or all the way to enlightenment at once by will alone. But taking a look at history, I think you'll agree that this seldom happens (Buddha for instance was born a prince and lived the first portion of his life in opulence, before *choosing* to live a more frugal lifestyle). Thus, the clearest barriers to spiritual progress for the person at the physical level are poverty (which causes the belief 'that if I only had money . . . ') and tyranny (which just causes a steady state of fear for your life).

Now doesn't that mean everyone has to become Bill Gates to move past the physical level? I seriously doubt it. I would probably say that all that is required (well really nothing is required, but the level that makes realization most likely) to realize that the pleasures of the physical realm are not the answer to it all would be what would be considered middle class in an industrialized nation. And

I would say that common sense and general experience bears this out. Do you know many people who are middle class who are worried constantly about basic physical needs? I've seen only a handful and of those, most of them came from a low class background, thus I would argue they're on the cusp. Most middle class people are concerned with physical things only as they relate to status or enjoyment (which are concerns of the second, or emotional level, of enlightenment).

So if money and a lack of tyranny are helpful in moving past the first level, what does a person need to move past level two? If you'll recall level two is a level of seeing a larger context to life than just a physiological process. We live, and hopefully succeed, and thus are rewarded. Whether it be by some form of karma, or by a just God for following his rules (in this lifetime or the next). Happiness is very important in this stage (as it *should* be in all stages). But it's a happiness based on success. And with level two, it's much the same as level one, to move past it you must realize that what you're after, success, isn't really where eternal happiness lies—and usually the only way you're going to come to that conclusion is by actually achieving success, tasting its sweet fruits, but only then realize that there is still something else missing. Now here comes another problem, when someone realizes that success isn't the complete answer, many people are tempted to give into guilt over their success, believing they don't deserve what they have because they clearly didn't deserve happiness . . . after all they would have happiness if they deserved it, says the logic of level two. With that guilt comes the possibility to backslide. Describes the spiritual problems of this planet for the last few hundred years or so, doesn't it?

So what we need, for level two people at least, is a system that allows people to succeed in business, the arts, sports, or whatever it is that people do. We also need a system that encourages some way to not backslide once success has been reached.

"The choice is not between order and liberty. It is between liberty with order and anarchy without either. There is danger that, if the court does not temper its doctrinaire logic with a little practical wisdom, it will convert the constitutional Bill of Rights into a suicide pact."—Supreme Court Justice Robert H. Jackson

Now, we could move onto what makes the transference from level three to four, four to five, and so on, most likely, but really there would be no point. These are primarily mental and spiritual journeys. They do not require the outside trappings of the physical world, one way or another. A person can move from three to four either having been born into an upper class family in New York, a middle class family in the Midwest, or even to a lower than dirt family in North Korea. Granted getting shot by secret police might put a slight hamper on things in the short run, but it actually acts as no barrier to spiritual growth. Problem is, as I've said, I'm convinced that the vast majority of the world has yet to reach level three. I think a healthy portion is on the cusp, but they're not there yet.

Therefore, as far as government is concerned, it, at present[29], can only be concerned with removing the obstacles for levels one and two. To do that it must ensure three things 1) liberty 2) an environment for economic prosperity and 3) and environment that allows not just prosperity but personal success. So those are ends. What are our means? Well the easy answer is democratic republicanism and near laissez faire capitalism. I'll bet anything you're rolling your eyes right now. "Yeah like that's an answer . . . democracy and capitalism?" It is. But you're just going to have to give me some time to define in detail what I mean.

But before we do, we need to know how to best judge what the best course of action for a government to take is. In this respect, I find five questions necessary to ask about any action that a government has to take.

1. Is the action leading to a positive, neutral, or negative end?
2. Is the action unethical or ethical?
3. Is the benefit this action provides removing a material or spiritual obstacle, or both?
4. Is this a long-term benefit or short-term benefit?
5. Is the action benefiting a large number of people or a small number?

Ideally, we would want ethical means that lead to long-term spiritual and material benefits for everyone. However, while enlightenment might be that simple,

---

[29] A world where most everyone is at level three will have radically different government problems. If we're really lucky our grandchildren might see that world . . . but I seriously doubt you and I will, so I'm not going to concern myself with it.

this world never is. Often it's more of a choice between hurting this group to help that group. Human nature of levels of one and two think more short term and materially (just look at all the ridiculous things that congress spends money on).

Now to deal with the first two questions, ends and means, we have all heard that the ends do not justify the means. Granted. You can't immediately rationalize every evil act by saying you had good intentions or even good results. And while we would all prefer good ends and ethical means the problem is that many times in dealing with government it is quite often a choice between good ends and unethical means, or ethical means and unfavorable ends. That's why we have the necessary evil of government in the first place; we believe a few unethical means are better to reach a good end than living like saints and killing ourselves off for it. However, ends don't just come in positive and negative ends; there are also ends of an act that can have no discernable change, in other words acts that work to enforce the status quo. Now what must be avoided at all costs is a negative end. So we would prefer a positive end with ethical means, and settle for a neutral end through ethical means. However, when ethical means will only lead to a negative end, then a necessary evil is, well, necessary. Government for instance is tolerated for this very reason; anarchy, while not limiting people's freedom through foolish laws, leads to chaos and violence, more suffering, and a far lower chance of anyone progressing to a higher level. (You would think that it goes without saying unethical means that lead to negative ends are obviously unacceptable, but then how does one explain the Democratic Party platform . . . or parts of the Republican platform when I stop to think about it).

So how do we separate positive, neutral, and negative ends? First, we need to make the distinction between spiritual and material ends. Giving a person $100,000. Material. Giving a person more choices in their life to exercise their freewill to the fullest. Spiritual. Now, some of you might be thinking didn't I already say that some amount of money to get over the fears of level one and two (and for all I know three and four). I did, but do not mistake the psychological difference between being given money and having the opportunity to earn money. Being given money is more than likely to keep a person in the mindset that they have no control over their lives and that they are the victim of fate and other forces beyond their control. Spiritual benefits are, more than anything, things that can only be viewed as opportunities, although those opportunities usually manifest into progress in a material benefit, but not immediately. Material benefits can usually be measured almost immediately in very specific terms. Now obviously an end that creates a material and spiritual benefit is best. However, a positive benefit or neutral state for spiritual ends must be attained, even if the cost is a negative material end. And if I have to explain to you why spiritual ends are more important than material ones, I'm amazed you have the reading skills to have made it this far, it kind of comes under the category of self-evident truth.

When talking about not impeding the opportunities of free will, we would actually solve a lot of the problems that come up in the first place. But reality and human nature is seldom so simple as what is obvious as on the page of a book. So, after we have established that a

Republicans and Reincarnation

positive or status quo must be established or maintained we sometimes, sadly, have to come into the realm of unethical means. Furthermore, there are just situations where you have a negative somewhere and you have to choose who will receive the benefit and who will receive the cost, again nothing can make this ethical, it's very unethical, but not facing or making such a decision would be even more unethical.

First and foremost, unethical means must never be used to create positive material benefits. Material benefits are by their nature short lived—they do not last, they do not succeed, because people do not escape the problem that caused the situations where unethical means are used to increase material circumstances. A person's fears about wealth are not allayed by winning the lottery (or more to the point by getting a welfare check), they are still there, perhaps shifted or buried, or whatever Freudian defense mechanism you want to pick, but those fears have not been confronted and moved past. A welfare check doesn't stop someone's fears; it only reduced the free will of someone else.

This now comes directly to the issue of long term versus short-term ends. If unethical means have to be taken, it should be for long-term ends. Too often, and believe me I will give numerous examples later in the book; unethical means are taken by governments to only correct problems on a short-term basis. This is a process that absolutely needs to stop. What else needs to be stopped is the logic of the needs of the many outweighs the needs of the few or the one. Often the government will take rights, property, opportunities, in other words free will, away from a small group to in their words give more to this or that larger group. Now obviously if it's a question of do we help one or twenty thousand in the exact same degree, obviously we should help more, but the rights, the spiritual goals of even the smallest minority should not be sacrificed unless the spiritual growth of everyone is at stake (seldom, if ever, does such a situation occur). As I've already stated spiritual ends, of even a single person, should not be placed in jeopardy because of the material needs of even the entire population of the world.

So to sum up:

No negative ends, even if it means unethical means. (Such as war to end tyranny)

No negative spiritual ends, even if it means negative material ends. (Quitting your job rather than violating your principles)

Unethical means only to prevent a negative end.

Long-term goals over short term. (The needs of the minority must never be sacrificed for the wants of the majority.)

The needs of the minority must never be sacrificed for the wants of the majority.

Now as I've already suggested democracy and capitalism accomplish the goals. Let's start with capitalism.

Chapter 5

ATLAS AND A ROBE: GIVING MONEY VERSUS STEALING MONEY

"It is not from the benevolence of the butcher, the brewer, or the baker, that we expect our dinner, but from regard to their own interest. We address ourselves, not to their humanity but to their self-love, and never talk to them of our own necessities but of their advantages. Nobody but a beggar chooses to depend chiefly upon the benevolence of his fellow citizens."—Adam Smith

Money. What is it? Is it the root of all evil as some may say? No. Why isn't it? Because the actual line is "the love of money is the root of all evil." Anyone ever tells you that money is the root of all evil, slap them, and tell them to go learn to read. And we'll get to the love of money shortly, but for right now, it's not getting us to an answer of what money is. For lack of a better definition, money is a tool. It is a tool designed to make the transfer of goods easier than through the previous barter system. With money you don't have to haggle as much as to how many pigs are worth how many wool sweaters (now you just have to haggle over what one sweater or one pig is worth . . . makes it much easier for those of us who hate working with fractions) because now we have a set amount of money, a price, set to everything. As the economist Thomas Sowell has said, "Prices are important not because money is considered paramount but because prices are a fast and effective conveyor of information

Cris A. Pace

through a vast society in which fragmented knowledge must be coordinated."[30] In other words, it just makes life easier.

But if it's only a tool, why is it so important to so many people? Cars are tools that get you from point A to point B; you don't see anyone obsessing over . . . okay bad example. Hammers? No, I've seen too many guys fawn over their tool kits. Clothes? Nope I've seen both sexes obsess over those. My point here is that people will obsess over tools, sometimes when they're not important (unless we want to get down to toothbrushes and thumbtacks, and I'm sure there is someone with OCD out there who has an obsession with those). But more than these other things I will admit that money is an exceedingly valuable tool, more useful than a hammer, a car, clothes to protect you from the environment (or make an impression) than any other tool. Why? Because it can get you all those other tools. Money is important because it's the most fluid tool, able to be converted into anything at a moment's notice if you have sufficient amounts of it.

A person would be a fool to not realize that there is a certain safety that comes with that. If you have enough money, you're prepared to combat the majority of things life could possibly throw at you. The problem comes in when the tool becomes more important than what the tool can do. Remember the line is "The love of money is the root of all evil"—not money, but the love of money. As such, it is only a tool and a tool is neither good nor evil, only its use can be judged as being good or evil. We're all too familiar with the evil uses of money, modern media makes sure of that, but what are the good uses of money.

---

[30] Sowell, Thomas, *Knowledge and Decisions*. Basic Books, Inc.: New York, NY, p. 80

Republicans and Reincarnation

For anyone who just said, "only charity and helping others," thank you for playing, but you're WRONG! Remember first and foremost that you are here for yourself. You can't help anyone in this world until you yourself are in a good place. Until you reach level two you are in no position to help someone get out of level one. And as I've already said you need some money to move from level to level (or at least at the lower levels). You need to have money, to buy those simple necessities like food and shelter and transportation and pieces of crystallized carbon set in gold for the woman you love. The things that keep you alive. Then there is that new DVD or that book everyone is talking about, sending the kids to college, more pieces of crystallized carbon for her. The things that will keep you sane. Then there come the things that make you happy. Can money buy those? Yes . . . yes it can . . . in a way.

I assume you've reread those last sentences at least once, to make sure you didn't miss anything. No you didn't, I said money can buy happiness, in a way. And for this I will move to two of my favorite books for example, *Atlas Shrugged* by Ayn Rand and *The Robe* by Lloyd C. Douglas. Now I'm sure some of you thought I was about to bring up Adam Smith's *The Wealth of Nations*, have no fear that is going to come up a bit in this chapter, at least implicitly[31], so back to the two books I did bring up which will in turn illuminate two larger concepts that Smith himself touched upon. I would say that a

---

[31] In fact at an early point in the development of this book I was going to call this chapter "So Atlas, Christ, and a guy named Smith walk into a bar . . ." but it sounded too wordy, and the punch line was too far removed from the title to still be relevant

majority of well-read people have at least heard of either one or the other, but I'll give a brief overview in case you missed one or the other. *Atlas Shrugged* is a story of all intellectual, creative, and productive people in the world (the successful business leaders, great artists, competent workers, etcetera) going on strike to protest the fact that all the lazy, ignorant, and all around worthless flotsam in the world (welfare recipients, second rate businesses that survive only on government dole and graft, most politicians) believe they have a right to live off the works of other people—to show these people are wrong—they are not entitled to the works of others without working for it themselves. It is a *laissez-faire* capitalism opus, even despite its lack of stylistic subtly (Rand prefers to beat her readers over the head with a single idea until only the most mentally challenged could possibly not get what she's saying) and a rather illogical adherence to atheism (not to mention its almost inhumanly unemotional characters). Not everything in the book is correct. Far, far from it. But, in spite of its flaws, it does lay out a very workable groundwork for the ethical basis of capitalism—it's a good place to start with philosophy, but should not be considered a final word on any subject. The other book, *The Robe* by Lloyd C. Douglas, is the story of a young Roman Tribune, forced by circumstance to be one of the executioners of Jesus, which begins for him a spiritual journey to learn about the man he killed and in the end results in his conversion. Throughout the book issues of charity and love come up constantly in the concept of ethics (discussion that are disturbingly lacking from too many churches in the world nowadays).

These two books could not possibly be more different from each other if they tried. One speaks of the virtues of

Republicans and Reincarnation

capitalistic selfishness, one the virtues of Christian charity. However, they are oddly enough speaking of different sides of the same coin. That money is only a symbol and only its use is good or bad. That money is only used well when it used to purchase individual personal happiness. Let's start with *The Robe*.

From Money To Charity

"With nothing better to entertain him, Marcellus sat down on the edge of his cot, with the robe in his hands, and indulged in some leisurely theorizing on the indeterminate value of this garment. If you computed the amount of skilled labor invested by the woman who wove it on a basis of an adequate wage per hour for such experienced workmanship, the robe was easily worth thirty shekels. But not in Sepphoris, where she lived; for the local market was not active. In Sepphoris it was worth twelve shekels. A stranger would have been asked fifteen. Marcellus had made it worth twenty. Now it wasn't worth anything. "He would give it to Miriam, who had no use for it, and it still wouldn't be worth anything until she donated it to someone who needed it. At that juncture, the robe would begin to take on some value again, though how much be difficult to estimate. If the man who received this excellent robe should be inspired by it to wash his hands and face and mend his torn sandal—thereby increasing public confidence in his character, and enabling him to find employment at a better wage—the robe might eventually turn out to be worth more than its original cost."—The Robe, Lloyd C. Douglas, Chapter XV

In the middle of a book on spiritual faith and conversion, you find this passage, almost worthy of being a section in Adam Smith's *Wealth of Nations*, discussing the fact that things only have as much value as someone is willing to pay for them. But where most economists would end their discussion of the fact that things do not have intrinsic value beyond what a buyer is prepared to shell out, Douglas does something radical and goes far beyond where most economists think. Charity. I'm not saying charity isn't brought up in economic theories, it often is, the transfer of property, how it has an effect on the overall economy, is it good for the economy, how to boost charity? All are discussion points brought up even in your basic 100 level college government or economic courses. But I have yet to hear an economist speak about what charity does to the value of an object. This is most likely because as a corner stone of modern economic theory an object is worth only what is given in exchange for it (this too applies to simple cash donations) when given away it is effectively worthless, completely useless until the receiver puts the item or cash back into the flow of the economic system and sells or exchanging that piece of charity. However, this violates a simple rule of Adam Smith's analysis of all transactions.

In *Wealth of Nations* Smith noted that all transactions benefit both parties. If I give a store ten dollars for a DVD, it isn't that I've made off well with a DVD that is worth more or that the store has ripped me off. It is not the case that one side comes out better and the other side in screwed. Smith noted that in all transactions, both parties come out better for it. I get something I want and didn't have before, and the seller makes a profit on previous investment that can be either reinvested or used to purchase something that they want. But in the end, as long as neither party is trying to defraud the other person, every willing transaction in a capitalist system is ultimately going to benefit ***both*** parties of the transactions. Which of course brings us back to charity.

From Charity to Happiness

"It can happen everyday you just have to want that feeling! And if you like it! and you want it, you'll get greedy for it! You'll want it everyday of your life! and it can happen to you I believe in it now I believe its gonna happen to me now I'm ready for it and its Great its a good feeling its better than I have felt in a long time. I'm ready."—Bill Murray as Frank Cross at the end of Scrooged describing how he now feels about giving, not just at Christmas, but everyday.

Be it donating money, goods, or labor, certainly one side of the charitable act benefits, the receiving side. But does the act of charity exist as the only honest transaction in the world that only one side benefits from? No, not at all. It's just that one isn't getting money or something tangible or physical from this transaction. What one gets from the act of charity is happiness. For instance, to go back to *The Robe,* take the following exchange between two men discussing charity and happiness:

"'Take little Jonathan's case, for example: if nobody had learned about his giving the donkey to the crippled lad, would he have been secretly rewarded?'

'Of course' declared Justus. 'If no one had known about the gift, Jonathan's heart would have overflowed with happiness. You wouldn't have heard him wishing that he had kept the saddle.'

'But the child had no way of keeping the matter quiet!' expostulated Marcellus.

'True' nodded Justus. 'That was not Jonathan's fault, but his misfortune.'

'Do you think that peculiar radiance of Miriam's can be accounted for by her having kept her secret? In her case, she was not the donor. She was the recipient!'

'I know,' agreed Justus. 'If the recipient doesn't tell, then the donor is rewarded in his heart. It is thus that the recipient helps him to obtain his reward.'"—The Robe, Lloyd C. Douglas, Chapter XIV

What this exchange is expressing it that charity does give the one giving something in return, happiness. Yes, money can buy happiness. Granted this quote is also expressing that the giving party can be paid also in praise by others if the charitable act is known by others, but if the charitable act is kept between as few persons as possible it is paid back only by the happiness that one has done a good deed. Now does this mean that any act of indiscriminate charity is paid back with happiness? Not really. The poet Kahlil Gibran may have critiqued that some people say "'I would give, but only to the deserving.'" when stating why they don't give much in the way of charity, but that does not mean that you should be throwing your money around all helter-skelter. Charitable money should only be given away in such a way as you think it could be possibly used for the betterment of the receiver, not because you're just supposed to give it to people, irrespective of who they are. To use an extreme example: give to the bum on the street asking for change once is fine, twice is fine, but after a year or more of every day seeing the same man asking for change day after day, never showing any sign of trying to use that money to better himself and to place himself in a position where he doesn't have to beg, that's not charity, it's insanity.

But for most things when you are not knowingly just throwing away your money or other forms of property, but rather putting it to some use that you truly believe will help others, it not only helps the person who receives your charity it helps you. Call it karma, or payback, acts of God, or merely psychology, but charity makes you feel better. More than that, but if you dedicate a great portion of your time to helping others then you will not only be happy but you will find two other side effects to your acts. The first is that since the whole universe tends to work on a karmic basis, you will find that you will not only be repaid in your own happiness, but that your own luck and success will increase . . . but this isn't a book about getting rich quick or how to increase your own personal happiness, it's about increasing the happiness of everyone so back to our main point. So, onto the second odd side effect.

Charity and happiness are in many ways currencies like anything in the material world they are exchanged and produced. But unlike most forms of currency charity and happiness have an odd tendency of going in two directions and not stopping at a single transaction. This comes into play in the last example I am going to draw from *The Robe*. In one of the final chapters, the story's main character, Marcellus Galieo has converted to Christianity and decides to forsake his position as a wealthy member of the Roman upper-class, resolving to spread his new beliefs not only through simple story telling, but to actually put its lessons into action (an act sorely lacking in just about every religion).

Marcellus travels to a large plantation in Italy that harvests melons, grapes, and other such fruit. It is presented as fairly accurate for the age. The workers in the field while not slaves are certainly in little more than indentured servitude; paid little more than a subsistence wage. As to be expected, they're less than thrilled with theirs lives or their boss, but not in out and out rebellion. Marcellus joins them in their job and through subtle acts of optimism and charity, begins to improve not so much the working conditions but the outlook of the workers. Please note that I don't mean he was that overly bubbly and deliriously happy as a Kindergarten teacher on her first day of school, syrupy sweet, chipper on a Monday morning worker that every other office seems to have, and everyone in the office, justifiably, wants to slap—Marcellus was subtle in just appearing to enjoy his own work and not gripe about it around others. But he does it intentionally and it spreads. Marcellus is quickly promoted to the position of the accountant/secretary, for the man who owns the fields. Marcellus is still his giving self, although he shows no subservience or humility in the presence of his new employers, who is initially shown not to be the nicest of men but by no means an overblown evil robber baron caricature that the Democratic Party likes to portray all business owners and employers as. Through both blunt and subtle ways he brings his employer closer to his family, and then convinces his employer to show some small acts of generosity to his employees, which in turn becomes bigger and bigger acts of charity, until finally the whole community is united, business is more profitable, and there is no longer animosity between the classes (and as it is a book about Christian faith, Marcellus has succeeded in converting everyone). The point here is

Republicans and Reincarnation

that simple acts of kindness have a way of compounding themselves and spreading like a plague when given the proper deliberative care. Now I am not naïve enough to believe that an entire town and everyone in it can be radically changed into better people by the act of only one man in the matter of three months (and I don't think Lloyd Douglas was that naïve either) but it's a parable, it meant to show what can happen, even if the reality has to be taken to an extreme to make its point.

The point here is that charity is in essence a double-edged sword. Not only does it provide you with great happiness but it also provides the people around you with an example and a positive influence to do better themselves. Now should you do this only because you will benefit others, not in the least, the main reason you should do this is because it benefits you. The New Age spiritual text *A Course in Miracles* says that generosity "means giving away in order to keep."[32] Translated to more colloquial human terms we give away our time, our energy, our money because it means something to us, and thus it means something to us when we give it away, thus we feel we have done something, and what we keep in return (goodwill, happiness, or favors) is worth more than what we gave away (thus it is a standard capitalist exchange wherein each participant comes out the better). *A Course in Miracles* continues, "The teacher of God is generous out of Self interest."[33] It is not wrong to give things away because we know they will bring us joy. It is right because it will bring us joy. And that's the only reason it's the right thing to do. The greatest indicator of our lives is whether we feel pleasure or guilt from an act. Deep in our souls is

---

[32] *A Course in Miracles: Manual for Teachers 4.IV.Generosity. Line 1.5*
[33] Ibid. Line 2.1

the voice of God, this is so because we are at some level still connected directly to God, and if we're sane then that voice is in our conscience and if we feel joy over something it is because we know that is in line with what we know, and what God knows, is right. And from charity and generosity come some of the greatest joys in the world.

From Charity to Self Interest

"There are those who give little of the much which they have—and they give it for recognition and their hidden desire makes their gifts unwholesome.
"And there are those who have little and give it all." These are the believers in life and the bounty of life, and their coffers are never empty."—The Prophet, Kahlil Gibran

As the quote above suggests it is not necessarily, what you can give away easily without thought or fear of loss that counts as charity. If you don't value what you're giving away, it doesn't really count as charity. Yes, you may be helping others, but that alone doesn't give you happiness in your own soul. If you just get to deduct what you gave off your taxes, it really doesn't matter in the long run. Now, the poet Gibran may object that "And there are those who give and know not pain in giving, nor do they seek joy, nor give with mindfulness of virtue" and granted he is right that giving should not be painful nor should it be done only because you're "supposed" to give because society or your religion says so. But he is very wrong to say that you not give because you are seeking joy. If you are not seeking, not receiving joy, there is no point in giving. Do you ever remember hearing about

Republicans and Reincarnation

Christ or Buddha, Krishna or St. Francis or any religious figure, not being joyful when they did a charitable act? I don't. Why? Because as Lloyd Douglas would point out in his other great book *The Magnificent Obsession,* giving is an act that brings nothing but happiness and joy. Be it giving of money or time, work or things, if it's not bringing happiness to you, then you're doing it wrong. Yes it may be something that enriches the world around you as a whole, as anyone who has seen *It's a Wonderful Life* can understand, but to hell with that. First and foremost, you should be happy about your generosity because it brings you trust, and friends, and most of all happiness. If you don't find happiness in the act of giving, don't give—sure, the world itself probably won't be getting better around you, but the fact is that unlike George Bailey in *Wonderful Life* the entire town doesn't hinge on your charity. Understand it's not the act of charity that spreads; it is the emotion of happiness that you exude that passes from one person to another. That, and that alone, is what changes the world for the better.

So where does this leave the government in terms of charity? Actually nowhere. You didn't give any of your money to the government willingly. Whether it's spent on programs you agree with or not, you don't give your money to the government first and foremost because you want to, you give to them because they have fines for more of your money, prisons to send you to if you don't pay those fines, and guns to shoot you with if you resist going to prison. Granted it seems only insane people refuse to pay their taxes (probably because sane people can do the simple cost-benefit analysis of not paying their taxes) but what happens when those insane people start up a compound up in Montana and then refuse to pay their taxes? The FBI and

ATF show up with no shortage of weapons to put lots and lots of holes in those nut jobs. Because they're nut jobs? Of course not, if it was because they were insane, Hollywood and the U.S. Senate would have been put under siege long ago; no it's because they didn't pay their taxes (okay they usually present a danger to others as well, but so do the Senate and the IRS, but I don't see the FBI laying siege to those nut jobs . . . although one could easily make the argument that would be a much better use of resources)[34]. You pay your taxes because, in the end, the government takes them by force. Now when this is for legitimate ends (police, fire department, military, courts, etcetera) it is a necessary evil. The things we need the government to do do have a very monetary price. But these services cannot be considered an act of charity because you had no choice in the matter of whether to give or not. But is it even a necessary evil when it is in effect the government giving charity, say as in the case of welfare? Well it is here that we turn to Ayn Rand's novel *Atlas Shrugged* for guidance.

The Guy Who Holds the World

"Your fear of death is not a love of life and will not give you the knowledge needed to keep it. Man must obtain his knowledge and choose his actions by a process of thinking, which nature will not force him to perform."—Ayn Rand, Atlas Shrugged

---

[34] The best use of resources might be that SEAL teams be sent to the IRS with orders to exterminate with extreme prejudice (as I believe the military puts it) . . . yeah who wants to bet I'm getting audited after this book gets published?

Republicans and Reincarnation

As I've already said, governments are necessary evils. Without them chaos reigns, fear rules supreme, and material and spiritual ends are both an afterthought after the simple need to avoid death. But, per the quote above, avoiding death is not life. Think of it this way, just because you're not in debt does not mean that you're filthy rich. Nor is sustaining life (making sure you can perform the biological function), really truly living (living with happiness). Why is this a necessary distinction to make (again)? Because of where government comes into play. Government as a necessary evil is supposed to be there to protect the sustaining of life, not provide the fullest enjoyment of it, because the fullest enjoyment is a function of the individual mind and the soul (two things that any and all government bureaucracies lack in the extreme). However government often goes beyond its proper function, and, rather than sustain the conditions for life it tries to improve those conditions, which actually always backfire. But before we deal with the specifics of why government power doesn't work, let's deal with the philosophical groundwork for why government shouldn't intrude on the rights of men—and for that we shall turn directly to Ayn Rand's *Atlas Shrugged.*

To start with, I will first say I am not the strongest supporter of Rand the world has ever known; I'm more of an apologist for her. The more I learn about Rand the more I think she was crazy, or at least very troubled, and the more I learn about her followers (and followers is the right word because far too many of them take anything she said as Gospel truth the way a Southern Baptist takes the story of Genesis) just plain disturb me on some levels. But while I would never take her as the final word, she does make many exceptionally valid points about the nature of government, and the nature of government run amok. *Atlas Shrugged* is just this. It presents a world where the government is slowly devolving into a completely communist/socialist state tyranny[35], and by virtue of this decline destroying everything that made civilization great in the first place[36]. It is dystopian in the sense of Orwell's *1984* or Huxley's *Brave New World* in the sense it shows a government taking too much control of people's lives, but *Atlas* is different in a few very important ways. The first is unlike those other novels it shows how such a world could come about—it also suggests that such a world will not exist for long for two reasons. The first is the heroes that Rand presents—a rag tag collection of artists, ethical business leaders, and engineers—are suggested as being the hope for the world when the socialist system collapses; and that is where Rand differs most—unlike Huxley's and Orwell's nightmares Rand correctly shows that such a system will collapse in on itself if left to its own devices (just like those great bastions of socialism called France after the Revolution and the Soviet Union). But while waiting for said collapse (and actually helping it out so they can start from scratch sooner than later) the heroes of the story make several observations about the nature of government.[37] So let's get back to government.

---

[35] This is of course a redundant phrase for any socialist state is by its very nature a tyranny.

[36] It is also quite disturbing at how prophetic she turned out to be. Many of the things that come out of the mouths of her villains in her book written sixty years ago seem to now be coming out of the head leaders of the Democratic Party.

[37] I have chosen these quotes carefully, and while I would say one should read *Atlas Shrugged,* at least once in their life, do

Republicans and Reincarnation

From Self-Interest to Government

No, I do not want my attitude to be misunderstood. I shall be glad to state it for the record. I am in full agreement with the facts of everything said about me in the newspapers—with the facts, but not with the evaluation. I work for nothing but my own profit—which I make by selling a product they need to men who are willing and able to buy it. I do not produce it for their benefit at the expense of mine, and they do not buy it for my benefit at the expense of theirs; I do not sacrifice my interests to them nor do they sacrifice theirs to me; we deal as equals by mutual consent to mutual advantage—and I am proud of every penny that I have earned in this manner. I am rich and I am proud of every penny I own. I made my money by my own effort, in free exchange and through the voluntary consent of every man I dealt with—voluntary consent of those who employed me when I started, the voluntary consent of those who work for me now, the voluntary consent of those who buy my product. I shall answer all the questions you are afraid to ask me openly. Do I wish to pay my workers more than their services are worth to me? I do not. Do I wish to sell my product for less than my customers are willing to pay me? I do not. Do I wish to sell it at a loss or give it away? I do not. If this is evil, do whatever you please about me, according to whatever standards you hold.—Hank Reardon, Ayn Rand, Atlas Shrugged

---

not construe anything Rand said that I do not quote to be something I necessarily agree with.

The above is a businessman's defense of violation of a government statute that "regulated" (read "prevented") him from selling a superior product because his well-connected competition could not come up with a product of equal quality. The quote makes a clear observation that in a capitalist system all commerce is an act of mutual agreement between individuals. It is not out of selflessness that he does what he does, just as it is not out of selflessness that most people do anything in the real world. We work because either it makes us happy or because we're getting money that will buy us the things that will make us happy (hopefully both). But most of all it points out that the money that this man possesses was earned. A commercial for the financial firm Smith Barney used to state, "We make the money the old fashioned way, WE EARN IT." Whether it is the old-fashioned way or not, it is the preferred way. Only three classes of people don't earn their money: thieves, welfare recipients, and the government. Now which one of these is unlike the other? Now for those of you who said thieves, I'm so sorry, but we do have some lovely parting gifts for you. The one that does not belong is the welfare recipient on the dole. This person at least is being given money they didn't earn. The thief and the government take money from people by force, although the thief at least has the courtesy not to try and tell you it's for the good of society.

Rand several times makes the point that there are only two ways to deal with people: by force and by reason—and most importantly "Force and mind are opposites[.]" The common thief and the government do not acquire their loot through any amount of reason. Yes, you use reason on your part by choosing to give your

Republicans and Reincarnation

wallet over to the thief rather than be shot, just as you demonstrate reason by paying your taxes instead of going to jail, or paying the extra money for the driver safety class so that you won't have to pay more in insurance fees (the legal term for what the government does there is called extortion, if you don't have a corrupt court system and police force to back you up, it's illegal—if you do then it's only immoral).

Now a Classical Liberal would point out that the government has to gather money somehow—it's the necessary part of necessary evil. Still this is only for the legitimate ends of a government, and not a penny beyond the cost of those legitimate ends is the government entitled to. Why? Because you earned that money. It is an extension of your mind, your work, your effort, your being. They have a right to money to defend your rights, because that is reasonable, it is moral, but beyond that it becomes immoral. As Rand put it, "morality ends where the gun begins."

So where are the immoral efforts of government actually taking place? It is in taking money that it doesn't deserve.

"The only proper purpose of a government is to protect man's rights, which means: to protect him from physical violence. A proper government is only a policeman, acting as an agent of man's self-defense, and, as such, may resort to force only against those who start the use of force. The only proper functions of a government are: the police, to protect you from criminals; the army, to protect you from foreign invaders; and the courts, to protect your property and

> *contracts from breach or fraud by others, to settle disputes by rational rules, according to objective law. But a government that initiates the employment of force against men who had forced no one, the employment of armed compulsion against disarmed victims, is a nightmare infernal machine designed to annihilate morality: such a government reverses its only moral purpose and switches from the role of protector to the role of man's deadliest enemy, from the role of policeman to the role of a criminal vested with the right to the wielding of violence against victims deprived of the right of self-defense. Such a government substitutes for morality the following rule of social conduct: you may do whatever you please to your neighbor, provided your gang is bigger than his."—John Galt—Ayn Rand, Atlas Shrugged*

Now the above quote does outline a classical Liberal view of the government. Police. Courts. Army. Basic defense. Just accept right now that we're never going to have a government that does only that. It would be nice, if for nothing else than our tax burden would probably not be above 10 cents for every dollar you earn (the entire tax burden of federal, state, sales, and all those little taxes on telephones, gas, etcetera—you're currently paying somewhere around 40-50 cents on the dollar, or more). However, government has grown far beyond that, and as much as I would wish to curtail it, and I'll explain why, the conservative in me knows that a violent radical change of eradicating large portions of the government would be ridiculous if not disastrous. (Even Ayn Rand knew this, as she preceded her changes in the world of *Atlas Shrugged* by what was effectively a second Dark Ages). Change should never be drastic, unless absolutely necessary. Still, before we can even possibly get back

Republicans and Reincarnation

around to that wonderfully simplistic and unobtrusive government we first have to see how we got the god-awful mess that we have today.

I could go back to the early days of the republic when after the first surplus of money for a fiscal year, Congress decided to spend the money on improving the conditions of roads between states, or how Jackson completely ignored the Constitution and its intent in creating a republic and not a mob democracy, or even Lincoln's setting bad precedent through the ignoring of basic Constitutional rights because he had significantly larger and more pressing problems to worry about; however, all these are mere rain drops compared to the torrential flood and "multitude of New Offices" that Roosevelt and the Great Depression created and thus "sent hither swarms of Officers to harass our people and eat out their substance."[38] The Great Depression was a time of despair and desperation. Nearly the entire western hemisphere of the world was suffering from economic depression and a good portion of this part of the world was desperate for any change. Germany, Italy, and Spain were so desperate they turned to fascism as an answer. The United States and the United Kingdom (among others) merely turned

[38] Some might think a comparison between FDR and King George III here is unfair, and you're right it might be. I have no reason to suspect that George would send a boatload of Jews back to Nazi Germany knowing full well what would happen to them because it was politically expedient. Nor do I believe George would make a deal giving half of Europe to possibly the one tyranny worse than the one we were fighting at the time. And so, for the insult of this comparison, my humblest apologies to King George III for comparing him to one of the worst excuses for a human being in all of history.

to the milder evil of socialism[39]. Government control of the economy became the name of the game because of the Great Depression. Farm subsidies for instance: paying people not to grow crops . . . not to mention government burning of crops to raise their prices—all this while people are starving; we still pay people not to grow crops, I'm sure those starving kids in Africa I see on the late night commercials must love that. Public works project: building sometimes worthless roads, bridges, and dams—we're still building useless roads most recently publicized was an attempt by Congress to build a bridge in Alaska that effectively went nowhere; this bridge was luckily killed, other such wastes of money weren't. Social Security: a program doomed from the beginning—put in money, get that money back and then keep drawing for another twenty years after that stealing money from your children (if a private citizen tried to put Social Security into practice they'd be arrested for marketing a pyramid scheme). Basically, the origin of most government waste of money and time can be tracked back to FDR and his New Deal. Not that everything they did was a bad idea, mind you, for instance the FDIC program, the government insuring individual bank accounts to prevent a run on a bank, was an excellent program fitting into the function of government: effectively low cost to protect me from other people being so stupid that they all try to run and get their money out of a bank which doesn't really carry that much cash on hand—the program really

---

[39] The technical term is a "mixed-economy" suggesting part socialist control of the economy, part capitalist freedom. However "mixed-economy" has such a whitewashed, politically correct sound to it. Maybe a new term should be found. Socialism-Lite?

Republicans and Reincarnation

doesn't do much, doesn't violate anyone's rights, doesn't cost much, and other than offering an illusion of security, which is all that is needed for stability, it should give no power to the government.[40] But the problem is that these incursions into the economy during the Great Depression have been used to justify larger and larger intrusions of the government over the lives of citizens. And this is two fold for not only is there the intrusion (telling me that I can only send a letter legally through their inefficient monopoly, taxing foreign imports to make domestic products more appealing despite inferior quality, telling me how much I can donate to the candidate of my choice, or telling me how fast I can drive on an empty highway) but also in the taxes levied to enforce these laws which again restricts my freedom.

So the question then becomes what was the justification for this expansion of government? Who was crazy enough to think that the governments that were partly responsible for creating this depression (While there is a natural boom and bust cycle to economics, what should have been a very bad recession was made a Great Depression through poor government monetary policy, the raising of trade tariffs, poor government loan policies, and leadership in Washington being so nonexistent as to

---

[40] You might like to argue with me that FDIC is not just for show and more substance than I suggest here, but I will in a couple of chapters point out that the recent use of the FDIC program and the government takeover of banks was in great part the fault of the government itself. If the federal government hadn't been a major cause of the current recession, then banks wouldn't have collapsed.

help cause panic[41]), that the very people who caused the problem would possibly be qualified to fix the mess they created? Who could possibly have been insane, ignorant, or just plain dumb enough to think the children with hammers who broke the complex machine that is the economy were qualified to fix it? John Maynard Keynes and his ideas of Keynesian Economics would be the one to blame.

Before I explain Keynes and his mad, mad ideas, I must apologize for the fact that this is going to be quick, to the point, and completely without the depth that the subject probably requires. I tried. I really did. I went through a dozen drafts trying to explain it all—but it was either quoting massive passages of economists like Friedman and Hayek (just go read their books), or just being so god awfully boring you'd be put in a coma. If you want a <u>full</u> explanation of why Keynes is wrong I

[41] This is one of the other functions of government, to offer leadership. While leadership is not anything substantial and more appearance it is exceedingly important. And this is one of the few points I will concede to FDR, although his actual policies may have hurt this country in ways we still haven't recovered from, he had the sanity to understand as a leader he had to appear as a leader and be calm so as to calm other people down. A modern parallel might be seen in New York and New Orleans. On 9/11 Rudy Giuliani didn't have the power to truly affect much, but he appeared as a leader and thus appeared to those around him as if he did have the power to control everything, meanwhile the city was literally falling down, but as afraid as the public was, New York did not devolve into absolute chaos. On the other hand a complete lack of leadership and panicking at all levels of government in New Orleans led to absolute anarchy with Hurricane Katrina.

Republicans and Reincarnation

have some lovely suggested readings at the back of the book, otherwise here is the short version.

Keynes, correctly noticed that part of a recession is that when the economy worsens, or appears to worsen, people stop buying things and start saving, this in turn actually causes the economy to slow down, which causes cut backs on the factories that are making those things people aren't buying, and I'm sure you can see how this creates a vicious cycle which ends in a recession (it's like the opposite of supply side of economics). So if people just kept buying things you might not get a recession. You can buy your way out of a recession. The problem is that most people tend to cut back on spending when they think the economy is on a downturn. Few people think, "I've only got $15 in the bank account maybe I should go see a movie tonight" (or at least few people who think ahead do). But if we had more money we would be more willing to spend money, and the cycle would cause the whole economy to rise. So how do we get more money into the hands of people? (Here is where Keynes makes a really insane move.) Let's have the government give out lots of money!!! (Let's not cut taxes; let's spend like crazy). Keynesian economics refers to it as priming the pump, shoving money into the economy by providing aid to those not earning money (welfare, social security) and giving jobs to people who otherwise didn't have jobs either because of the economic downturn (most of the works programs during the Depression) or simply because they're too incompetent to get a real job (employees of the IRS, the Department of Education, the House of Representatives). The Keynesian idea is that this will get the whole economy started again. Followers of Keynes' wacky ideas view the economy as a well, you have to "prime the pump", pump it several times getting the air out before the water begins to flow out of the pump with little effort. The pump metaphor is very good for those who endorse Keynesian principles, because they like to see government as the hand that needs to keep pumping to keep the water flowing, if you stop pumping, the water will stop. This ignores those little things like the fact that economies work quite well without any government intervention (Hong Kong under the British); one could probably argue that from an anthropological standpoint, economics in the sense of division of labor and trade preexisted anything we would call a government. But not those Keynesians—no to them we need government, we can't survive without it, and we certainly can't be trusted to let the invisible hand run the economy, like, oh, it did for hundreds of years with a steady upward movement for the masses.

The better way to look at what government intervention in the economy is not as a hand pump on a well, but a different water metaphor—rivers and dams. Rivers can rise and fall, the boom and bust of an economy. And sometimes those rivers flood which in my metaphor could be comparable to recessions and depressions. So rather than deal with the occasional flooded basement a dam is built. But this dam is the control of the government over the economy—so it's more like a dam built out of sand and rock than out of concrete and the flood gates are watched over by the same people who built the dam, so they have no clue as to how much water to or not to release. This can result in longer periods without floods (longer boom periods) but it can also lead to, if the dam ever breaks, (and keep in mind it is being run by dunces), in even greater floods

Republicans and Reincarnation

(like Great Depressions or the economy during Jimmy Carter's Presidency[42]). Or the flood can be kept going longer than it would naturally occur, the recession or depression last longer than it should had the government not interfered (see FDR, Bush, and Obama). So instead of slowly letting the water out, the government, in their typical genius of Keynesian just builds the dam higher and higher to where the economy has become overly dependant on their presence. It becomes intractable because the minute you take away the government support the economic troubles that never had a chance to work themselves out return. For example, several times during the Great Depression FDR attempted to disband large portions of his work programs, but had to reinstate them quickly because he was not willing to let the economy work itself out which takes time. The worst examples of government control getting too out of hand of course come from the failure that is communism. Economies are too complex and too intricate to be run by people in a central planning department, but communists tried to control every aspect—that worked out real well for them (death, destruction, mayhem, giant pictures of unattractive tyrants).

And herein lies the problem of government control. The economy is too complex a beast to be under the control of any number less than everybody in the economy. Like it or not but the "invisible hand" Adam Smith described, the collective intelligence of 6.5 billion people each making

---

[42] One of the few examples of a president having an almost immediate effect on an economy. Granted Ford didn't leave office with the country in terrific shape, but it didn't take Jimmy long to do every possible thing wrong and cause a major recession.

their own economic choices, is the only thing that can account for every factor in the economy. Yes, it has ups and downs, but what in the universe doesn't? But the more you try to give power over the economy with its trillions upon quintillions of unknowable variables and conditions, the more a group of people, no matter how well educated and well meaning, are going to make a mistake that would have merely been corrected over time naturally had nothing been done. And the nature of the beast is that when a mistake is made, not to pull back and realize you were wrong to interfere in the first place, but rather to give more power over the economy. This is the issue clearly depicted in *Atlas Shrugged* (and possibly modern American history). The government takes more and more power; the situation gets worse and worse until it's more about protecting government power than about doing what's right. (Don't believe me, first think about one reason why we keep the Department of Agriculture around, there isn't one, then think about how much holy hell would be raised if someone actually suggested on the floor of Congress of disbanding that insanely outdated creation).

In the end, you could be left with something like the following conversation, if you're lucky[43]:

"You can make it [the economy which was failing under socialist policy] work."

"How?"

Mr. Thomson spread his hands out. "I don't know. If I did, I wouldn't come to you. It's for you to figure out. You're the industrial genius. You can solve anything."

"I said it can't be done."

"*You* could do it."

---

[43] If you're not so lucky you end up with the implosion of the Soviet economy.

Republicans and Reincarnation

"How?"

"Somehow." He heard Galt's chuckle, and added, "Why not? Just tell me why not?"

"Okay, I'll tell you. You want me to be the Economic Dictator?"

"Yes!"

"And you'll obey any order I give?"

"Implicitly!"

"Then start by abolishing all income taxes."

"Oh, no!" screamed Mr. Thompson, leaping to his feet. "We couldn't do that! That's . . . that's not the field of production. That's the field of distribution. How would we pay government employees?"

"Fire your government employees."

"Oh, no! *That's* politics! That's not economics! You can't interfere with politics! You can't have everything!"

Galt crossed his legs on the hassock, stretching himself more comfortably in the brocaded armchair. "Want to continue the discussion? Or do you get the point?"[44]

Those hell bent on controlling of the economy never want to see it is their actions that muck up the system and that more action on their part will only do more harm.

From Government to Happiness

"Happiness is the successful state of life, pain is an agent of death. Happiness is that state of consciousness which proceeds from the achievement of one's values. A morality that dares to tell you to find happiness in the renunciation

[44] Ayn Rand, *Atlas Shrugged,* New York: Random House, p, 1100-1101

> *of your happiness—to value the failure of your values—is an insolent negation of morality. A doctrine that gives you, as an ideal, the role of a sacrificial animal seeking slaughter on the altars of others, is giving you death as your standard. By the grace of reality and the nature of life, man—every man—is an end in himself, he exists for his own sake, and the achievement of his own happiness is his highest moral purpose.*
>
> *"But neither life nor happiness can be achieved by the pursuit of irrational whims. Just as man is free to attempt to survive in any random manner, but will perish unless he lives as his nature requires, so he is free to seek his happiness in any mindless fraud, but the torture of frustration is all he will find, unless he seeks the happiness proper to man. The purpose of morality is to teach you, not to suffer and die, but to enjoy yourself and live."—John Galt—Ayn Rand, Atlas Shrugged*

So once we admit that government can't properly run an economy better than the laissez-faire model. This model still has the government protecting you from outright theft and fraud, abuse and the degradation of slavery, not to mention death and dismemberment. And laissez-faire economics does require regulation and oversight of the private sector, just not absolute control. But as Supreme Court Chief Justice Marshall observed "the power to tax involves the power to destroy." In fact, with modern government that's about all taxes do. They destroy trade. They destroy businesses. They destroy jobs. And with all of that they destroy an individual's options on how to use the money that they have earned. Which in turn can destroy happiness. I can hear the objection already, there are lots of people with lots of money and

Republicans and Reincarnation

they aren't happy. I don't contest that. I am only arguing that happiness is an act of choice, and if a government is taking away the ability to choose things, choices that individuals earned, it is impeding that happiness. You know the right to pursue happiness. You might have heard of it. No one in the government can promise you, or is promising you, happiness, but you should have the right to pursue it. Money won't get you everything, but it will open many of the opportunities. Opportunities like the ones of charity I described earlier.

Money doesn't buy happiness. This is true. But it does buy the preconditions for happiness. From Aristotle's *Nicomachean Ethics* to Maslow's theory of the hierarchy of needs, money and wealth are requirements for happiness. Immediately following those requirements is the requirement of security and safety, the idea that the money I have will be there tomorrow. An over active government makes that impossible. Not only is there the fear that the wannabe Gestapo we call the IRS will come and take money from us, but it also comes in with the problem that an overactive government chips away at our concept of free will. In a world ruled by capitalism, yes the economy goes up and it goes down, but I alone am the one who navigates my course through these troubled and calm seas because they are governed only by the laws of invisible hand and human nature, my free will determines my outcome. With an over active government, it appears to many people that their fate is determined by policy of the ruling party. They see themselves as victims of forces beyond their control. Now this is false, but fearful people will latch onto to something to blame to relieve themselves of responsibility for their own destiny. Will these same people be afraid in a world governed by capitalism? Yes, of course they will. But they will not have a government to blame or act as parent; they will not be able to put a face or name to what makes them afraid to face their own free will. And a fear such as that is easier to dispel, and increases the chances of them reaching the next level. Rather with an active government they can point to politicians and say those people are to blame, and have proof to back up their fears, making them so much more difficult to do away with and thus again block the path to happiness.

"Socialism is a philosophy of failure, the creed of ignorance, and the gospel of envy, its inherent virtue is the equal sharing of misery."—Attributed to Winston Churchill

Still, despite my best efforts, I can already see several objections against capitalism. They are very old, very common, and very ignorant. However, they're also very difficult to kill. History, statistics, logic, and common sense haven't killed these asinine objections to capitalism—because all those things have time and again PROVEN that only capitalism works. I know it's arrogant to think I'm going to kill them once and for all in the next few paragraphs (in fact I know I won't—Socialism is more like a wacky religious cult: all faith no proof) but I have to do it, if no other reason than to show that these challenges do have rebuttals.

Objection One: Doesn't capitalism just allow the rich to get richer and the poor get poorer?

"Over the decades [from 1973 to the present] the percentage of American families with incomes over $75,000 has tripled.[45]*"—Thomas Sowell, Economic Facts and Fallacies.*

Ah, one of the most common and asinine critiques of capitalism. However, the detractors of capitalism can offer little in the way of a legitimate case. Not that they don't try. In an article to the Financial Times entitled "Why America needs a little less laissez-faire", Democratic former chairman of the House financial services committee Barney Frank had the following to say:

"As we prepare for this autumn's election, the results are in on America's 30-year experiment with radical economic deregulation. Income inequality has risen to levels not seen since the 1920s and the collapse of the unregulated portion of the mortgage and secondary markets threatens the health of the overall economy." [46]

That's the best that the capitalism's critics can offer. Rich people are rich and idiots who got adjustable rate

---

[45] Okay this statement is kind of worthless unless I state that, first the U.S. population has not tripled in that time (from 211 million to just over 300 million) and, second, the figure of $75,000 was a figure adjusted for inflation.

[46] Barney Frank, Financial Times.com January 13th, 2008 http://www.ft.com/cms/s/0/d001b2c6-c20a-11dc-8fba-0000779fd2ac.html

mortgages actually had the rates adjusted. The second argument is the more ridiculous of the two, but it ties into the whole poor get poorer myth. The mortgage crisis, while bad, was also in great part due to people just for some insane reason walking away from their mortgages and letting banks foreclose even when the banks were willing to work with them. Nor was it something affecting innocent bystanders, it was affecting people who took an adjustable rate mortgage, a move universally recognized to be on par with buying stock on margin and treating the lottery as your sole retirement plan. Although if you are one of those people who got an adjustable rate mortgage, please contact me, because I have some lovely bridges to sell you for rock bottom prices. Furthermore, this is not an example of the capitalism market running rampant to destroy average citizens—it's one of those natural low periods in the cycle. That's life, no one seems to complain about the unreasonably high moments (although the rational people get out of the market when it is too high) but somehow when it's unreasonably low they shouldn't take responsibility. Of course we could have the government come in to try and prevent those little recessions and the occasional minor depression, but then as I said you'll get one of the Great Depressions again. I'll take the recession with its "subprime housing crisis" or "internet stock bubble burst" over a rerun of the 1930's. But given the left's continuing calls for "bail outs and stimulus", I'm betting on having to suffer the latter.

The second argument, that the income gap is too wide, while not as ridiculous, is certainly more egregious and frankly is below the intelligence of anyone we should let serve in Congress (although it does show the intellectual depth of other icons bearing Mr. Frank's first name). Yes, the rich are getting richer. It tends always to work that way over time. But the poor are getting richer too! But, says Frank, the rich are getting richer faster than the poor. He goes on to complain that while the top 1% has had their after tax incomes double that "average earnings for the vast majority of workers have fallen in real terms." Wow. Really? Real wages have dropped during the recession. I'm shocked. (And this of course is when, as far as I can find on the Bureau of Labor Statistics says yes 2007 saw a dip in real earnings, however, it's been a steady average growth over the course of the Republican controlled Congress which is what Frank argues caused the dip in real wages . . . even though the Democrats controlled Congress at the time of this dip). Will there be a dip in real wages, assuredly, at some point; recessions are inevitable in any capitalist economy. But here's the thing, the real wage of workers will go up. If you look at history, when you average out the highs, lows, and midpoints of any capitalist economy they have wacky tendency of always going up, up, up. Let us not forget that we live in America, where our poor are the envied of the world. The rich are getting richer, but the nice thing about capitalist economies is that the poor get richer as well. Just consider for a moment that most people in America, poor included, own a car, own a DVD player, get their 2,000 calories a day (America is famous for getting more than their 2,000 calories a meal), have access to free emergency health care (that's right any ER has to treat you in an emergency case even if you can't pay), have access to free public education, and the list could go on. Yes, no one in this country would like to be poor, but in the grand view of things, the poor of a capitalist (semi-capitalist in actuality) country are not doing terribly in the grand scheme of things.

Another problem with this argument is that it views a person's economic class as something static and unmovable. As the economist Thomas Sowell is fond of pointing out when talking about economic class "most people in the bottom 20 percent move ahead over time to rise into higher income brackets."[47] Your average high school graduate earns next to nothing right out of the gate, but, even without a college degree, they are likely to make it securely into the middle class by their 40's. Give or take, people tend to double their incomes between their 20's and 30's and to make about $8,000 more every ten years (that's adjusted for inflation) during their prime earning years.[48]

By no stretch of the imagination are the poor getting poorer over time. When you really look at it almost everyone gets richer over time under a capitalist system (so long as the government doesn't destroy that system). Thus in this single respect of fulfilling material needs capitalism lessens suffering for those under it. And while it may have its dips and downs it is a wholly positive trend that in the long term benefits more people, for longer periods of time.

---

[47] Sowell, Thomas, *Economic Facts and Fallacies.* Basic Books: New York, NY, p. 153

[48] U.S. Census Bureau—Alternative Income Estimates in the United States: 2003 http://www2.census.gov/prod2/popscan/p60-228.pdf

Objection Two: Doesn't capitalism let rich countries exploit poor countries?

But, alas, you say, even if the poor are getting richer over time, that's only in the industrialized world. Capitalism exploits and steals and destroys those poor developing countries around the world. All of our economic growth comes on the backs of the third world . . . or whatever such nonsense and blatherskite protesters outside the WTO meetings are chanting.

Once again this is just not so.

Yes, companies go to developing nations around the world and set up factories in these countries because it's cheaper. They pay the workers in those factories pennies. They, a good deal of the time, employ child labor. It's all very terrible when you see it on the evening news. But, as is often the case with news outlets, they're not revealing the whole story.

Let's start with those pennies they pay those workers in those countries. Those pennies a day are still far above the average wage in those third world countries. Working in those factories will often put the worker in the a pseudo equivalent of the middle class in those developing countries—probably why people clamor to work for multinational corporations in those third world countries.

Do they employ children? Yes, less often now because of all the bad press that such a practice gets, but let's look at the long-term effects of child labor. Child labor in these developing countries tends not to last a whole generation. Why? Because with one or both parents and a kid or two working, then the younger siblings get to, finally, be in a position to go to school, rather than everyone having to beg subsistence. School leads to better jobs. Better jobs leads to better money, and being able to send all your kids to school.

Think about this. Japan, South Korea, Taiwan, India, and China—these are all countries we used to send our low paying factory jobs to. Now these are all economic powerhouses, some of whom we were afraid would overtake us in the 80's and 90's, some of whom we are afraid will over take us within the next decade. These used to be the places of sweatshops and low-end production, now they're centers of industry, technology, and first world standards of living (or will likely reach it within the next decade or so). Yes exporting jobs does terrible things for those developing nations . . . like give them a middle class. A middle class that soon demands laws to protect the money they earned. Then demands democratic reforms to decide how those laws are made. Allowing the prerequisites for economic development and stability and democracy in the long run . . . how can we sleep with ourselves at night for shipping jobs overseas.[49]

Now this also tends to bring up the point that these countries are stealing the jobs of Americans. Any politician who suggests that American jobs are going overseas as something terrible for the U.S. economy should be shot on the spot for gross ignorance. You know what would be worse for the U.S. economy? Having to pay the price of goods that were made on overpriced American union salaries. Not to mention that those same politicians would then want to send economic aid money to those

---

[49] For a further discussion of this process of how economic development can lead to democracy please read "In Defense of Globalization" by Jagdish Bhagwati

countries we didn't send jobs to. So you would be paying 10 times the price for basic goods plus your taxes would go up to subsidize another failing foreign economy . . . . I fail to see how this is better for the average American citizen.

Objection Three: Doesn't capitalism just encourage avarice?

> *"Avarice, the spur of industry."*—David Hume
> *"Those areas where people are motivated the most by greed are the areas that we're the most satisfied with: supermarkets, computers, FedEx."*—Walter E. Williams[50]

And while the above quotes are quite true, more to the point, greed isn't only good, it's natural. Wanting more is human nature. If you meet someone who says that they don't want anything else they are probably one of four things: 1. Lying. 2. A conman out for your money. 3. An enlightened soul (and even then I would wait to see the holy light or a couple of miracles . . . besides even the enlightened souls want more in the sense they want all souls to join them). 4. Mentally disturbed.

So does wanting more, in other words greed, get encouraged by capitalism? Not really, it was there whether capitalism is present or not in every normal human being. The only difference between capitalism and every other form of economics out there is that capitalism actually

---

[50] Quoted in the article "Greed is Good" by John Stossel, http://townhall.com/columnists/JohnStossel/2006/04/26/greed_is_good

allows people to get what they want if they are willing to work for it.

Now, the more accurate question is "does it encourage avarice"? Avarice is wanting more than one could ever use at the expense of others or without regard to what is ethical. Lots of times people use the word "greed" when they mean "avarice"—just an unfortunate fact that the English speaking world is rather slipshod with vocabulary. Greed, while it is generally assumed to mean not caring about ethical implications, is actually more on par with the term rational self-interest. A person can be greedy and still be ethical. They want more, but they're willing to work for it. Capitalism allows them to do that. Avarice on the other hand is the caricature of Dickens' Ebenezer Scrooge. Lie, cheat, steal, pinchpennies all for the purpose of amassing wealth for the sake of wealth. So, does capitalism encourage avarice?

No. Doesn't take their numbers down either. Conditions like avarice are a personal problem that stem from psychological issues (and I would argue more deep-seated spiritual and karmic issues) and are seen in every cultural and economic system on earth. Now capitalism does allow those who are avaricious to hoard more money I'll grant you, but that's a dollar value. The fact is that capitalism actually drastically decreases any possible effects of the avaricious.

To look at this, let's look at someone who is avaricious in a socialist country. The only way they are going to make the obscene amounts of money their desires require is by either bribing government officials or being one of those government officials taking graft. Either way, the money from this transaction is considered illegally earned by the country's laws (even if the business in question is actually

Republicans and Reincarnation

ethical) and thus must be hidden from public view. In comparison, an avaricious person in America can safely and publicly store all of their gains (unethically acquired or not) in banks or in the stock market. That money has a habit of spurring more investment by the bank or the company which was just invested in, which then works out to economic expansion, etcetera, etcetera, etcetera. Further, in a capitalist society, the avaricious person must produce something that people want and/or need. If you have no product to offer anyone, it's unlikely you're going to hoard much in the way of money because capitalism has a way of weeding those people out. In a socialistic society, as long as you have the right connections, you've got a job whether you're any good at it or not (well at least until the whole thing comes crashing down). Or try avarice in a third world nation. We call these people warlords. Since there isn't much money, they have to have the next closest thing: land and power. Gun battles, civil wars, genocide . . . Oh, yeah, this is better than capitalism.

To recap 3rd world avarice: Robert Mugabe.

Socialist avarice: every nameless corrupt bureaucrat bilking you for everything you're worth.

Capitalism avarice: Donald Trump.

Now which one of these is the worst?

But here's a more important feature of capitalism. People are actually more generous under it. According to the Charities Aid Foundation, Americans give approximately 1.67% of all our GDP, compared to more socialist nations such as the U.K. (.73%), Canada (.72%), or France (.14%).[51] Further as pointed out in

---

[51] Charities Aid Foundation, International comparisons of charitable giving November 2006, http://www.cafonline.org/

Arthur C. Brooks's book *Who Really Cares*, "no European country reaches American volunteering levels—indeed, most don't even come remotely close."[52]

Is capitalism the sole reason Americans are more generous with their time and money than their more socialistic European counterparts? Of course not. There are numerous factors of culture and sociology, but the fact is that capitalism (or at least more capitalism than we generally see in Europe) is not encouraging avarice, but rather charity.

Objection Four: Doesn't capitalism create monopolies and thus destroy competition?

> *"Some regard private enterprise as if it were a predatory tiger to be shot. Others look upon it as a cow that they can milk. Only a handful see it for what it really is—the strong horse that pulls the whole cart."—Winston Churchill*

As anyone who has ever played the game will tell you, it takes an inordinate amount of time to establish and hold a monopoly, often so much time and effort that when dealing with the concept off the board game no one is dumb enough to try it. Further the unfortunate fact is that most monopolies, when they do exist, exist only because the government is the one maintaining them, rather than letting capitalistic competition create a more efficient alternative. How many monopolies

---

pdf/International%20Comparisons%20of%20Charitable%20Giving.pdf

[52] Brooks, Arthur C. *Who really Cares*. Basic Books: New York, NY, p. 121

Republicans and Reincarnation

currently exist in the U.S.? Not many but a few come to mind. Amtrak. A business more known for crashes than for effective or cheap transportation. (And before you bring up the railroad monopolies of the late 1800's, please remember that those monopolies were enforced by a government being bribed and bought by the railroad barons. If government hadn't gotten involved in the first place, it probably wouldn't have felt the need to come in later, when the bribes became smaller, and break up those monopolies.) Or we could look at the government instituted monopoly of the U.S. Postal Service (with their iron clad monopoly on delivering letters and riddling customers with bullet holes); the few areas that have been wrenched from post-office control in terms of parcel delivery has led to a quick growth in competition (UPS, FedEx, DHL) which even though by federal law they can't undercut post office rates they still provide better, more reliable, and less deadly service. God alone knows how much more efficient mail could be if we just got rid of the post office's monopoly and the laws that allow them to be the only ones to offer the "cheapest" plan.

So government-protected monopolies are inefficient and are subject to competition the minute government withdraws its protection racket. What about non-government-protected-monopolies? First, I can't think of a company with a true monopoly, but let's look at some that were incorrectly called monopolies. As some of you may remember in the early '80's the government broke up AT&T because they had a monopoly into the "Baby Bells." This did allow Sprint and MCI to compete more effectively, I'll grant you . . . at least for a few years. Then the nature of competition and advances in technology made the break up of AT&T a rather pointless gesture with the invention of the cell phone, and now with a new cell phone company seemingly popping up every couple of years, not to mention cable and DSL all but making traditional phone companies useless. (Now just think what could happen if government didn't protect cable companies pseudo-monopolies).

Then of course there is that great evil of Microsoft. The evil monopoly that will over run the world with its evil evil Windows. Oh wait, a bigger hindrance to Microsoft taking over the world seems to be how universally reviled Vista seems to be for is its ineffectiveness (Yes, I am typing this book on a Mac). Forget any government antitrust case, I've never seen a defection to Mac (and other platforms) in my life like I've seen since Vista came out—people I know who would have rather died than buy a Mac ten years ago are now asking me if I like mine because they're thinking of getting one. I doubt I will see a major change in this for the immediate future. The fact is that monopolies, when they do occur, in the modern world will likely soon face stiff competition from a new innovator, unless they have government protection.

Or remember all the hype over the monopolies of internet browsers. Is this even a remotely relevant concern anymore?

Capitalism, which despises that kind of protection, tends to reduce monopolies, not encourage them. Why? Because if there was enough money in a field to want a monopoly over it, then there is enough money to make someone else want a share of it too. If there's not enough money in that field, no one cares if there's only one company.

Objection Five: Doesn't government funding of research spur new advancements?

> *"You've never worked in the private sector. They expect results."*—Dan Aykroyd, Ghostbusters

I once heard a joke that went something along the lines of, "If God had to deal with congressional oversight it would only be Tuesday afternoon, God still would not have separated the sea from the heavens, and we would already be over budget." Yet despite this universal knowledge that any government project costs more than it should (while the $500 hammer is an exaggerated urban legend, nothing with that many levels of bureaucracy is exactly procured at cost) and the speed at which government moves is generally recognized to move somewhat slower than a snail on Thorzine, people I know still argue that the government should be involved in research. They argue without such government intervention science would certainly not progress.

Let's put that argument to the test. Most of these arguments currently center around funding for medical drug research. They argue since companies don't make much in the way of profits on a drug they won't research such drugs because the costs of research and development are so high. But why are the profits of a drug not worth it? Because the government has said that a company can only hold onto a drug patent for a certain number of years (hideously shorter than any other patent in any other field) thus reducing the company's possible profit. They do this because, they argue, that a company will gouge the price if they are the only ones with the patent to that drugs (this of course ignores the fact that other companies will reverse engineer a similar drug, which is difficult with drugs but not impossible, and that drug companies gouge us now because they can only make a profit for so long, whereas they lower the price if they were guaranteed money for decades to come). So then the government subsidizes the medical research to make it worthwhile. So rather than pay the higher price for the drug itself, I pay through my taxes (probably a significant amount more due to government inefficiency) for the exact same drug. (Worse yet I'm in my 30's and still healthy so I'm only paying for other people's drugs). So we pay more in taxes to fund a problem caused by government interference . . . somehow I'm failing to see how the government is helping me as it claims.

Now the second most common claim I hear in favor of government funding into research helps society is the space race of the 1960's. It gave us microchips, microwaves and Tang. All valuable to society I'll admit, but it ignores the fact that microchips did preexist the space race, as did the technology for microwaves. I'll grant you that the development for these things in commercialized form may have been delayed a few years (although let's keep in mind that computers sat around for over another decade before truly becoming a revolutionary catalyst for society). But let us also keep in mind that the space race to the moon was not the typical government project. Most government projects just do things because the government wants to do them. The space race operated on a more capitalist model—in other words we had competition. We had to beat the Russians; we had to out think them in every way possible to get to the moon first. Now since we can't have major competitions like that with other countries on a regular basis, capitalism seems the best alternative to government inefficiency when it comes to spurring technological advance.

Objection Six: Why should the business owners get all the profits when it's the employees who do all the work?

When doing research for this book I was a little shocked to find this complaint still prevalent among pundits and bloggers, not to mention implicit in the arguments of many journalists and commentators. I found it odd because this is essentially the central argument of Marxism, and I thought that even the semi-educated in Western civilization had given up on this insanity. But for the sake of those out there who don't bother to ever think things through, here once again is why this is a ridiculous argument.

This argument against capitalism, in an expanded form runs thus. Business owners who own "capital" (i.e. businesses, factories, farms, etcetera.) hire employees to do work. The employees work creating a finished product (food, toys, tools, anything that you buy in the store). The product, which has been created, is then sold for a price above what the worker was paid to make it. This surplus value is kept by the owner of the business as profit even though said owner did no work. Having done no work, or so the argument goes, the business owner is not ethically entitled to any of the money made from the finished product, thus their profit is really just stealing from the poor foolish worker. This asinine argument goes on but I'm sure you get the gist of it.

The reason why this idea is so dim-witted is that it makes the incredible assumption that only the physical labor done by someone is of value. The ideas that came up with the product, the drive and leadership to build the business, the management skills to keep the factory running, the genius to innovate new ways of doing things are all given no value. Only the physical labor is given value. Physical labor, something that machines and animals can do is given value, but the work of the mind and soul is given no value. Is it a shock with an idea like this that standards of living are so low in socialist societies, since they only seem to view man as an advanced animal and not as the thinking, feeling, reasoning being that he is?

Still one could argue that the physical labor is more valuable than the mental work (I'm not saying someone with a fully functioning brain would argue this, I'm just saying some mildly psychotic cable news pundit could). So who is more valuable the manager and owner or the workers? Who needs who? I will briefly return to my discussion of Rand's *Atlas Shrugged* because this is one of the central questions of that work. In the novel, all the owners and managers of real skill go on strike, and without them the world falls apart. Those on strike are doing quite well in the book because they know how to use their minds and how to use them to live life in a comfortable and still successful manner. People whose contributions are mental usually possess the ability to do physical work, but it's not as efficient because it's not what they do best. Those who are unhappy with being just physical workers should try using their brains, because in a capitalistic society there is nothing to stop them from doing so if they have a good idea.

Objection Seven: Capitalism is Unsustainable.

Further, I'd heard a related point about how capitalism is unsustainable because there are limited resources in the world, hence all growth in capitalist countries is bound to stop and eventually come crashing down. This ignores the idea, clearly supported by history, that ideas have the unlimited ability to use, reuse and reconfigure the world around them into endless new forms of supplies. When it comes to really needing new things because supplies are low, I'm sure that necessity will continue to be the mother of invention and under a capitalistic system where there are advantages for doing so we will figure out how to keep the world strong and growing for as long as we need it.

Now I'll grant you there are times when innovation doesn't outpace resources (the Dark Age) but these times are rare. And I'll grant that with 6.5 billion people on the planet we may be approaching one of those times of stagnation, but that does not mean that there is only a zero sum game to be had.

Objection Eight: There are still poor people.

But there are still poor people, critics whine. Yes, yes there are. But under capitalism there is usually this thing called meritocracy. People tend to rise by their merits when that's all they're judged by and those who are poor and stay poor generally, yes there are exceptions, but generally it's because of flaws in them not the system. Believe me I've had high school students who were far from the sharpest tacks in the box doing fine for their 20's and will probably continue a moderate rate of growth well into retirement.

Character, intelligence, drive, or talent. If you have even one of these you can make it into the middle class of any capitalistic society. Really, you can. Yeah, there may be hiccups and years where you're not doing so hot, but I seldom see really, really smart, talented, driven people on the side of the street begging for change. As callus and politically incorrect as it is to say, while there is no shame in being poor, there is a lot of personal shame involved in staying poor, and it is the person not the system that is broken because some choose to not use the opportunities life presents them to their advantage.

Objection Nine: But voters want the government to do something about the economy when it fails.

"Your representative owes you, not his industry only, but his judgment; and he betrays, instead of serving you, if he sacrifices it to your opinion."—Edmund Burke

Please tell me when what was popular became what was right. The Founding Fathers often spoke of the "tyranny of democracy" when drafting the Constitution; not a day goes by nowadays that I don't see why. I believe I was quite clear earlier in this book why the will of the majority is not always a good thing, but I will reiterate just a few points here.

First the government is nowhere near competent or quick enough to deal with something as complex as the economy. Further, any government is supposed to provide the greatest benefits to its people for the long term. Government intrusion into any economy is predicated on short terms gains only, often with long-term consequences. For all its short-term ups and down, capitalism provides the greatest and most stable gains over time. Thus the momentary whining of the public should never be a justification for ruining the economy in the long run.

Objection Ten: Doesn't the economy do better under Democrats who you claim to be against capitalism?

A common complaint I've heard goes as follows: "Like we want another Republican in the White House . . . we had deficit spending in the 80's and 2000's and only had a good economy in the '90's." The suggestion here is that only under Democrat Bill Clinton was the economy worth a damn and that Republican presidents ruin the economy. This judgment however makes numerous assumptions about how an economy works. First it assumes only a president has control over the economy. Completely incorrect assumption to begin with—it further ignores those great moments in economic history as when Jimmy Carter was one of the few presidents who did have a very direct effect on the economy. Anyone who thinks Democrats know how to run an economy should remember how Jimmy didn't[53].

The next assumption this makes is that the only aspect of the economy is deficit spending. Deficit spending is not the only aspect of the economy the government can control. It controls a lot of things, spending to be only one of them. Regulation and taxation just as important to the

[53] Many of his economic decisions were so incompetent one wouldn't expect a toddler to have ideas that stupid. Then again, we already know how adverse an effect Amy was on Jimmy's foreign policy decisions.

smooth running of an economy. Any real conservative would always argue for more cuts to spending. Which brings us to assumption number 3: the president controls that spending. Actually it's congress that controls spending, and if we're going to only give credit to the economy based on who controls spending (which I am not advocating because it is a gross simplification of the complex monster that is the economy) then weren't the 90's in the hands of a Republican congress (I also seem to remember Clinton governing mostly from the center and not the far left, but that's just me). Democrats every year propose far more in spending than their Republican counterparts, and let us not forget those all encompassing black holes of spending Medicaid, Medicare, Social Security, and Welfare (which is where most of your tax money goes) were Democrat plans.

So, yeah, Reagan had deficit spending (it was his spend happy Democrat Congress at work) mainly because he thought foreign policy was the most important thing and he cut the deals he needed to get what he wanted to on what he thought was most important at the time. Bush had deficit spending too, but I would be hard pressed to call W. an economic conservative (actually I'd have to be high on LSD to make a statement that preposterous).

The fourth assumption is that the 80's and early 2000's were bad economies. I looked for stats that show the 80's to be a terrible time . . . they weren't especially when compared to the 1970's. And the first half of the 2000's which have consistently shown economic growth quarter after quarter only appear bad because they're just not growing as fast as the 1990's. Hey, economic slow downs will occur even if all government policies are perfect (which they're not).

Republicans and Reincarnation

The fact is that all things being equal it's been a decent, not spectacular (when you add in the last couple of years), but decent run for the economy for the last three decades and neither Republican nor Democrats deserve that much praise for it, because most of their efforts have worked to impede the economy and not improve it (yes I'm blaming both parties here).

Objection Eleven: The invisible hand, which capitalists say guides the economy, doesn't exist.

Now very recently[54] I heard the complaint that the invisible hand that Adam Smith states controls the market doesn't really exist. The proof for this preposterous argument is that once the fields of energy and housing were deregulated the invisible hand did not come in to stabilize and balance these markets. This is a ridiculous argument because the invisible hand, when left alone, keeps everything balanced—balanced here is to be defined like the tides or your sleeping habits, a pattern of high and low where extremes are avoided for the most part; boom and bust are natural. However, when you mess with the invisible hand, it has a tendency to slap you silly for your arrogance. Regulation tries to keep systems from experiencing even the slightest amount of busts, even those minor ones that keep the inferior business practices from growing too large, however it also keeps you from having the really good booms as well. The theory here is that if you can keep the busts from happening then more people will make money in the long run (despite the fact that the regulation itself cost numerous times what you

---

[54] I was actually in the middle of writing chapter 12 when I had to come back to write about this act of idiocy.

save from losing in those busts). To go back to my sleep metaphor, regulation is like shoving caffeine into yourself to keep from going to sleep. It will momentarily bring up any depressed system for a while but after that short period of time more and more caffeine or regulation will be needed to maintain that high, and even then you just find yourself stumbling along awake, but performing poorly. So then you remove the caffeine/regulation . . . as any college student will tell you, you have a brief second wind . . . and then crash. Sounds a lot like deregulating stories you've heard recently. Now is your crashing after an all-nighter a bad thing? No it's your body resetting the system to normal. The economic bubble bursting is the invisible hand resetting things back to where they should be. But if you really want to avoid future crashes, don't over-regulate and needlessly interfere. These crashes and recessions aren't proof that the invisible hand doesn't exist, they are proof that the invisible hand does exist and it will enforce its balance with a vengeance when you mess with it.

Objection Twelve: Your plans will put thousands of government employees out of work.

Yes, yes it will, I always viewed that as one of the benefits to my plans. But this objection does ignore two points I have been making. First that the reduction will be over a long period of time (except for the IRS, we're firing them all at once). And that I maintain the economy is going to grow as the government contracts, usually growing faster than the government shrinks. So while there will be transition time between, it's not like I'm destroying all unemployment benefits all at once, and government employees I recall get severance pay. Further the objection seems to suggest that these government employees are completely unqualified to get jobs in the private sector . . . well, there might be something to that—but all the more reason our tax dollars shouldn't be paying them.

Objection Thirteen: Don't we have, as a government, an obligation to help those less fortunate? Those less gifted? Those in need?

And here we come to the crux of all arguments against capitalism. The humanity argument. The argument that the government must help those in need and create a society, as Marx put it, "from each according to his ability to each according to his need." Because if the government doesn't help them, who will. And because this is the crux of the idiocy and evil behind the hatred of capitalism, I'm going to need a whole chapter to deal with it.

Chapter 6
WHEN ROBIN HOOD AND HIS MERRY MEN GO BAD:

Why Government Shouldn't Spend Your Money Even When The Best Intentions Are Involved and Why it Really Helps No One.

This is the horror which Robin Hood immortalized as an ideal of righteousness. It is said that he fought against the looting rulers and returned the loot to those who had been robbed, but that is not the meaning of the legend which has survived. He is remembered, not as a champion of property, but as a champion of need, not as a defender of the robbed, but as a provider of the poor. He is held to be the first man who assumed a halo of virtue by practicing charity with wealth which he did not own, by giving away goods which he had not produced, by making others pay for the luxury of his pity.—Ragnar Danneskjold—Ayn Rand—Atlas Shrugged
"We were told four years ago that 17 million people went to bed hungry each night. Well, that was probably true. They were all on a diet. But now we are told that 9.3 million families in this country are poverty-stricken on the basis of earning less than $3,000 a year. Welfare spending is 10 times greater than in the dark depths of the Depression. We are spending $45 billion on welfare. Now do a little arithmetic, and you will find that if we divided the $45 billion up equally among those 9 million poor families, we would be able to give each family $4,600 a year, and this

Republicans and Reincarnation

added to their present income should eliminate poverty! Direct aid to the poor, however, is running only about $600 per family. It would seem that someplace there must be some overhead."—Ronald Reagan, "A Time for Choosing" 1964

Oh, where to start? So many useless programs and budget expenses in a government. Federal, state, county, city governments all taking and giving money. Thousands of dollars going to bridges that people don't want or fruit market analysis, museums that no one actually wants or building weapons that the military doesn't actually want. Then of course there is that most worthless of all budget expenditures of the government: the salaries of the members of the United States Congress. All in the name of being of benefit to the public, helping those in need.

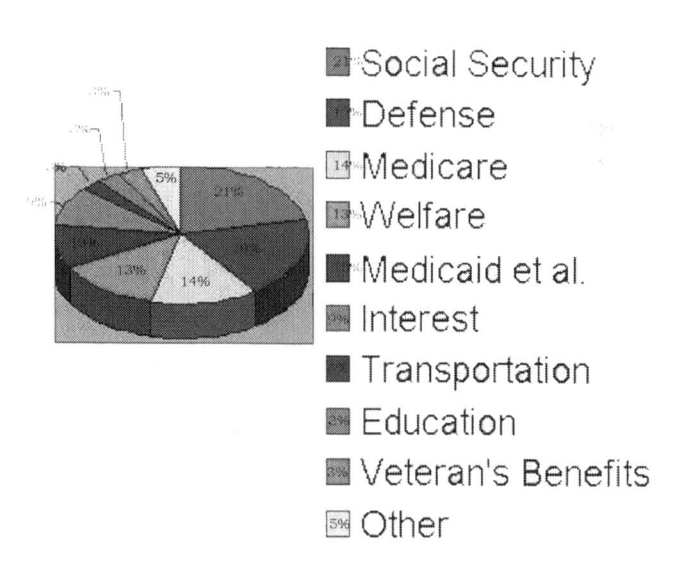

- Social Security
- Defense
- Medicare
- Welfare
- Medicaid et al.
- Interest
- Transportation
- Education
- Veteran's Benefits
- Other

Cris A. Pace

Well, according to figures of government spending that were before everyone got stimulus happy[55], the 2007 fiscal year budget went as follows: Social Security received 21% (that's 21% of about 2.8 trillion dollars, or give or take about 588 billion dollars), National Defense took 19% (although I have been told that this number does not include the cost of the occupations in Afghanistan and Iraq), Medicare 14%, Welfare 13% (the Washington Post article I took these stats from calls it "Income Security", isn't that such a nice and pretty term for paying people to lay around on their ass), Medicaid and other Health programs 10%, Interest on the Debt 9%, Education 3%, Veterans Benefits 3%, Transportation 3%, and Other 5% (Other contains such unimportant things as the Justice Department, and the Department of Energy . . . you know those guys who are protecting the nuclear power plants).

How much of that is going to help people? If we lump Social Security, Welfare, Medicaid and Medicare together we get 58%[56] of the budget ($1,624,000,000,000) spent on helping the less fortunate out. Or given that there are

---

[55] http://www.washingtonpost.com/wp-srv/politics/interactives/budget07/category.html

[56] One might wonder if taking that 58% spent on Welfare and 3% spent on Education and switching those numbers might solve two problems with one stone. Because, hey, if the little brats were educated appropriately maybe they could get real jobs and not need welfare. And while I'm sure my public charter school teacher's salary bank account would be more than willing to tolerate a few years of that experiment, I will be the first to admit that the problems with American education are far too deeply seated, too firmly structural, and too clearly philosophical to be solved by just throwing lots and lots of money at the problem.

about three-hundred-million people in the United States that's just over $5,000 for every man, woman and child in taxes; now since we know that every man, woman and child isn't paying taxes . . . some of them are getting welfare and social security and such, the actual bill per person comes out to a little more on average, and that's only what goes to welfare.

Now I could rant and rave and provide figures against all of this. I could cite long boring analysis that boils down to the obvious that when welfare reform of the 1990's went into place, more people got off welfare (who would have thought that if you stopped paying for everything that people might actually be forced to get a job). Or the fact that everyone of my generation knows that social security is a broken system that doesn't need to be fixed, it needs to be slowly dismantled and gotten rid of because there is simply no way to make it actually solvent. But these are all pragmatic arguments and would lead some foolish people out there to just try to think of ways to make these systems solvent and workable rather than just get rid of them. So more important than the pragmatic arguments about these systems being completely unfeasible, let's go for the more important truth: *That any system of government welfare or income redistribution is not merely inefficient, it is unethical, immoral, and borderline evil because all it does is perpetuate a system of dependency and poverty (both economic and spiritual).*

Still my bank account would like to argue that 58% on education couldn't possibly be worse than what we're doing now.

Cris A. Pace

Robbing Peter to Pay Paul vs. Peter giving to Paul

"The inherent vice of capitalism is the unequal sharing of blessings; the inherent virtue of socialism is the equal sharing of misery."—Winston Churchill

Let's look at two hypothetical systems.

System 1:

Peter is rich. Very rich. The government takes what it considers a reasonable amount of money (which has nothing to do with what a reasonable person would consider a reasonable amount). Let's say 31 cents on the dollar. The government then takes that money and spends about 18 cents, of every dollar Peter makes, on Paul. So what is the point of this system? Supposedly it's to help Paul improve his station in life. We take money from Peter because Peter can afford it. So now let's looks at this. Through the questions we established earlier.

1. Is the action leading to a positive, neutral, or negative end?
2. Is the action unethical or ethical?
3. Is the benefit this action is providing removing a material or spiritual obstacle, or both?
4. Is this a long-term benefit or short-term benefit?
5. Is the action benefiting a large number of people or a small number?

Republicans and Reincarnation

I'm going to take these in reverse order, so bear with me. This is hurting at least on face value a smaller portion of the population (not really, Peter as representative of "the rich"[57] is actually a fairly large portion of the population) to help a larger portion of the population (again not really, Paul as representative of those on the dole is a relatively small portion of the population[58] . . . but we're going to play in the opposition ballpark for the moment). So at least the argument (no matter how flimsy it is) is that few people are hurt and lots of people are helped.

But how are they helped? Is this a long-term benefit or a short-term benefit? When we talk about this we have to think about what Paul will do with that welfare check. Now I couldn't find figures on how many welfare checks are spent on capital investment or college tuitions, but given the fact that until the 1990's welfare reform the number of people leaving the dole could not be described as a mass exodus, I think it's a safe assumption that not much of that money was being used to better Paul. Quite

---

[57] Of course this isn't accurate as it is more like the top 50% of wage earners that liberals like to define as "the rich" . . . so ask yourself do you personally make more than $45,000 . . . if you do, then many in Congress define you as "the rich".

[58] Unless you count all those elderly people who were somehow too stupid to have any understanding of saving for retirement, and rather chose to live like leaches off people who actually have jobs and know what the stock market is for, but one has trouble feeling sympathy for someone who had over forty years to plan for the inevitable and didn't do anything about it. And if you tell me they expected the government to be there for them . . . well that makes me lose even more respect for them. Even the Sheriff of Nottingham wasn't dumb enough to think Robin was going to give the money back to him when he retired.

frankly it's human nature. People value things by what they sacrifice to get it, by the amount of work that goes into it, by what had to be done to earn it—thus money just thrown at you without strings has little value. As such it will be spent on things of no lasting value. Yes there are numerous examples of people who climbed their way out of welfare, and I applaud these people for the strength of character to fight human nature's more lazy and apathetic tendencies, but no one can be foolish enough to say that these few examples are indicative of the whole—nor ignore the fact that many of these people who have gotten themselves out of the cycle of poverty are some of welfare's harshest and most vocal critics. Thus welfare in general is at best a short-term fix; it by no means attacks the root of the problem.[59]

So it helps lots of people, but is only a short-term solution. Now obviously this has material benefit (at least for Paul, to hell if it actually depresses the economy as a whole) but does it actually have any spiritual benefits? Sadly, and rather obviously, the answer is no. Peter gets none of the spiritual benefits described in the previous chapter that come from giving, because he did not give by choice, the money was taken from him against his will. Nor is Peter also likely to give to charity now, or at least not as much, because human nature is that once that money has been taken, then that person feels that they've already given, when they haven't. In fact if anything this leaves Peter more negative and bitter toward humanity as

---

[59] I'm actually going to exclude all job training and education problems from this critique as those do actually attack the root of the problem and do exhibit long-term thinking. I have no problem in theory spending money on those . . . although I'm sure the money itself could be spent more wisely.

Republicans and Reincarnation

he now sees money stolen from him and given to people who are less than deserving and not using said money to better themselves. This is likely to make Peter more bitter toward humanity around him, more cynical, and overall a worse human being. So it's actually a spiritual negative. How about for Paul? The answer is again in the negative. Paul feels no need to earn this act of charity; it was given to him by an unfeeling, cold, heartless institution, not another human being. The insult to self-esteem alone comes as a spiritual negative. More often than not the psychological effects of such a handout will make Paul feel even in less control of his life than before because now that he must depend on the government for his existence—this increases his feelings of powerlessness, increases fear that he is not in control of his existence and rather a mere victim of fate and circumstance. In short another spiritual negative.

Finally is it ethical? No! The phrase is "to rob Peter to pay Paul" for a reason. It's stealing money from a human being by force. I know I don't pay my taxes out of the goodness of my heart; I do it because I don't wish to go to jail or have a standoff with the FBI and ATF. I'm pretty sure that's the same reason you pay your taxes. They have jails and guns, a lot of them—certainly more than I would like to make a standoff against. So in the end it's theft. A clear violation of "Thou shalt not steal" or its numerous variations in every religion on earth, and New Agers are no different on this point. Stealing is stealing; it's a complete and total violation of any conception of ethics I can think of. Now we do honor the myth of Robin Hood, but not because he was a thief, as someone once tried to disprove my point that we never believe theft to be a good thing. Notice that if you actually look at all the legends, it wasn't that he robbed from the rich and gave to the poor (a more modern socialist reinterpretation) but rather robbed from the robbing tax collector and gave back to the people who had actually earned the money. His heroism isn't in the theft, it's in putting his life on the line to get back for people what was stolen from them, what was originally theirs (which is what we would like to think the police do when they put their life on the line for us).

But don't the ends justify the means you ask—to which I respond: did you read the previous paragraphs? Even if there were cases where the ends justify the means, I can't see how stealing hard-earned money from people is justified by short-term material benefits and long-term spiritual and economic harm. The welfare system in all its myriad forms is actually harming the spiritual growth of everyone it touches. Unless you were an atheist you couldn't possibly support it, and even then to believe that this system pragmatically worked you'd need to be an atheist and a moron to . . . (Or am I being redundant there?)

System 2:

So let's say that starting today we started reducing all welfare entitlements. Making them harder to get, requiring more oversight of the people who get them, and requiring even further time constraints in regards to how long you can be on the program. In terms of social security this would be cutting benefits, raising retirement

Republicans and Reincarnation

ages and begin to either privatize or simply eliminate[60] through a phased out process. Now you might be wondering why I'm not suggesting this second system as being one of completely wiping welfare, social security, Medicaid, and Medicare simply off the face of the earth. The answer would be that for better or much much worse, these programs have unfortunately become part of the country's society and while they do eventually need to die, just cutting them with a machete, while greatly satisfying, will cause short-term chaos, and long term societal scars. Welfare, like heroin, is not an addiction that one just quits cold turkey.[61] There does need to be a large initial cut to show we mean business of somewhere in the ballpark of 10% cuts right off the top—but this needs to be followed by a 10 to 20 year plan of phasing these programs out of existence.

So assuming we do the right thing, and cutting these programs back with the intention of eventually leaving them only as significantly smaller local programs or just out and out killing them. What are the benefits and losses?

First, how many people are helped? While I'm sure we all agree that supply-side economics doesn't work quite as well or as quickly as everyone thought it did back in the

---

[60] Even privatizing the system is the government still saying you're too incompetent to handle your own money ... which I'll grant you, a good portion of America does fit into that description, but it's still the government calling you stupid ... this from an organization currently run by some of the biggest buffoons the world has to offer. A statement about pots and kettles comes to mind.

[61] Interestingly enough, welfare also shares the quality of heroin of leaving its users emaciated, soulless shells of their former selves.

'80's, but it does work, albeit its effects take time to work through. When the economy improves everyone benefits, and when you cut government intrusion the economy improves . . . eventually. But the fact of the matter is that more money in the hands of the people is still more money circulating through the economy and not being lost in some bureaucratic nightmare land that creates nothing but red tape and paperwork and thus doesn't really add anything to the flow of the economy. More money, more things being bought. More things being bought, more profit. More profit, more investment. More investment, more jobs . . . you know how this goes. So certainly this will take time, but then again that's what we conservatives like—long-term fixes, not short term band-aids. Further if we do this properly as a long term rollback of funds people receiving these handouts should have time to plan and adjust to the changing environment (like doing things of such a radical nature as getting an education, getting a job, or actually saving for retirement . . . I know it's radical thinking, but I believe it just might work for most people). So there is no harm to this group either. So everyone makes out with the status quo if not better.

As I already said these are long-term benefits. Long term the economy does better, more people have jobs, more people have control of their lives, and if we don't fall in the trap of socialism again, this is a self-perpetuating system. Yes, long term we will have recessions, can't do anything about that, but they will work themselves out, and if people begin to learn how to save properly and educate themselves properly to be able to move from career to career if needed they will not need to worry.

But more than these advantages, this puts the control of a person's life back in their own hands. A major spiritual

Republicans and Reincarnation

benefit. For both Peter and Paul, the government is no longer butting into their lives more than it needs to. This will reduce the likelihood of fear in their lives. It will also increase the feelings of security since for Paul survival depends on himself now, and for Peter there is less worry about how much the Brownshirts at the IRS will be taking this year. Further, as I pointed out previously, more money in Peter's hands will increase the odds and amounts that Peter will give to charity, and this charity will come from living human beings who care about people not the cold, mechanical system of welfare. With this charity to Paul comes the emotional and ethical ties that will force Paul to in some way to be worthy of the gift he has been given and improve himself.

So materially, psychologically, spiritually this provides long-term benefits to the majority of people. But is it ethical? Well we're not stealing from anyone, so there it's ethical. And as I stipulated this program has to be carried out slowly, so were not just uprooting people from the system they have become accustomed to . . . But I hear one last objection about it being ethical coming from the far left: That people have a right to health care or a livable wage, or a right to care from the government in old age and that to deny them that right is unethical.

The crux of this argument is that everyone has a right to these things. If you believe this you A) have not the foggiest conception of what a right is and B) are just as confused about ethics. No one has a right to health care or a livable wage or even happiness. What you have a right to is that the government will not overtly deny you the chance to achieve, to earn, or to buy these things. But neither the government, society, your neighbor, nor your brother owes you these things. You have rights to what you come into this world with: Life, Liberty, and the ability to pursue happiness (emphasis on the pursue). Nor is anyone ethically required to provide these things to you just because you exist (except for your parents as long as you can't provide these things for yourself). First and foremost a person is ethically bound to seek their own happiness, not yours. Now we are ethically bound to help those in immediate need; the Parable of the Good Samaritan comes to mind, but notice that in that case the story revolves around people who are not victims of their own laziness but literally victims to the violence of others or circumstance completely out of their control. Yes we are ethically bound to help those people. We are even ethically called for to be generous and charitable, but keep in mind the entire concept of generosity and charity are dependant on the idea we are not bound to help people out of duty, law, or right . . . if we were it wouldn't be generosity now would it? Further generosity does not call for us to help everyone who would come and demand our help—that would bankrupt anyone and certainly lead to personal unhappiness, a very unethical end. Charity, to have true meaning and worth, must be to those who will use it for their own long term benefit and betterment, not merely short term waste, and anyone who demands the work and property of others as their own isn't someone who cares about personal betterment because this is indicative of a character that believes in not doing anything for themselves. Anyone with this sort of entitlement and need for instant gratification can never better themselves, because they cannot even conceive of what is required to better themselves[62]. Hence they are not worthy of the generosity or charity you would give.

Charity is ethical. But its generosity must be coupled with a desire to improve one's self, otherwise whatever work or money that is given is merely wasted. The claim that one has a right to other people's works is an affront to that belief and merely helps to instill a feeling of helplessness and that is irresponsible.

Yay Capitalism!

So to sum up. Capitalism provides long-term material and spiritual benefits to anyone who is willing to work for them. The more socialist a system becomes the fewer benefits to anyone, and the more harm both spiritually and materially to everyone.

A few caveats do apply. For capitalism to work, you first need a government with a good set of laws and an unbiased court system. Disputes will arise, and this is what government needs to be there for, to resolve disputes when they come up. Also there will always be those few who try to blatantly take advantage of others through theft or fraud. And we need a good set of laws, police, and courts to catch and punish them accordingly. But these facts are inherent in any definition of functioning capitalism.

---

[62] I would like to point out that this critique is not aimed necessarily at those who are poor, but rather at the demagogues and activists that propose such a system of entitlement and character flaws, who in effect create a system that encourages the poor to stay victims and not seek a better life.

Another requirement is an active press. Why you ask? Because sometimes the government isn't very good at enforcing its laws (what a shock that a bloated bureaucracy full of dim-witted politicians and their lackeys isn't very good at doings it's job.) Here is where the press, for all of its annoying tendencies, is good. When properly functioning, or even when it's not, the press is very good at finding fraud, theft, and deceit among those who would try to hide it. They help to keep everyone relatively honest. But since the freedom of the press doesn't seem to be in any trouble in this country (nor is the press's freedom from intelligence, sadly) I think we're okay in this area too.

And since so much of the preceding chapters have been so much theoretical philosophy I will end with some common sense suggestions that can be drawn from that philosophy.

1. The government needs to stop forcing by law businesses to provide health care. And it needs to remove the barriers that prevent insurance companies from crossing state lines. Individual competition will keep prices down.
2. Medicare, Medicaid, Welfare, and Social Security need to undergo an immediate 10% cut (well Medicaid and Medicare could live, or more accurately die, with an initial 20%-50% cut) followed by further long term and permanent cuts, somewhere around a 3-5% cut each year in social security and welfare to give people time to adjust to the changes (not to mention slowly increasing the retirement age requirements), and continuing the

Republicans and Reincarnation

10% cuts each year for Medicaid and Medicare (if you study the problem it is those programs along with the other government created monster, the HMO, that are what cause medical prices to be so high anyway).

3. Immediate 5% across the board income tax and corporate tax cut. Or better yet, how about a flat tax with no floor of about 12%. If you only make $20 then the government is entitled to its 12%. This way everyone has a stake in the system.
4. Cut all spending to research and art. These are things the private sector can handle on their own. With this must also come reform on patent law for drugs and other such developments to make these research opportunities once again valuable avenues.
5. A 90% pay cut for all publicly elected officials, plus a complete and total revocation of their health care and retirement benefits. Why? Because they're morons and I'm tired of spending money on the sort of crappy legislation they've been putting out. Won't do much to solve any budget problems, but it will make me feel good; it will make all of us feel good. And that's a good enough reason for me. And make them pay triple the taxes of regular people, while we're at it.
6. Every employee of the government (federal, state, county, city) take a 15% cut in pay, benefits and 30% cut in future pensions. This just has to be done. I actually would like to make it more, but military personnel and various jobs like FBI agent don't deserve that (they actually have a real function and do their jobs admirably, but if you start putting in exceptions, then everybody will get an exception and it loses the impact it needs). But the fact is that most

civil servants are paid better than their private sector counterparts for inferior work. That's not so much of a servant, as it is of greedy taskmaster. Government work shouldn't be a life—long job, it shouldn't be desirable and it should be competitive with the private sector. Oh and all elected officials need to take 50% pay cut and lose all pension funds. After that there needs to be a 10-year freeze on all salaries (that does not mean you don't get a raise if you get a promotion, it just means the amount for each pay grade will not increase for any reason).

7. After the pay cuts, every single department from top to bottom needs to cut its budget by another 15%. Given government waste this should be easy.
8. Stop messing with the interest rates! The Federal Reserve should learn that the occasional recession, actually is good in the long run. Because without the occasional recession you get the occasional depression. And maybe having someone in the Fed who has a clue what monetary policy is, unlike the current bunch, and maybe has read a book by Milton Friedman at some point would be helpful. Slowly take the prime rate up to 6% (maybe a quarter point every quarter) and then leave it there. Never touch it again for any reason whatsoever.
9. Someone really has to have the guts to go through the entire budget and kill every asinine pet project of the legislature and executive.
10. Tort reform. Yes that sounds very boring, but half the reason that things like health care cost so much nowadays is because this country is sue-happy and sue anyone for any reason. Even if they don't win they've cost the defendant a rather large sum of money in

legal costs. This country has to make it a little harder to sue somebody, because let's be honest here it's not McDonald's fault that Captain Ahab is now chasing many Americans with a harpoon, it's their complete lack of self-control. Tort reform could stop silly lawsuits like that, not to mention deprive thousands of lawyers across the country of money (excuse me while I ponder that idea in complete ecstasy . . .)

11. Federal minimum wage needs to be lowered by at least a dollar (disbanded entirely eventually, but one thing at a time). Everyone knows when you raise minimum wage you will increase unemployment and raise prices . . . it works the same in reverse.

12. Anything that can be privatized in the government should be. I have no doubt UPS and FedEx can deliver letters better than the US Postal Service. I have no doubt a private firm can keep national parks cleaner, with more interesting tours and gift shops, for much lower costs. I know for a fact freeways work better as privatized toll roads. All the government has to do is in addition to the initial lease fee; they get 5% of any profits the company makes off these services. Everybody wins.

13. Either through Constitutional Amendment or through Supreme Court decision the commerce clause of the Constitution has to be reinterpreted to only apply to commerce that actually does cross state lines, not that could theoretically cross state lines and not that aids in crossing state lines only that which does cross state lines and those actions which impede commerce crossing state lines. The commerce clause was meant only to stop barriers from being put up, not to allow the Federal government to put up restrictions.

14. All loans and grants that the government gives out need to be cycled back over the next 10 years to nothing. Yes that includes student loans. One of the reasons that college tuition has jumped over the last few decades is because the government kept increasing the amount it was willing to pay students, and amazingly college tuitions tended to rise by about the same amount. This will result in a year or two low attendance at colleges followed by a price collapse similar to the housing market. The good news is that after the market takes over on determining prices more people will be able to go to college. Will quality suffer, probably for a short while, but it will balance out in the end.
15. Federal open shop laws need to be passed thus destroying the government enforced monopoly that unions have. Also federal and state employee unions need to be abolished.
16. Corporate welfare of any kind needs to be stopped.

These are just a few ideas. I could come up with more, but I'm sure you get the idea. The other point I would make is that this is an all or nothing thing. You can't only do a few of these ideas, see them not create immediate economic growth and then claim they don't work. Changing one or two individual pieces doesn't make the system capitalism, it's still pseudo-socialism, and that is still doomed to eventual failure. Nor will the effects be immediate . . . the economy is a very slow creature and takes time (like decades) to fully adjust to change. But change, and I do mean measurable positive material and spiritual change, (not esoteric intangible change that politicians like to talk about so much), will come.

Chapter 7
CORPORATE WELFARE AND BAD LOANS THE BAD SIDE OF CAPITALISM, OR WHAT PEOPLE BLAME CAPITALISM FOR

Now that's all well and good you say, but we're in the middle of a recession. You can't go cutting the government left and right, right now. It would ruin everything! We need the government right now. Talk about cutting the government only after we get out of this crisis!

If these words, or similar sentiments, went through your mind at any point the in the previous chapters do the following: (1) Slap yourself (2) re-read the previous chapters because you clearly missed the point that government is the problem not the solution to economic woes.

Let's look at the current recession. Or more accurately what caused it, as we don't need to look at how the Bush and Obama administrations reacted to it—it goes without saying that Obama's Socialist tactics are doomed to failure.

What caused it? We could say it was the housing market collapse but that would be far too simple. Let's start tracing it from the present back to its origins (they're disturbingly similar).

Where are we right now? We're in an era of $700 billion bailouts of the corporations of the American Economy and $14 trillion deficits. $14,000,000,000,000.00! That's $45,000 for every man, woman and child in the United States. It gets worse when you start figuring in that not every man, woman and child is paying taxes. Even if we get out of the economy's way and let it recover it will take years to get the deficit back to a reasonable level. And what is that money that we're still giving out going to do—to help out businesses that are near collapse from failing, businesses the government thinks should be saved despite the fact that the economy and the invisible hand seem to say something else. In addition to giving away money in ways that make drunken sailors look like trusted investment advisors, it only adds insult to injury that the government is partly to blame for being in this situation in the first place.

So let's look at this whole debacle, and see who is to blame at each and every stage of the problem. Here is the major sequence of problems that caused even greater problems: (1) Bad business practices, buffeted by corporate welfare, weaken the actual strength of companies and coupled with unethical accounting practice which hide these weakness and simultaneously making them appear stronger than they ever could, (2) leads to an inflated economy, which is encouraged by a Federal Reserve hell bent on preventing inflation and keeping unemployment low, (3) this leads the government to push for an increase in the housing market as they believe if the economy is up, then more people should own a house, (4) which then causes an overly inflated housing market, which is further encouraged by government mandated bad loans to buy those houses, (5) which when the bubble bursts causes a housing market crash, (6) which causes a banking and credit collapse, (7) which causes all the problem in the corporations mentioned in point 1 to come to the forefront and show those businesses to be weak and thus collapse, (8) which leads to the current bailout cycle and recession.

Let's have a more detailed look at this and how at each stage government interference where it shouldn't be interfering, and noninterference where government has a capitalistic responsibility as the appointed judge/referee of the whole economic system.

(1)

For decades now government has been covering up bad business practices with what is called corporate welfare. Now usually under a fully capitalistic system when a business has bad business practices, such as investing in bad markets or hiring incompetent executives, or coming up with a product nobody wants to buy, one of two things will happen, either that business will learn quickly that what they're doing isn't working and change and begin to make a profit, or that business will collapse. The system of capitalistic economics is very much like the Darwinian theories of natural selection on this point. Those variations that give a species/company an advantage will promote growth, expansion, and life; those variations that do not grant a given species/company an advantage will lead to death and extinction. If you'll recall your high school biology class's discussion of population growth and evolution it would go something like this. You have a certain number of rabbits. Rabbits being rabbits, they reproduce at an exponential rate (this would be the equivalent of an economic boom) and suddenly you have tons of rabbits hopping around everywhere, and doing what bunnies do, if you know what I mean. However with the rabbit populations booming, this then leads to a boom in the local wolf population (the beginning of an economic slow down) because now the wolves are no longer limited by a meager food supply. The wolf population booms and starts eating every rabbit it can get its teeth into. Only the cleverest, fastest, healthiest rabbits survive, but on a whole the rabbit population drops like a rock (an economic recession or depression where all the weak companies, because of their poor policies, go the way of the Dodo). The wolf population in turn because of the limited food supply drops and soon the rabbit population, without predators to kill them all, begins to grow again and the cycle repeats itself. Without this cycle weakening mutations that are not beneficial would be allowed to continue in the rabbit population until it might make the entire population susceptible to disease or other possible causes of extinction.

Now where does corporate welfare come into this? Well, like many crazy early environmental efforts to eliminate predators from certain areas thus protect certain species of this or that, but which eventually led to only more environmental disaster, with the greater possibility for disaster to two or more species. For instance, whereas a single bad business policy will often be noticed quickly—even by semi-competent business leaders (or at least by the consultants they obsessively hire) it will be noticed—and just as quickly done away with. This is for a very simple reason: bad business policies lead to less money. Under a situation where the government isn't handing out money for nothing to businesses, businesses keep an eye on all of its policies to see what works and what doesn't because they have a profit to make.

Republicans and Reincarnation

Businesses that don't adjust stop making profits and soon go out of business long before they become very large or very important to the economy. But here's the odd thing when the government is giving away money or favors or protective tariffs and legislation to companies (call whatever you will: corporate welfare, subsidies, bailout, paying people not to grow crops, legislation that gives existing companies an advantage, or just plain idiocy) weird and terrible things start happening. When the government was paying roughly 92 billion dollars a year[63] in 2006, before bailouts and stimulus, to companies, low and behold companies do stupid things with this money. And that $92 billion doesn't even begin to count the corporate welfare supplied by legislative and tariff protection. As I said before people don't use welfare money intelligently, the same goes for corporations. When it's other people's money they're spending they stop pinching pennies, as all good businesses should do.

But business, even if they know they're doing stupid things with government money, know they just can't admit to the public, the government, or worse, their stock holders, that they're doing stupid things that won't work in the long run. At this point every incompetent businessman gets down on their knees and thanks Satan for the existence of the IRS. Ever look at the IRS tax code? Decoding a Braille message written in Navajo code talk would be easier to decipher. And with this lovely mess of insane laws, rules, codes, and legal decisions come an accounting system to match. An accounting system that lets you print reports that move money

---

[63] 2006 figures from the Cato Institute The Corporate Welfare State: How the Federal Government Subsidizes U.S. Businesses by Stephen Slivinski. http://www.cato.org/pubs/pas/pa592.pdfstitute

around in such a obscure and mystifying way you can be a business without a penny to your name in reality and look like you are worth billions on paper (Enron). Now I'm sure you're thinking that you were sure you saw Congress correct those problems. Didn't they charge the executives of those companies with multiple crimes? (Yes, but not with their accounting practices). Didn't they charge Arthur Anderson, the accountants of Enron? (Yes, for shredding documents, not for their accounting practices . . . it's more the PR scandal that followed that destroyed Arthur Anderson . . . but not enough to stop almost every employee of Arthur Anderson to just form new companies with new names and do the exact same thing they did before). Didn't Congress pass laws after all those debacles? (Yes but not a single law that reformed the tax and accounting practices). Because, believe it or not, Enron's accounting, as dishonest and unethical as it was, was and still is completely legal. Under any sane definition of capitalism, government is supposed to set the rules for which we play by to make sure that no one is cheating someone else . . . yet in this specific function of government the U.S. Congress has and is still failing to accomplish their actual responsibility. They would rather give out money in a very socialistic way, than actually do their capitalistic duty and reform the tax code and by extension accounting procedures and say that this or that form of accounting is not only unethical, but actually illegal. But that would actually point out that corporate welfare is actually helping ruin companies, so we can't have any of that.

(2)

So, for a time, these companies which are bleeding money through bad policies encouraged by government welfare, and hidden through government sanctioned practices, appear to be doing well, doing so well that their stock jumps up in price. This is called a bubble. Where the price of things is actually higher than they should be because of the emotional enthusiasm of the market rather than logical conclusions of what things are worth.

These bubbles cause the economy as a whole to shoot up. Now even under a system without government interference you would have a bubble here and there—they just wouldn't be as large or as frequent. However you know what else comes with economic growth? Well if you ask the people at the Federal Reserve they will say inflation and low unemployment. In fact, based on incredibly outdated economic theories, the Federal Reserve believes that inflation and unemployment are tied together and that when one is high the other is low and that to control the two the government has to take control of such things as interest rates and investment to make sure that inflation doesn't get out of control or that unemployment doesn't get too high.

A few problems with this. The first is that while there is a mild correlation between the two figures, one does not control the other. If I were to plot inflation rates and unemployment rates on a chart it would look like a scatter plot rather than a nice correlation line. There are simply too many other factors in the economy to say that one controls the other.

The second is that the Federal Reserve thinks that it can control these issues . . . and it can in the short term. It can control it through the supply of money in the economy, which if anything is far more effective and has few negative effects (so obviously they don't use this method, or if they try they don't use it well) or they can do it through the more dangerous (but faster, and in our society of instant gratification faster is always better) changing of the interest rates. The interest rate control has usually quick effects on the economy—affecting the rates on loans, the ease at which loans can be acquired, how attractive stock investment is compared to government bonds. But with every change in the interest rate ripples begin in the economic system that are often hard to predict and the ripples have a way of creating further and further problems; and like the little Dutch boy, the government has only so many hands to deal with the problem.

Notice that the last few years involved the Federal Reserve under Bernanke raising the rates to avoid inflation to points where anyone with an adjustable rate mortgages couldn't pay their loans partly because inflation happened anyway, and then Bernanke cut rates to historic lows to avoid unemployment (which was partly caused by his unexpected raising of rates, and it didn't do anything to help unemployment)[64].

---

[64] Especially ironic when Bernanke is on record for agreeing with Milton Friedman that poor choices by the Federal Reserve caused the Great Depression. Guess he didn't learn that history repeats itself. "Regarding the Great Depression. [Milton Friedman is] right, we [the Federal Reserve] did it. We're very sorry. But thanks to you [Friedman], we won't do it again." ... or maybe he will. http://www.federalreserve.gov/BOARDDOCS/SPEECHES/2002/20021108/default.htm

So once again government interference is screwing things up. But before that happened with the economy still up, the government did some other really stupid things.

(3)

Since the Carter administration, there has been a major push to get more people to own houses, as owning a house is a sign of wealth and provides secure wealth that can be used as an insurance against economic hard times. After all, if you own your house, and then have a hard time paying the bills, all you have to do is take out a mortgage and pay it back when the economy goes back up. So the government as usual put the cart before the horse, and rather than try to find ways to improve the economy so more people earn the wealth to buy a house, they just skipped to the last part and created the Community Reinvestment Act (CRA) which focused on getting people who couldn't usually qualify for a home loan a loan (to hell if they actually have the income to pay it off). But during the Clinton Administration Department of Housing and Urban Development (it was 1995 so the Republicans in Congress are equally to blame here) it gets worse, because during that time period the CRA is revamped to allow for this fascinating thing called the subprime loan.

Long story short "[t]he Clinton Treasury Department's tough new regulations in 1995 compelled the banks to engage in far-riskier lending practices or receive a failing CRA grade."[65]

---

[65] The Heritage Foundation: The CRA Cover Up. http://www.heritage.org/Press/Commentary/ed101508b.cfm

(4)

No really, if banks and mortgage lenders didn't make these incredibly stupid loans to people who couldn't pay they faced fines, lawsuits, and bad PR. When you have the Departments of Treasury, Housing and Urban Development, Commerce, and Justice all screaming at you you're not likely to disagree (especially considering Janet Reno's penchant for bloody FBI standoffs). The only advantage to the bank was that they got to give out these loans on an adjustable interest rate, so if the Federal Reserve raised the interest rate on money it lends to banks, banks got to raise the rates on these people with the subprime loans (people who couldn't afford a higher rate, because if they could, they would have qualified for a fixed rate loan . . . it's utterly astounding that no one in the field saw this disaster coming).

This situation is further encouraged by the existence of Fannie Mae and Freddie Mac. Fannie Mae and Freddie Mac are two of the strangest companies in all of existence. Created by the government to buy and sell the loans of mortgage lenders on what is called the secondary market and all the liability that comes with them, and to hold them for profit or sell them to other banks, Fannie and Freddie are both government run institutions and privately held/publicly traded companies (and the bang up job this kind of arrangement did should make you very worried about current practices of the government buying stock of American corporations to keep them solvent). Now banks and investors can buy from mortgage lenders on the secondary market without Fannie or Freddie, but these two companies help to expedite the process (not to mention exacerbate the problem). They are set up to compete with each other to buy and sell loans; this competition theoretically will keep loan prices down. But since they're both run by the government through the Department of Housing and Urban Development (HUD), one wonders how much competition is really going on (it's like playing a game of chess with yourself, no true competition is going on; or more accurately since this is the government, it's like a lobotomy patient playing chess with themselves).

How do Fannie and Freddie work into this? Well the government through numerous Departments and officials guaranteed that Fannie and Freddie would buy up all the loans that were sold thus the mortgage lenders would be out nothing in making these incredibly risky loans.

So lenders are forced by law to make loans to people who can't pay their loans; these loans are subprime (meaning you're a bad loan risk) or adjustable rate loans; the Federal government promises it will buy the paper for these loans from banks so the banks are in the clear.

But then banks, investment groups and Fannie/Freddie, start buying more of these loans and selling this idea to their investors as a good investment because it will have a high yield of return (because high yield over a short term promises have always been a safe investment—S&L scandals and the roaring '20's come to mind). So banks feel free to offer even more and more of these loans. (Just the whole issue of banks making loans, Fannie/Freddie buying them then selling back to banks as investments plans should have told someone something was rotten in Denmark). Remember when you couldn't turn on the TV without five commercials for a mortgage lender coming on during every break, this was about that time. Sell loans to everyone. Bad Credit. No Credit. No Problem. Give everybody a loan! No income whatsoever—no problem. There's a subprime loan for anyone dumb enough to take one.

(5)

Strangely enough now that everyone and their cat can now get a loan for a house, low and behold, everyone starts to buy houses. Now what did your Economics teacher tell you happens when demand rises on a product? That's right prices go up, up, up. So now we're not only giving loans to people who can't afford to pay them back, but we're giving loans on inflated house prices as well. And we're making lots of these subprime loans.

And remember all this time, as privately held companies Fannie and Freddie are trying to make money for their investors. And the only way they make more money is by trading in more and more loans. This reaches a point in the early 2000's where over 90% of their loans are adjustable rate loans to people with no ability to afford their loans should that rate move up or any of their other costs go up.

Then add to this some banks were being sued for not making enough loans to minorities on the claims of discrimination. However, these claims seem rather specious since,

"If the lending discrimination theory were correct, it would mean that blacks had to have higher credit-worthiness than whites in order to have their loans approved. That in turn would imply that subsequent default rates among black borrowers would be lower than white borrowers. But empirical evidence from census data did not suggest a racial difference in default rates among the approved borrowers."[66]

But relevant or not banks are forced to make even more loans to avoid being sued.

So now we're at high amount loans, lots of mortgages, and borrowed money all over the place. This in turn inflates the rest of the market because when people took out that second mortgage on the house at the adjustable rate; did everyone pay off their debts? No. Did everyone put their money into investments in something safe? No. People went out and bought stuff. Added to this America's obsession with credit card debt and keeping up with the Jones, everything from the mid-90's until the current recession was a buyer's paradise. Don't believe that Americans were purchasing anything they could get their hands on? Well, ask yourself if they weren't, how did the stock market recover so remarkably quick (a couple of years) after losing one of the world's most important financial centers (the World Trade Center)?

And it gets worse, Fannie and Freddie were engaging in that same Enron style of shady accounting that made them look even better than they were (how good could you really be when all you hold is loan papers on over priced houses with promises of repayment from people who aren't in a situation to pay?). This did not go completely unnoticed by everyone. There were even some attempts at regulating these two companies (by Republicans of all people, but in the end every party deserves blame because nothing was done about this). But that didn't go forward. Mainly because of people like Barney Frank (you may remember him making comments two chapters ago

[66] Sowell, Thomas, *Economic Facts and Fallacies.* Basic Books: New York, NY, p. 181

about how deregulation was always a terrible thing and it's the government's responsibility to redistribute wealth, so clearly we're dealing with someone with the mental acumen of Sean Penn in "I am Sam"):

> *Frank was nearly as bold: "These two entities—Fannie Mae and Freddie Mac—are not facing any kind of financial crisis," Frank told the New York Times then. "The more people exaggerate these problems, the more pressure there is on these companies, the less we will see in terms of affordable housing."*[67]

So let me get this straight the guy who wants to regulate the entire private sector because it can't be trusted, thinks regulation of a government organization is uncalled for because it would hurt its business. And yeah, affordable housing—Inflated prices, inflated overpriced predatory loans, which will only leave people without a house, without money, and without a credit score. Yeah, really affordable.[68]

(6)

Then some problems cropped up.

---

[67] National Review "Frank Talk" By David Freddoso http://article.nationalreview.com/?q=ZDExZTIxY2RkYjYzN2QyM2YxOWEyO GFlZjZmMzAxNDU=

[68] But Barney Frank doesn't deserve all the blame . . . while I could even select other names, like Chris Dodd, or Barrack something or other, in the end everyone in the government is to blame for either being against regulation or for not raising holy hell over this and making it the key issues of the last decade. And we're all to blame for sending morons like this to D.C.!

Republicans and Reincarnation

While there were numerous causes, one of the most visible causes was that the price of oil rose dramatically. This is partly due to the fact that China was buying up every drop they could get their hands on (possibly to inflate the price and thus hurt the U.S. economy) and partly because a good chunk of the oil market is controlled by a rather greedy and corrupt government sponsored cartel (once again showing that monopolies cannot exist without government sponsorship) called OPEC. (OPEC's membership oddly enough tends to make the yearly who's who of countries where civil rights, liberty, or human dignity are not in vogue). So oil prices went up. And so did gas prices (as if you didn't know that).

Now since everything you buy at the store has to come from somewhere it's not just your gas bill that's going up, it's the stores, and their suppliers, and their suppliers and so on. So everybody raises their prices just a little to compensate for the loss. So you've now got higher gas bills and higher grocery, clothing, and everything else bills. In other words, INFLATION. Now if you've got a middle-class or better job your yearly salary is probably also being increased to compensate for the rise in costs (in harder economic times it probably will not be enough to keep you ahead of inflation, but you aren't being dropped like a rock either); if your company didn't you'd probably go somewhere else and then, while no employee is irreplaceable, taking time to find a new one, training them, seeing if they work out or not, tends to cost more than your cost of living adjustment to your salary; so it's just good business to give you your raise. It's an advantage of understanding that we live in a meritocracy and if you have marketable skills you'll be safe in life[69].

But back to they pesky Federal Reserve—they hate inflation. So what do they do? Raise the interest rates to prevent inflation (way to go boys on thinking this one through).

So now we have people who were credit risks before, with higher transportation costs, higher food and everything else costs, and now thanks to the higher interest rate, higher loan payments to make. The bad loans, the interest rate, and a portion of the inflation—all are the government's fault (keep in mind Point 1, that the economy is already being inflated by corporate welfare).

So with those adjustable rate mortgages actually make a semi-rational decision (not a good one, but a rational one). When you have three bills: food, gas to get me to work to pay for food and housing and gas, and my loan payment—which one is the one that is the least pressing? That's right people stopped paying their loans. Now one person here or there doesn't pay their loan for a month (or twelve) it's going to be annoying for the bank, but not the end of the world. But when most of their clients stop paying all at once . . . well that's a different story.

(7)

So banks do what banks always do when you don't pay your home loan. They foreclose. But everybody who wanted a house already got a great subprime loan, so there is no one to buy at the inflated price, so to get someone to buy the prices come down. This in turn lowers the

---

[69] Oh, if we could only get teenagers in high school to understand this basic fact of life.

value of the entire housing market. Suddenly people find themselves paying a high interest $300,000 loan on a house worth $200,000. Not surprisingly more people stop paying their loans.

This in turn brings us back to Fannie and Freddie. They had guaranteed the loans. They said that if the loans go bad they'd pay the bank the difference so the bank doesn't lose anything. Problem is that they were promising government money . . . government money they didn't really have in their own bank account. Suddenly Fannie and Freddie have more outstanding loans they've guaranteed than they can actually pay off in their wildest drug induced dreams. (And remember that they've been cooking the books as well). So what happens to Fannie and Freddie stock that's publicly traded? It goes from being a really good buy to a value where you'd have better luck getting some money for the paper your shares are printed on. And with the emotional nature of the stock market, if two major companies fall, then the prices of a lot of companies fall. The bubble has been burst—the inflated economy is over (but the inflated prices for everything else are here to stay).

Fannie and Freddie are bankrupt, and suddenly they can't guarantee all those loans. So now, all those banks and investors are stuck with loans that aren't getting paid off and foreclosed houses that can't get sold. Now as we all know banks don't keep their money in giant piles—as much as we like to think that Scrooge McDuck's money bin is out there somewhere to swim in, deep down we all knew that the money we give to the bank is reinvested in other places . . . like real estate.

But now that real estate is effectively worthless, so the bank's stock becomes worth a little less than it had before . . . so much so that the banks go under. In steps the government again. Rather than letting the banks just fail, pay out the FDIC insurance on the accounts and letting the assets of the bank go up for auction to the highest bidder (which would have resulted in the papers on all those loan being bought for rock bottom prices, prices so low that whoever bought them would be making a profit and thus be more financially secure) the government steps in and takes over the banks, keeping them up and running. It's like scientists finding an animal in the wild with genetic mutations that don't allow it to survive on it's own, but helping it live through some sort of medical treatment, thus guaranteeing those genetic flaws are continued to the next generation (not like we'd actually like to tell banks that they need to clean up their acts, no, the government will always be there to help).

So Freddie, Fannie, and a whole host of banks are bankrupt and under full government control. It's no shock that people are pulling back on investment and, depending on the day, the stock market is in near free fall (nowhere near as bad as the Stock Market crash that caused the Great Depression, but still a recession is caused). Further with poor economic news, let's be honest here, we all pinched those pennies just a little closer. With that came the fact that we bought less, and thus most companies did more poorly in terms of profits.

(8)

With profits down, companies are less likely to hire new people to replace those who are leaving/retiring/being fired, let alone opening up new positions. This in turn results in slightly higher unemployment (for those of you screaming about how high the unemployment rate is, please keep in mind that unemployment in the single digits is really not that bad in the grand scheme of things).

This hit to companies comes to multiple companies multiple ways, but few examples are as glaring as the auto industry.

GM, Ford, Chrysler were all hit with the recession to the point that they would likely collapse. Why? Not just because the economy slowed down and they had a bad quarter. No. That's like looking at a coroner's report and seeing that final cause of death was drowning and then blaming the victim's death on not being able to swim, when in reality the cause of the drowning was the lungs filling with water, caused by pneumonia, caused by the flu coupled with a weak immune system, caused by years of poor health habits. Often what finally does a company in is not necessarily the root cause of its failure. So what's the problem with the American automaker? Overpaid executives are one cause, I'll be the first to violently defend upper management making millions upon millions of dollars if they're doing their job which is making the company money—if they're not doing their job, which given the companies economic woes they clearly weren't, these rich idiots deserve to have their houses, and all other private property, repossessed by their own companies on grounds of failure to comply with their contract. Next, they do make inferior overpriced cars. But why do they make inferior overpriced cars? Well, mainly the American laborer is to blame. Workers in American car companies are all union employees. They are guaranteed over priced wages for jobs that a machine could do at a fraction of the cost. They bind car companies to hire and pay so many employees. "GM has a $73 hourly wage cost including benefits and overtime."[70] $73 an hour for unskilled labor! No wonder the education system is beyond repair in America. What incentive is there to go onto graduate high school with high grades and then get a college degree which earns you on average $80,000 (which comes about to about $38 an hour) when you can get a union job and never have to learn anything but stand on an assembly line. The fact is that American car companies are overstaffed and overpaid all because of the unions they have to deal with (those would be the same unions that refused to even discuss lowering employee levels or wages as the car companies are heading for bankruptcy). And this isn't a problem just facing the auto industry, unions in every field "add costs and discourage productivity"[71] causing we the consumer to pay for higher priced lower end goods . . . which in turn, oh yeah, causes people to buy less, helps lower the economy, and contributes to our current situation. So to the American union worker let me personally thank you for your part in our current economic situation. !@#$%^&.

Now, am I arguing for getting rid of all unions? No, without them being there, business, given how intelligently they're currently acting, would probably go back to all of their pre-union practices if they could. No we do need to keep unions around to keep the other side honest. However let's be honest the way unions

---

[70] Williams, Walter E. "Bailout and Bankruptcy" http://townhall.com/columnists/WalterEWilliams/2008/12/10/bailouts_and_bankruptcy

[71] Heritage Foundation: "Do Americans today still need labor unions?" by James Sherk http://www.heritage.org/Press/Commentary/ed040108c.cfm

treat their members nowadays make the robber barons of days gone by look like saints. However the union's government sheltered protection racket needs to be stopped. The government guarantees through closed shop laws that unions have complete tyrannical control over their employees contracts, work, salaries (of which they take an obscene portion)—which really means that the government guarantees artificially and insanely inflated wages for work performed by minimally educated and minimally skilled workers.

But really, what's the worst that could happen. So one or two of the big three automakers goes out of business, either their American competition (bolstered by a lack of competition) or their foreign competition will buy the factories and equipment and continue to use them. But that move would foster growth, as it would mean the businesses practices that work best, that offer the products people want at affordable prices would survive. The government saving such a company only ensures continued inefficiency, poor products, and stagnation.

But more importantly this is just a symptom of a larger problem. If these companies had not been on corporate welfare in the first place, they would never have simultaneously made years of bad decisions, been forced to plan more carefully in the first place, never made poor products, and wasted millions on corporate bonuses to upper management for wasting money like the government was just giving it out for free (oh wait they were).

Besides it's so much easier for the government to take over GM and make up lies slanderous lies about the safety of GM's competitor, Toyota. I'm sure there was no conflict of interest there.

(9)

This brings us to the current era of trillions of dollars in stimulus and bailouts—otherwise known as corporate welfare on lots of steroids.

So let's review the government mistakes that led to this one last time:

- Corporate Welfare
- Encouraging bad accounting practices
- Messing around with the interest rate
- Allowing banks to make bad loans
- Forcing them to make bad loans
- Backing bad loans
- Protecting Union overpriced wages
- Taking over banks
- Encouraging economic stagnation
- Taking control of failing companies
- Using the power of congressional hearing to slander those companies competitors

And then there is what they didn't do that they have not just the power, but the right and responsibility, to do under capitalism:

- Enforce ethical accounting practices
- Regulate government run organizations like Fannie Mae and Freddie Mac

So, given all that, that the government when given an opportunity to do the right thing will always do the opposite, does anyone think that another $700 billion is going to fix anything? Will an extension of unemployment benefits help? Will forcing everyone to buy a healthcare plan help? *Or is it more likely only going to delay the inevitable, which, when it does come, will be worse because the cycle you saw above will have yet another chance to run itself through.* The fact that we are in a bad recession is not an excuse for government interference, it's a giant neon sign screaming to reduce, not increase, government intervention in economic matters it should have no part in.

Oh and how can I forget the icing on this cake? Many states, to pay for their myriad of socialist welfare state programs that go way beyond the actual rights of a government in any Classical Liberal since, are raising taxes because the economy is low. So, to pay for their foolish Keynesian priming of the pump to get the economy started again, these states are going to take more money out of people's pockets. Is it just me or does that seem to be doing the exact opposite thing that you need to do at this point in time. Shouldn't government expenditures be cut back and taxes lowered to encourage a slowed economy? Or am I using logic again, which as we all know is anathema in the government.

In the final analysis recessions, and even the very occasional depression, are natural. Not just natural, they're a necessary part of the system. A natural check developed against bad business practices, old production models, and inefficient systems. As America moves past the 20th century, its power as a production center has and needs to drop, because the economy has moved beyond just production of things. Sadly politicians can't understand any of these points. They stop the natural culling methods of the system, which allows inefficiency to survive long enough to become a serious problem and are keeping outdated businesses around and preventing new innovations from filling the place of the old companies that die out.

Is it just me, or is not so much capitalism that is the problem, but rather, the government thinking it can do better than capitalism.

Chapter 8

LET SLIP THE DOGS OF WAR: JUST WAR AND THE REASON IT SHOULD AND MUST BE USED.

"No cause is left but the most ancient of all, the one, in fact, that from the beginning of our history has determined the very existence of politics, the cause of freedom versus tyranny."—Hannah Arendt

Now, around this point I'm sure you've thought about, at least once, the most glaring (or at least what seems to be the most glaring) contradiction in these two philosophies of conservatism and New Age belief: war (or you might have just been very, very bored by the economic stuff, sorry about that). New Age beliefs are almost always in favor of peace and harmony. Modern conservative beliefs are fairly aggressive with its "let's kill them before the psycho tyrant kills us" logic. How can one possibly reconcile one with the other? The answer: very easily.

All you have to do is admit one thing and that is that peace, in a political sense, is not the absence of conflict. Just as the absence of conflict in one's soul is only the first step to spiritual enlightenment not the last. The last is presence of love and knowledge. A similar truth exists with peace in the political sense, as a wise man once said, it is the presence of Justice that defines peace.

Thus we are left with the question of how to seek this justice and two possible avenues seem open to us. On the one hand we could attempt to make our own country (or countries) a bastion of justice, a shining beacon for the rest of the world to imitate and hope that it will spread from there. The second is to deal with the world as a single entity and seek out and destroy the worst examples of injustice one at time, correct them one at a time, and then move onto the next worst. The first is more passive, the second more aggressive, let us deal with each at a time.

Essentially I have already detailed what needs to be done to make this country the "shining city on the hill" envisioned by colonist Jonathan Winthrop, and later quoted by Ronald Reagan. Capitalism with all of its freedoms and laws creates the society that is the envy of the world[72]. Much of the world is taking up these practices, albeit slowly, and not necessarily in the most effective order (usually laws protecting property rights should come before McDonald's, but so long as the end result is a capitalist system that protects the rights of the individual, I think we can all live with the hiccups, annoying though they may be). But the fact of the matter is that capitalism alone is not enough to bring every person to a material level of living where they more easily move to a higher spiritual plane. There is something that

---

[72] Some may wish to argue with me on that statement to which I point out that no country on Earth has the number of immigrants coming to our shores wishing to be citizens of this country. It is then not hard to understand why Western Europe and Canada with slightly more socialistic tendencies, but still essentially holding to the core beliefs of Liberalism, are the next most popular countries to come to.

is far more malignant than poverty, because it is often the cause of poverty and fear wherever it exists: tyranny.

I can already hear the snorting of a few on the far left. The objection will go that tyranny is not that much of a problem anymore[73]. With the exception of North Korea and a few other third world nations, tyranny doesn't exist anymore; the cry goes to my face along with a look like I'm a Neanderthal that doesn't quite understand the world I'm living in. Or, even better, the only real tyranny nowadays is the hegemony of the United States—I always love to hear that bit of inane drivel.

But modern liberal ranting aside, let's look at the state of tyranny versus Classical Liberal defense of human rights in the world today. Now while doing research for this chapter someone said I should go by the U.N.'s Human Rights Council and what the U.N. has to say about countries being tyrannical or not. But while I know many liberals love to defer to the insanity of the U.N. (I'll have a whole chapter on them later) let's just look at a few points: The U.N. security council has Russia and China on it with permanent seats that have veto power . . . because that's logical, a body that should theoretically be there to stop the growth of tyranny, yeah, let's give veto power to two of the worst examples of tyranny in the world.[74] Or the U.N.'s Human Rights Council, let's

---

[73] And I can also hear the objection from the more sane quarters of the population: Why is he putting this in here? Why, you ask, because I have actually had arguments with people who really felt that essentially tyranny died with the Axis at the end of World War II and that all countries could now deal with each other through rational means.

[74] Yes and I do mean both Russian in both its communist and its current corrupt pseudo-fascist stages.

look at some of the members of this august body: China (which has redefined the terms human rights violation and genocide to the point where they may soon become the national pastime in China), Russia (where the lines between government, mafia, and bloodbath is never really all that clear), Cuba (a country where people would rather risk almost certain death swimming more miles than a human being should be capable of in an inner tube, just to leave that hellhole), Saudi Arabia (where women are valued somewhere below dirt), Pakistan (very recently a country headed up by a dictator, a somewhat benevolent dictator, but a dictator nonetheless; it's also a place with such a reverence for life that most of Al-Qaida is thought to be hiding in Pakistan without fear of being turned over?) I could name a few others but you get the point that giving weight to the Human Rights Council and anything it does is much like asking Charles Manson to baby-sit your kids for the weekend.

So then anything directly from the U.N. is out. That was a given. So who do we now turn too? Well there are three lists that are generally quoted. The yearly *Freedom in the World* published by Freedom House[75], *The Economist*

---

[75] www.Freedomhouse.org. Freedom House, in their own words, is "non-profit, nonpartisan organization, is a clear voice for democracy and freedom around the world" and state they make their judgments of countries based on political right and civil liberties. They judge all countries to be in one of three categories: Free, Partly Free, Not Free. For instance it's 2007 report list 92 countries as being free, 65 as being partly free, and 52 as being not free. All figures will come from their 2007 report. Freedom House has its critics, but who doesn't.

Magazine's *Index of Democracy*[76], and *The Economic Freedom of the World Index* put out by the Heritage Foundation and The Wall Street Journal[77]. So the question is, is tyranny really still a problem? Well looking at all three lists here are the countries that are unquestionably free[78]: Australia, Austria, Canada, Cyprus, Denmark, Estonia, Finland, Japan, Germany, Iceland, Ireland, Luxembourg, Mauritius, the Netherlands, New Zealand, Sweden, Switzerland, Taiwan, the United Kingdom, and last, but not least, the United States of America. This comes to about 715,862,600[79] of the people currently living in the world. That's 716 million out of 6.5 billion (about 11% of the world). But maybe it's just that most of the world is in that middle ground. Well let's look at

[76] http://www.economist.com/media/pdf/DEMOCRACY INDEX 2007 v3.pdf. This list goes more on how democratic the process is, judging such things as universal suffrage, and having a competitive multiparty system. They list countries in four categories: Democracies (28), Flawed Democracies (54), Hybrid Regimes (40), and Authoritarian Regimes (55). Again all figures are taken from the 2007 report.

[77] http://www.heritage.org/research/features/index/. Their methodology is given in extensive detail, but as the title suggests it's dealing with economic figures. Their determination is whether a country is Free (7), Mostly Free (23), Moderately Free (51), Mostly Unfree (52), and Repressed (24)

[78] My criteria is that they are listed as Free by Freedom House, Democracy by The Economist, and have a score of higher than 70 out of a possible 100 from the Heritage Foundation and the Wall Street Journal.

[79] Population estimates are taken from the CIA World Fact Book July 2008 estimates. https://www.cia.gov/library/publications/the-world-factbook/index.html

how many countries and people are living in tyranny[80]: North Korea (with a whopping 3 out of 100 on the Index of Economic Freedom), Cuba, Zimbabwe, Libya, Myanmar, Turkmenistan, Belarus, Iran, the Republic of Congo, the Democratic Republic of Congo, Syria, Angola, Chad, Togo, Laos, Vietnam, Russia, Equatorial Guinea, China, Uzbekistan, Rwanda, Tajikistan, Algeria, Azerbaijan, Pakistan, Swaziland, Tunisia, Kazakhstan, Qatar, Saudi Arabia, the United Arab Emirates, Oman, the Ivory Coast, Bhutan, and Eritrea. And this rather extensive list of places you'd never like to visit gives us a population estimate of about 2,236,797,124. That's right about 2 BILLION people are living in near or complete tyranny. Or, for every free person on Earth, there are three people living under tyranny. And don't forget the other 3.5 billion in that gray zone in between.

So, I think it's a safe bet to say that tyranny is still a problem in the world; arguably one bigger than economic problems since many economic problems are caused by the way dictators like to run their countries as if it was still

---

[80] To make it on this list I require a Not Free from Freedom House, a Authoritarian Regime from The Economist, and lower than 70 on the Index of Economic Freedom. There are a couple of exceptions here though. Russia is listed as having a hybrid regime, not an authoritarian regime by The Economist, but it also has one of the lowest economic scores in the world (49 out of 100) so they made it on the list. Further, the Ivory Coast, Bhutan, Eritrea, and the Democratic Republic of Congo weren't rated by the Heritage Foundation and the Wall Street Journal, so they actually don't have economic scores, but one can safely assume that this lack of score probably has something to do with the kind of hellish existence that goes on in these places.

the 13th century (but they do love having lots of brand new guns . . . makes terrorizing the masses easier).

Still some say that tyranny isn't the problem it used to be. They look at the world and say, "well they're not as bad as Hitler." Really? China has killed over a million Tibetans, subjugated over a billion people, run over protesters with tanks, funded and backed regimes in North Korea, Pakistan, Vietnam, Laos, Cambodia, has given nuclear material to Pakistan and North Korea, has publicly stated its desire to conquer another free nation in Taiwan and would probably take down South Korea and India (just for starters) if they had the chance. Iran from its nut job president to its more powerful Ayatollah has called for the mass genocide of every citizen in Israel, not to mention being the primary supporter of terrorists in Iraq. Dictatorial governments in Sudan and the Democratic Republic of the Congo starve, mutilate, rape, and hack to pieces their citizens. And this is just a sampling of the evil in the world.

But they're not like Hitler. Why because they haven't hit that magical number of six million? (Actually they have and then some, but let's ignore that for a moment).

It is this disgusting, willingly turning away, this apathy, this regard for numbers of people, not the quality of life and the reduction of suffering that we must first stop. Before we can hope to end tyranny . . . we must end our own apathy. We must rise up and say "no more." It doesn't have to be shouted, or screamed, but it must be said. It must be realized that no matter the cost this sort of evil must end, and it must end within our lifetime. We have the power to stop it, to give hope to those suffering, to give a rallying point to spark revolution and coups that will oust these vile excuses for governments and human beings. It will not require military action over the entire world, because dictators only understand fear and fear that they will have to deal not only with their own people, but with the free nations of the world will keep them in line, it will force them to give show elections in their countries which will turn against them and become real elections. This will form, although with undoubtedly many hiccups and false starts, laws and systems of government.

But what should we do about it?

Now I'm not suggesting that since we think attacking tyranny is a good idea we should declare war on the ten worst dictators in the world tomorrow with all the same restraint that I show by buying up every CD an artist has ever produced when I find one song I like. No! We're conservatives. We show consideration and restraint. We're slow and deliberate. We think things out. We plan. Planning for not only how to get rid of the current regime quickly but how to rebuild the country over the next decade or more until it is next to on par with us (unlike some other dimwitted administrations[81]). Occupation is something that has to occur after a war, and occupations take lots of time—and when done properly (Germany, Japan) yield nice friendly nations with capitalistic and democratic natures . . . when we don't stick around after we invade a country and don't clean up the mess we made it leads to countries sane people would usually avoid and

---

[81] Yes I supported the invasion of Iraq even though we should have first tightened up the situation in Afghanistan even more. But arguably we were only cleaning up the mess we should have originally cleaned up in 1991 if we hadn't had a complete incompetent wimp in the oval office at the time. That and how was I to know that absolutely no planning whatsoever was given to what to do after Saddam's army was beaten.

bear some resemblance in their governments to levels of Dante's Inferno (Nazi Germany, Mexico, Cuba).

I see three options: ignore it, diplomacy, or active intervention.

Let's deal with American foreign policy up to the present with its schizophrenic attitude toward ignoring the problem and see how well that's worked for us in the past.

U.S. Foreign Policy in the 20th Century

"[America's] previous attempts at isolationism were successful. Unfortunately, they were successful for Hitler's Germany and Tojo's Japan. Evil is an outreach program. A solitary bad person sitting alone, harboring genocidal thoughts, and wishing he ruled the world is not a problem unless he lives next to us in the trailer park. In the big geopolitical trailer park that is the world today, he does. America has to act."—P.J. O'Rourke, Peace Kills: America's Fun New Imperialism

As a brief refresher course let's look at the last century or so of U.S. foreign policy. Coming off our crazy Manifest Destiny kick, Americans swung into a full isolationist mode in the early 20th century[82]. So much so that when people started dying by the thousands in WWI we chose

---

[82] I start with the 20th century because this is the first time in history that technology allowed the world to be small enough for any country to legitimately be involved in the affairs of another country anywhere in the world. Had such technological advances been available a century earlier I would probably also be complaining that someone should have come and invaded

to do nothing. Thousand of soldiers—British, French, Italian, German, Austrian, to name a few—suffered in trenches with some of the most horrific conditions modern warfare has to offer. But it's not America's problem so we do nothing. The Ottoman Empire (ally of Germany and Austria) begins genocidally slaughtering Armenians, Assyrians, and Greeks so brutally the Allies actually issue a statement using the words "crime against humanity" for the first time (so I doubt everyone in America was ignorant of this). America still does nothing, because still not our problem. Then one of our ships gets torpedoed while going through a war zone, so now it's our problem. We come in with enough troops to end the war (if we had come in years earlier it would probably have ended the war then and spared thousands upon thousands suffering and death, but, oh, that's right it wasn't our problem at the time).

So World War I ends. President Wilson has a good idea in the form of a world organization to oppose tyranny and support democracy around the world, the League of Nations, but the isolationist quickly take power again in America and decide not to be a member of the organization. I'm not saying American participation in the League would have stopped World War II from happening, but explain to me how it would have hurt. So in the end the League of Nations is filled by almost nothing but countries that have pacifist views that will cower when anyone with a gun shows up.

The first major failure of this war weary League and America (both parties are equally guilty) is allowing the continuation of the Red Army in the former Russian

the United States for it's slavery policies and genocidal treatment of the Native Americans.

Empire. World War I ended officially in 1919, but the Russian Civil War didn't end until 1923, yet no one even really offered to help the White Army put down the communists (good call, because the Soviets didn't cause any problems over the next 70 years or so). No, rather than actually take out the root of the problem at maybe the cost of a few thousand more lives for Western nations, here in America we chose the policy of going into a hysterical fit over the fear of communists in our country, mobilizing every federal and state power to track down what turned out to be nothing more than a few dozen radicals with access to gun powder and a rough skill in making bad mail bombs.[83] So we'll use police powers against our own people over the fear of a foreign nation but won't actually deal with that foreign nation we fear, because it's not our problem.

The next few years brought up other things that weren't our problem. The Spanish Civil War, which allowed the country to fall to fascism. Italian aggression and empire building in Africa, but not our problem. The growing Maoist Army in China, not our problem. Invasion of China and Korea by Japan, not our problem. And dare we forget all those things Germany under Hitler did that weren't our problem. Crimes against humanity each and every one of them. Not even counting the Holocaust, literally millions of people are being killed, raped, enslaved, and tortured. Americans can't be that stupid to not know anything about this. Yes, many chose not to learn anything, just as nowadays many don't bother to read about what goes on in the Sudan, because we know

---

[83] I'm not saying there weren't Soviet agents ever in America, there were, but odds are they didn't become entrenched until after the Russian Civil War was over.

deep down if we knew we would be morally required to act, but American ignorance was one of choice, not one of lack of information (also much like how after we went into Germany all we found was a country filled with "Good Germans" who never knew what was going on in the concentration camps). And if all American's were really that ignorant of these things, then how does one explain the very few Americans who went to all these wars to fight against fascism, to fight for what they believed to be right. They had to learn about it somewhere.

But these things weren't our problem.

Then once again a weird thing happened. Low and behold after nearly every other nation who opposed fascism had fallen or was under siege, all of a sudden the fascists turned their eyes to us and it became our problem. Who could have guessed that an ideology founded on conquering the world would ever come to American shores. Completely unpredictable. So once again it suddenly became our problem again, and we went in and took down most of the bad guys. Then we went back to isolationist tendencies. Now some history buffs out there will call me crazy, because Truman's post war policies could hardly be called isolationist—after all, we helped rebuild Western Europe and contained the Soviet Union. True, we contained the Soviet Union. This was isolationist in itself. Let's go back to the day immediately following Japan's surrender and look at the situation. You have Soviet Russia preparing to take total control of Eastern Europe as a "buffer zone" between them and Germany. Even at this point in history everyone knows Stalin is a worse butcher than Hitler. The bulk of the Soviet Army (devastated far more than the rest of the Allies by the war) is racing across Asia hoping to get a

Republicans and Reincarnation

foothold into Japan and thus more land to control, thus leaving everything up to Moscow with minimal defenses. Gen. Patton (certainly not the most stable of men, but a strategic and tactical genius nonetheless) has this wacky plan to push the Russian army in Europe back to the Russian border if not destroy it completely. It was August, giving us at least a couple of months before those infamous Russian winters set in. Oh, and America was the only country that was a nuclear power at this point. It wouldn't have been bloodless, but had the Allies decided to attack Soviet Russia it wouldn't have been a long war, nor would it's outcome been in the favor of communism. But we chose once again to not deal with a problem until it affected us.

We create the U.N., but then give two of the most evil governments in the world veto power to stop any action intended to stop their tyrannical ways.

Some more things that weren't our problems after that. Eastern Europe is placed under a dictatorship as brutal and bloodthirsty as the one we just liberated them from. China, with Soviet help falls to communism. Tibet, after asking for U.S. help, receives no help and falls to Maoist butchers. The Soviet Union becomes a nuclear power (yes we did recognize that as our problem, but the fact is if we had recognized them as a problem a few years earlier, they wouldn't have been around to become a nuclear threat). And after some half-hearted[84] fighting we allow the communists to take North Korea (it's not like allowing that one would ever lead to problems). Cuba also falls to communism, but not directly our problem, until low and behold communists from one part of the

---

84 I'm insulting the politician who made war policy, not the soldiers who fought.

world start giving communists in another part of the world nuclear missiles.

So isolationism is not looking like a good option at this point to anyone who can count hundreds of millions tortured and killed as a direct result of it, but the U.S. still can't give up it's isolationist way. So we now try a kind of halfway isolationism. The use of the CIA to work behind the scenes and the use of the U.S. military only in "police actions." The problem with police actions is if you have rules about when and where your troops can fire back at the enemy, and what lines they can cross, and just generally the falling short of fighting a real war then all you end up with is a lot of U.S. soldiers in body bags and a wall in D.C. commemorating the fact that despite being excellent soldiers, who never actually lost a real battle, politicians will make their deaths completely worth nothing by just leaving countries like Vietnam to communist governments.

Then Khmer Rouge takes over Cambodia and does things that might turn a Nazi's stomach, but again, not our problem.

All this time it would take a whole book to recount all the bloody things being done in Africa that weren't our problem.

Iran falls to a dictator whom we don't support, falls to a dictator whom we do support, then falls to a radical Islamic cleric who no one in the world of the sane is not disturbed by. Our president at the time of this final change of power decides it's best to be weak, and let them hold American hostages until he leaves office. But then again this is the same man whose grand stand against the invasion and resulting crimes against humanity in Afghanistan by the Soviets was best combated by boycotting the Olympics. Way to take a stand, Jimmy.

So we learned not to use police actions. So still not actually wanting to fight real wars, because it's not really our problem, we just start arming people in their wars against our enemies. People like the rebel soldiers in Afghanistan to fight the communists (this guy named Bin Laden comes to mind), and people like Saddam Hussein to fight off Iran. I wonder if that policy ever came back to haunt us?

Oh wait, it did. Hussein invades other countries; we kick him out of Kuwait but leave him around for the next generation to deal with (incompetently I might add).

Our genius plan of dealing with the collapsing Soviet Union is to support whatever dictator comes along in the Balkans, which once again leads to genocide and U.S. troops having to go in under the cover of the U.N. (really wasn't even our idea, it required Tony Blair twisting Clinton's arm to get U.S. troops to go). And I'm still trying to figure out what drugs were being passed around when it came to our policies involving Russia itself, but the result was what it always is, let's not get involved.

Then let's try and help out in Africa, until a few bullets get fired (in a war zone of all places, who could have predicted that) and it's decided that's it's better for a few soldiers to have died in vain, than to actually clear Somalia of the warlords.

Afghanistan falls to psychotic religious fanatics, not our problem. At least until the New York skyline gets a permanent makeover.

Is it just me, or does it seem that all of these things that aren't our problem have a bad tendency of becoming our problem, and rather big problems at that? Ironic because they weren't necessarily always big problems, in fact they would have been more easily dealt with problems back when it wasn't our problem.

And let's look at another pattern that seems apparent to me, when what wasn't our problem becomes our problem we go in long enough to stop the current problem without sticking around long enough to make sure it doesn't happen again. The few places we have stuck around (Germany, Japan, and the Balkans seem relatively stable at the moment, I'm hard pressed to think of another one as so many in this country want to abandon Iraq and Afghanistan at this point . . . I wonder if actually doing anything would lead to even bigger problems in the long run?)

So no matter how you want to look at it isolationism on any country's part, but especially one as large as the U.S. seems to lead to three things: (1) Torture (2) Death (3) and problems that become so big they do become our problems.

So doing nothing is out.

But just because doing nothing isn't in our best interest, this observation doesn't mean much, it's a pragmatic assessment. So the question becomes: Is doing something ethical or is it simply a necessary evil dictated by pragmatics?

"I swore never to be silent whenever and wherever human beings endure suffering and humiliation. We must always take sides. Neutrality helps the oppressor, never the victim. Silence encourages the tormentor, never the tormented."—Elie Wiesel

What causes an isolationist attitude? Indifference.

Indifference is not just some forgivable vice for not stopping the evil they know nothing about (and sadly too many in this world intentionally keep themselves ignorant; how deeply unethical this is, only their conscience can know for sure). But to know about the evil in this world and do nothing . . . well there is a term for this: depraved indifference. It is a state where any decent human being, who, when they know of evil or injustice being committed, they have an ethical responsibility to act to prevent that evil being committed and to not do so is not only unethical but evil in and of itself. Now, I'm sure no prosecutor would take it to that level in a court of law, but I'm not talking legality—I'm talking ethics (it's truly deplorable that these two fields have next to nothing to do with one another). But I get the feeling I'm going to need to justify that previous statement, so let's break it up.

(1) Knowledge of evil requires action
(2) To not act is an act of evil itself
(3) This action must work to prevent or stop said evil.

(1) Well, I guess, even before I can prove that knowledge of evil requires action I should define what I mean by evil since it is such a vague term. What I mean by evil at least for this chapter is any act by a person or group that unquestionably violates the most basic natural rights (life, liberty) of any person with malice aforethought. Murder, genocide, rape, child molestation, and prohibitions on religious freedom, legally enforced racism and misogyny—all are forms of what I would call evil. Now should these kinds of things demand action to stop these things on the part of someone who knows about them? This seems to be kind of an easy one, doesn't it? But for those a little unclear let's start with the smaller more immediate acts. If you see someone being murdered or raped, you help; be it scream your head off for more help or take more drastic, and perfectly justifiable action you do something to stop the act from happening. This is that whole "Good Samaritan" story; you help those who are victims of other people when you come across them.

Now while we might think that, "yes, we must act for those acts of evil in our immediate presence, when those acts are not directly in our line of sight we are not morally required to do anything." Wrong. Now, for individuals the only thing you must stop are those things that are within your power. You can't be expected to worry about the murder on the other side of the country, nor are you even conceivably morally responsible for not doing anything about it. You simply cannot be expected to take part in righting every single injustice in the world; it's much like what I was saying before about charity: if you gave all your time and money to charity you wouldn't be happy, and if you worried about those acts of evil outside your immediate knowledge you wouldn't have the time to be

Republicans and Reincarnation

happy either. So while it may be ethical and just, you are not required to assault a murderer like O.J. Simpson or any of his legal defense team with a aluminum bat across the head (even though they may ethically deserve it), this is only an ethical imperative for everyone that actually crosses their path on the street.

Now the next level up are the laws. Are you ethically bound to support laws that stop such crimes as these from occurring? Yes, because it is within your power to do something. For instance in the past decades certain laws have spread from state to state on the issues of child molestation. Megan's Law, Jessica's Law, Amber Alert laws, these are laws going after the only crime I can think of as more morally depraved than genocide. Quite frankly I don't really care about the argument's constitutionality of these laws, because ethically nothing will be sufficient until every state has passed a law that an act of child molestation has a mandatory life imprisonment without the possibility of parole[85]. To not support laws like these gives more freedom to a group of things that resemble people, but through their actions have certainly lost all claim to any rights whatsoever. These are souls that are so encased in fear that I doubt there is any hope that they will be able to be rehabilitated within a single lifetime. Now when you get into laws that are less clear than this it is still a moral imperative for you to support that which your reason and faith leads you to believe is the ethical course.

Now what about those even larger crimes—genocide, crimes against humanity . . . are you required to do something about that? Or is this like a singular murder

---

[85] I don't support the death penalty, but child molestation constantly makes me question that stance.

that can't have an ethical duty to do something about it when it's out of your direct experience? And it's not comparable to passing laws because these are the kind of things that happen outside your country's jurisdiction, isn't it? Well, since things like this are more governmental and for any government in the modern day there is no such thing as too far from their direct experience, then you, as a person that makes up the body politic of your government, are morally required to do something about them. These are crimes that not only affect the people that are suffering through them; these are crimes whose influence tends to spread when not stopped. History bears out that tyranny, genocide, and the like, are like cancers—they spread and kill everything they touch until they are dealt with. Dealing with them sometimes may be painful, but the alternative is worse.

For instance let's go back to the obvious example of the Holocaust. No serious person can honestly believe that the German public was completely ignorant of what was happening to the minority communities in their country. They may be correct in stating that they didn't know the full extent of what happened in the death camps (no one could ever be expected to envision the level of depravity in those places) but I doubt a whole country believed that the Jews, and Gypsies, and homosexuals, and political dissidents were being driven off to pleasant country clubs. They knew. They knew it was something unpleasant and probably morally depraved (they had to know it was morally questionable at best). Now imagine if the whole country had stood up then. No Holocaust. But that was their immediate vicinity.[86] But the same is

---

[86] On the flip side, I have known several people of the current generation who were raised in Germany, which now seems to

true of France, of England, of the United States, of all the countries that capitulated early on saying it wasn't their problem. Evil is evil and for governments in the modern age, space and distance is no excuse for letting evil continue, and for people who let their governments ignore such evil, they are just as responsible as the Nazi who operates the furnaces. Yes, I just said the so-called "Greatest Generation" and their parents were all guilty of the Holocaust . . . but they ended the evil you claim . . . to which I point out they ended it 6 million lives too little too late. When Roosevelt turned back the ship *St. Louis*[87], full of Jewish refugees trying to escape the horrors of the Holocaust, refusing to give them asylum in the US, forcing them to go back to Nazi controlled territory, he became as guilty as any Hitler, Mussolini or Stalin for the genocide. Nor was that an isolated act, but rather merely an example of the systemic U.S. indifference to the evil going on in the world. And contrary to the popular statement the "buck stops here" the President is not the one ultimately responsible—as an elected official it is the people who elected him four times to the office of President who bear the final responsibility. Now some could claim that Roosevelt had no choice because he was opposed by a heavy anti-Semitic population of the country (again not winning the American public any points), but isn't a leader, like the President, supposed

---

have an education system based on causing guilt over the actions of prior generations. I'm not big into the idea of the sins of the father carrying onto the son, so I'm not a fan of the German guilt machine because I truly feel most Germans know it was wrong and will never do anything like that again.

[87] http://www.ushmm.org/museum/exhibit/online/stlouis//story/voyage/index.htm

to lead, supposed to provide people with the evidence and reason to see what is right and true? So much for Roosevelt's leadership.

(2) This country was in a position to help during the Holocaust, if only to open our borders to refugees, and it did nothing. That is guilt. The legal system may not have fully caught onto this yet, but ethically and morally the failure to act in the face of evil is an evil in and of itself. The failure to act, when capable, is still an action and any action is bound to help somebody. So you're either helping the victim or attacker. Life doesn't always provide simple either-or situations, in fact it seldom does, but this is one of those black and white issues. To help or hurt, that is the only options available in such situations.

There exists only one exception for a country and that is that they are incapable at the time of doing anything. If, for instance, your military is busy in Iraq and Afghanistan you get a temporary pass on the genocide in the Sudan, because spreading yourself so thin that you'll just make everything worse everywhere is not going to help anyone. This however doesn't mean all those other countries that are not so busy, are off the hook.

(3) So if your only options are to aid and abet tyranny and genocide through inaction or do something to stop these acts of depravity, which one is the ethical action? Despite these seemingly obviousness of this answer, the so-called civilized world often seems to have a problem with this question.

So, thus we have ethical responsibility to oppose tyranny, genocide, and all forms of violations of the most basic human rights. But that still leaves us with the question of do we do it through diplomacy or military power?

"There are only two means by which men can deal with one another: guns or logic. Force or persuasion. Those who know that they cannot win by means of logic have always resorted to guns."—Ayn Rand

Now, contrary to the quote above, there are actually three ways of dealing with people. The preferable way is always as friends. Friendship has nothing to do with reason or force, but love and respect (this is a fairly consistent flaw in Rand's reasoning and pretty much the reason that her philosophies can only be used as a starting point). Regrettably however, nothing in the current state of the world suggest that governments can deal with each other out of friendship. Which again leaves only reason (diplomacy) and force (military power).

That previous question about choosing between diplomacy and military action really was meant to be rhetorical. Obviously diplomacy should always be the preferred method of dealing with governments. Only a lunatic would prefer using military action first and foremost. But therein lies the problem. People who commit genocide, who perpetrate actions of tyranny on their people have shown quite clearly that they prefer the sword to reason.

Dictators are people who have almost shouted to the world that they prefer force to reason. Think about it. A person who uses reason first can see that from time to time reason has its limits and force is required. But a person who prefers to use force as their first option is someone who cannot be reasoned with.

Still, diplomacy should always be the first call of action, if for no other reason than to show that we can use reason. But it cannot be the diplomacy of the past century—the diplomacy of appeasement. As I think my history lesson has shown appeasement isn't a limited mistake made at Munich letting Hitler have Czechoslovakia, it is a long-term problem because tyranny cannot be appeased. A line cannot simply be drawn in the sand and a tyranny be told not to cross it. Because, as I have already stated tyranny is a cancer. It is a malignant tumor. It is deadly to the tissue it surrounds. It spreads. By its very nature it can't help but spread. It must spread or it will die. And no living thing, be it a cell, an organ, a tumor, a person, or a nation, will choose death, even if living will cause suffering so long as the option for life continues. Yes people choose suicide, but because they feel life is no longer an option. Tyranny isn't the depression of suicide (although it may cause that) it is the evil of wanting more at the cost of others—more power, more force, more . . . A tumor will spread because that is its nature, and a person is left with two options when they have a malignant tumor: They can treat it or they can let it run it's course. Treatment is not pleasant. Cut the tumor out. Chemotherapy and god knows what else. It's hell on earth, but people choose it because life is more important. Life is worth a little suffering. All good things are. The second option, to let the malignancy run its course is the option of those who have lost hope. They feel that treatment is worthless, that the suffering is not worth it, that there is not enough life left to live. They feel what is left of their life is not worth fighting for.

Republicans and Reincarnation

Drawing a line in the sand, the diplomacy of containment, doesn't work. If it worked Communism wouldn't have spread from Russia to Eastern Europe. From Russia to China. From China to Tibet. From China and Russia to Korea. From Russia and China to Vietnam. From Russia to Cuba. To large portions of Africa and Latin America. And need I remind you when we're just trying to contain one philosophy we tend to make deals with dictators of just another brand of evil. I hardly call this a successful policy.

No, diplomacy cannot have the goal of merely containing; it must have the goal of constantly pushing the opposition to the next line. It should only be containment when we're busy with other more pressing problems. Will Rogers has been quoted as saying "diplomacy is the art of saying 'nice doggie' until you find a rock" and sadly this is the kind of diplomacy that is needed. But when those problems are finished then the next tyranny must be pushed back to the next line in the sand. Unfortunately, most diplomacy of this sort has to rely on threats, because while dictatorships may not be reasonable, they're not dumb either. They know they're being pushed back into oblivion and so to get them to concede to moving back to that next line in the sand the threat of force must be used as their incentive to go back yet another step. So this kind of diplomacy really has to make it worth their while to comply . . . usually along the line of do it or we'll annihilate you off the face of the planet. This does work from time to time. Remember when, following the invasion of Iraq, Libya suddenly agreed to take responsibility and pay the 2.7 billion for the 1988 Lockerbie plane bombing, and following the capture of Saddam Hussein, Libya turned over all of it's weapons of mass destruction technology (common sense says that there is some relation between these events, specifically that Colonel Qaddafi didn't want his country to be the next country on the list) . . . of course it didn't guarantee him perpetual rule either.

Some would say economic sanctions are a good tool to use in diplomacy. This exhibits a form of naïveté seldom seen in the world. Most places that are dictatorships are not exactly places where a first world standard of living is enjoyed by everyone in the country. Taking away their money is first off not really going to be noticed, and secondly only going to give the dictator in question more propaganda in their 'why we should hate America/The West' campaign. Rather economic incentives should be offered. Business deals, cheap products, so forth and so on. When a populace find out about the virtues of Western living they tend to want the laws and policies to match. A fun experiment would be airlifting flat screen TV's, cable satellites, and the generators to power them all over North Korea . . . I wonder how long Kim Jung Il would be in power after the North Korean populace found out the rest of the world wasn't still living in the 5th century B.C. The best possible result of economic incentives like this would be a bloodless revolution deposing the dictators, but I'll settle for a bloody one so long as Western nations are bright enough to politely offer their help in rebuilding the country once the fighting is over in order to prevent yet another dictator coming in. This helping to rebuild a nation is one of the biggest parts that we have often forgotten—look at Afghanistan, we have made next to no improvements in that nation's infrastructure, is it any wonder that we are having troubles in that country.

Now, as I said, most dictators while immoral and firmly entrenched in using force first, aren't dumb; they will do what is necessary to avoid military conflict because in the end the fact is that if all the democratic nations of the world joined together, nobody is strong enough to defeat them.

The Theory of a Just War

"Those who wage war justly aim at peace, and so they are not opposed to peace, except to the evil peace, which Our Lord "came not to send upon earth" (Matthew 10:34). Hence Augustine says (Ep. ad Bonif. clxxxix): 'We do not seek peace in order to be at war, but we go to war that we may have peace. Be peaceful, therefore, in warring, so that you may vanquish those whom you war against, and bring them to the prosperity of peace.'"—St. Thomas Aquinas, Summa Theologica, Second Part of the Second Part, Question 40, Article 1, Reply to Objection 3

Still, every so often, you will get the occasional madman who would choose to make a suicidal stand rather than simply hobble to their demise. And at the moment it's not so suicidal. So often in the last century, dictator after dictator has called the bluff of the democratic world and gambled on their reluctance to fight a war, and won. Too many have been allowed to continue to oppress and gut their own people, because the world won't stand up to them. Still, even if the free nations of the world did start acting ethically and choose to not back down to despots, what should be the criteria for going to war? Luckily there are already criteria in place: Just War Theory.

Just War Theory began thousands of years ago and can be traced back, like so many philosophical concepts, to Ancient Greece and Rome. However, it was first given explicit treatment by Middle Age philosopher St. Thomas Aquinas. Aquinas not only stated that war can be just and virtuous idea, but laid down the criteria for war to be considered as such. He had primarily three criteria: (1) That war is waged by proper authority, (2) that the cause of the war is just, and (3) that the side of the war that is to be considered just has the intention of doing good and avoiding evil.

Over the centuries Just War Theory has further been refined to include the following points: (4) that the war is treated only as an option of last resort after all other options have been expended, (5) proportionality, or that the benefits of waging such a war must greatly outweigh the harm and cost that war will inevitably cause, and finally (6) a likely probability of success must exist

So before we see if what I'm proposing as a change to U.S. foreign policy meets the criteria of Just War, lets make sure we're all clear at what I've been suggesting up to this point. That the U.S., and quite frankly all the free nations of the world, must draw a line in the sand and set a policy against tyranny; that we must "make the world safe for democracy" and work for the specific intent of ending tyranny and ensuring liberty to the entire world. That to accomplish these ends the powers of the free world must be brought to bear against tyrannies the world over. When possible through diplomacy and economic incentives to reform, but when necessary military force must be used to depose the worst tyrannies that are beyond reason. And finally, in opposition to over a century of Western shortsightedness and isolationism, that every country we invade and every nation whose revolution we assist

Republicans and Reincarnation

we stick around with monetary, military, and political support until they have become a stable and functional democracy, no matter how long that takes. And this policy is carried out without reservation, without stops, and without hesitation, until tyranny is a word only in history books and discussions of theoretical philosophy.

Is that a little idealist? No, it's incredibly idealist. But pragmatic isolationism just seems to be yielding a vicious cycle of genocide . . . so I don't know about you but my idealism seems more pragmatic than isolationism. But does my idealism meet the criteria of a Just War?

Proper Authority

"There has never been a single resolution about the decades-long repression of the civil and political rights of 1.3 billion people in China, or the more than a million female migrant workers in Saudi Arabia being kept as virtual slaves, or the virulent racism which has brought 600,000 people to the brink of starvation in Zimbabwe. Every year, UN bodies are required to produce at least 25 reports on alleged human rights violations by Israel, but not one on an Iranian criminal justice system which mandates punishments like crucifixion, stoning, and cross-amputation. This is not legitimate critique of states with equal or worse human rights records. It is demonization of the Jewish state."—Human rights scholar Anne Bayefsky, UN Conference of Anti-Semitism, June 2004[88]

---

[88] The United Nations: Leading Global Purveyor of Anti-Semitism, *An Interview with Anne Bayefsky* http://www.jcpa.org/phas/phas-31.htm

"Some of the world's most abusive regimes have won seats on the Human Rights Commission and used them to insulate themselves from criticism. Current members include Sudan, which is carrying out genocide; Nepal, whose absolute monarch has suspended basic liberties; and Saudi Arabia, where women have few rights. All are gross violators of the Universal Declaration of Human Rights, the commission's founding document."—New York Time Editorial, February 26, 2006[89]

Now the first thing you need in a Just War is a sovereign authority with the legal right to wage war. Many think that in the modern world that the only body with the authority to do that is the United Nations. Now, there are few people as supportive of the idea of a one-world government as I am[90], but as much as I like the idea, that government is not going to be found in the United Nations.

The United Nations is a corrupt, inefficient, Anti-Semitic, supporter of tyranny that has China and Russia as two of the most powerful nations in deciding how to deal with tyrannies (like themselves), and whose peace keeping missions in the Congo, Hati, Liberia, Sudan, Burundi and the Ivory Coast have yielded verifiable charges of rape, child molestation, and various other human rights abuses against the very peace keepers who were sent to end those depravities.

---

[89] http://www.nytimes.com/2006/02/26/opinion/26sun2.html?_r=2&n=Top%2fOpinion%2fEditorials%20and%20Op%2dEd%2fEditorials&oref=slogin&oref=slogin

[90] Preferably in the form of a confederacy of limited power that exists only to ensure the basic human rights of life, liberty, property, and pursuit of happiness are protected everywhere.

Republicans and Reincarnation

The U.S. and all its Western allies have histories that are far from spotless. But for the most part our greatest atrocities are in the past, and when individuals commit depravity under our auspices we are quick to bring the full force of the law against them. But the U.N., to this day, either ignores or revels in its evils. Ironically the U.N. is the kind of government the U.N. was meant to oppose.

And while nothing would make me happier to have a legitimate world body to deal with the issue of war[91], there is no such organization. And in the absence of such a government any legitimately established nation becomes a legitimate authority. What do I mean by a legitimately established nation? One whose people are free, one whose government is established as a Classically Liberal democratic republic (or at least a Classically Liberal constitutional monarchy like the U.K.). In other words pretty much those countries I listed earlier as free nations of the world. Obviously the more of those nations that work together, the better, but agreement between a certain number of nations is not required for legitimacy, or at least until a legitimate world government can be established.

Further, I would note that even Aquinas pointed out that any organization be it an external government or internal revolution serves as a legitimate opposition to wage war against tyranny. His justification for this was "A tyrannical government is not just, because it is directed, not to the common good, but to the private good of the ruler, as the Philosopher [Aristotle] states (Polit. iii,

---

[91] And I will deal with how to create such a body, and what it should look like in Chapter 13.

5; Ethic. viii, 10). Consequently there is no sedition in disturbing a government of this kind [.]"[92]

What I have proposed, an alliance of free nations to end tyranny, certainly fits the qualification of a just authority.

Just Cause and Right Intention

"Secondly, a just cause is required, namely that those who are attacked, should be attacked because they deserve it on account of some fault. Wherefore Augustine says (QQ. in Hept., qu. x, super Jos.): 'A just war is wont to be described as one that avenges wrongs, when a nation or state has to be punished, for refusing to make amends for the wrongs inflicted by its subjects, or to restore what it has seized unjustly.' Thirdly, it is necessary that the belligerents should have a rightful intention, so that they intend the advancement of good, or the avoidance of evil."—St. Thomas Aquinas, Summa Theologica, Second Part of the Second Part, Q 40, A.1, Answer

Honestly, I am hard pressed to think of a cause more just than the opposition to tyranny and genocide. A much bantered around definition of Just Cause on the internet is "Force may be used only to correct a grave, public evil, i.e., aggression or massive violation of the basic rights of whole populations."[93] Massive violation of basic rights

---

[92] Aquinas, St. Thomas, *Summa Theologica,* Second Part of the Second Part, Question 42, Article 2, Reply to Objection 3

[93] Although I will be damned if I can find two sources that agree on who said it first. I got this wording from, http://www.natcath.org/NCR_Online/archives/102502/102502j.htm

of whole populations . . . that would be a definition of tyranny and genocide? Thus to work to end these acts seems to be the very definition of just cause.

However, let me make a major caveat, the cause here is not to simply end the tyranny and leave. This is where right intention comes in. Our intention must not and cannot be just to end tyranny it must be to create liberty. This requires planning for the occupation and rebuilding that will inevitably follow any war. This is taking a near impossible task upon ourselves, I will grant, because creating a system that encourages liberty for a populace that has no experience with it, is a long, sometimes generational process. But anything short of this is merely going back to the old system of a cycle of wars and dictators. Any nation that leaves a country it has invaded before it has ensured that said country will not fall back into tyranny and chaos has fought an unjust war, and is thus guilty of a form of evil themselves.

Option of Last Resort

"The only thing necessary for the triumph of evil is for good men to do nothing."—Attributed to Edmund Burke

As I have already stated I would prefer to use the threat of war, diplomacy, and economic incentives before going to war. But sadly, while these things questionably seemed to be working to get North Korea to give up it's nuclear weapons program for a couple of years (yeah right?), I don't see these things working to actually free the people of North Korea, which should be our real objective.

Many people who talk about an option of last resort think only of last resort meaning that another country is invading or about to invade you or you allies without question. This view of last resort is isolationist and beyond selfish. It forgets that people do have a responsibility to help others when they can.

The option of last resort begins when a government begins to act in a way that violates the natural rights of its citizens or the citizens of another country. At that point a government has said it will use force before reason. The free nations must give, because we will choose reason over force, a chance to diplomacy. But a chance doesn't mean years of negotiations that lead nowhere. Negotiations of that sort mean that innocent people continue to suffer—diplomacy should seek to end the suffering of people without the use of force, not to just extend the suffering of the innocent without having to get your own hands dirty.

Diplomatic negotiation should go on for two reasons. The first is to give whatever country is intending to lead the charge against the tyranny in question time to prepare for their assault, seek alliances, and work out a detailed plan for all contingencies of both the war and the occupation that will follow. Hopefully this will give the intended invadee time to realize that negation and compromise would be in their best interest. The second reason to negotiate is because you're busy in other parts of the world and do not wish to over extend yourself. This form of negotiation should be filled with the implied statement, "Don't be at the top of our list when we get done with our current operations." And quite frankly if this became a continuously enforced policy of the free nations of the world, if a country had been doing nothing to clean up their act up until that point, they clearly weren't going to be open to reason the minute your military was freed up from its current assignment.

But to use the statement "last resort" to imply only your own personal safety is to say that the problems and suffering of others doesn't affect you—that it's not your problem. And I think we've seen the body count that line of reasoning leads to.

However, if what I'm proposing as foreign policy for the United States and the free world is adopted, I believe, that actually, few, much fewer wars will occur. The goal here is not to invade and over throw every dictatorship on Earth. The goal here is to frighten every dictatorship on Earth that they will be next on our list. This fear will cause them to make reforms in their countries—not a lot of reforms at first, just enough to not be dead last in the world. At this point you will likely see populations having viewed the free nations of the world supporting freedom. Yes they'll have a little more freedom because of the reforms, but more importantly they'll have hope. Hope that if they stand up in defiance of their country the rest of the world will not abandon them. How many revolutions haven't started because people don't want simply to be the next Bay of Pigs or the next Tiananmen Square? How many revolutions have started in the Middle East because the people there thought they might just stand a chance because it worked in that other country? What would happen if people over the world thought that the world would back their revolution, would provide support for their democratic movement before, during and after their initial actions? What would happen is you'd see a lot more revolutions against tyranny. And revolutions that want democracy are so much more effective in establishing democracy than having to go and force it on a populace . . . but that populace first has to have the hope that they can win such a revolution. In the wake of more stable classical liberal havens, the remaining dictators will likely keep pushing more and more reforms through to keep the population happy enough that they don't revolt. The problem with this for the dictator is that one day they'll find they've reformed their country into a nation that votes them out. Thus the last resort of war will be less and less likely, but only if we show that last resort means you will stop abusing your own populace or else, and not, don't attack us personally or else.

Proportionality

"I must study politics and war that my sons may have liberty to study mathematics and philosophy. My sons ought to study mathematics and philosophy, geography, natural history, naval architecture, navigation, commerce, and agriculture, in order to give their children a right to study painting, poetry, music, architecture, statuary, tapestry, and porcelain."—John Adams

"Ultimately, the best strategy to ensure our security and to build a durable peace is to support the advance of democracy elsewhere. Democracies don't attack each other."—Bill Clinton, State of the Union Address 1994

Do the benefits of my proposed complete warfare outweigh the costs of such a long-term policy?

The costs are so obvious I need only gloss over them: Massive amounts of money spent; human life lost on both sides during the course of war, occupation and rebuilding, totaling thousands a year if not more; the constant aggravation of fighting those who oppose the policy both in our country, in the occupied country and around the world; and a policy that despite this cost may take so long to institute we may not live to see it come to its final goal. Even if the costs are distributed across the entire free world, they are still steep.

But what are the benefits? For that I turn to another aspect of philosophy called Democratic Peace Theory. Dating back to Immanuel Kant's essay Perpetual Peace, and receiving more interest in the latter half of the twentieth century, Democratic Peace Theory states that with only the rarest of exceptions democratic nations do not have wars with other democratic nations (and the wars that are used as exceptions you have to have a rather broad definition of what counts as a democracy). The reason for this is that, by nature, democracies rely on reason first and force second, and thus in arguments with other democracies, they both come to the table using reason. They may not like each other, they may not always be ecstatic with whatever details they come up with to end their problem, but they will always find a means through reason to deal with each other.

So for every country that becomes a liberal democracy, that is one less country exceedingly less likely to go to war with the other free nations of the world. So let's look at what the end result of the policy I'm advocating is. A world where there are no tyrannies, where there are only democratic nations of varying levels of success. Now obviously this is a world where there is no genocide. Big plus. The number of people not dying on a daily basis not only counters the lives lost fighting to achieve this sort of world, but long term will far exceed the loss of life. Democratic nations are more economically stable . . .

economic stability means more and more money flows and economic growth spreads to all. So the investment of money is again not only counter balanced but exceeded.

But let's take a closer look at both of these points a little more deeply. With concern to the issue of sending innocent young men and women to fight and die in these wars. I have actually heard people complain that this makes us no better than the dictators who force their people to fight against us. This ignores a few exceedingly important points. Unlike these dictators we don't simply conscript people into an army and force them to fight, possibly against their beliefs. This complaint further ignores the fact that in most free nations, especially America, those who serve in the military are not conscripts or draftees, but rather volunteers who serve because they want to, because they believe in what their country does. Keep in mind the number of soldiers who appear on the news as saying they refuse to go to Iraq are limited, to the point where it's still news when it does, however one has to really search for a news story to find out that reenlistment rates in the military still meet or exceed their goals[94], probably because it is so common that it hardly comes off as something new. For a person to make the argument that their fighting and dying is a waste, that they need to be brought back, that the war they fight is unjust is to argue that they know better how to live that soldier's life better than that soldier does is sheer arrogance. Quite frankly I'm reasonably sure the soldiers would prefer to deal with hippies calling them baby-killers and spitting in their face, at least the hippies had spine to face the soldiers, while today's critics are so arrogant they deign it not necessary

---

[94] http://www.usatoday.com/news/world/iraq/2005-05-02-iraq-soldiers-reenlist_x.htm

to not even show their contempt and belief that they know how to live another person's life better than that person does to their face, but prefer rather to hide only in rallies, on cable news shows, in the halls of Congress, and in the Oval Office. If a person volunteers to go and free another people, how dare another person critique that person's free will and choices . . . But the complaint then comes that the military is only filled with poor people who enlist because they can't get a job anywhere else. This is so ignorant that it must be confronted right here and now. According to the Department of Defense about such claims:

"Many of the assertions about the class composition of the military have been based on impressions and anecdotes rather than on empirical data[. . .] All [reports] found that members of the military tended to come from backgrounds that were somewhat lower in socioeconomic status than the U.S. average, but that the differences between the military and the comparison groups were relatively modest. These results have been confirmed in recent editions of this report, which portray a socioeconomic composition of enlisted accessions similar to the population as a whole, but with the top quartile of the population underrepresented. While the socioeconomic status of recruits is slightly lower than the general population, today's recruits have higher levels of education, measured aptitudes, and reading skills than their civilian counterparts."[95]

[95] Population Representation in the Military Services, Fiscal Year 1999, Chapter 7 Socioeconomic Status in perspective. http://www.defenselink.mil/prhome/poprep99/html/chapter7/c7-perspective.htm. 1999 seems to be the last year that this report gave information on the socioeconomic background of

Let me translate this for you—the parents of the average person in the military are making slightly less than the average, but since the average serviceman is more educated than the average civilian, and education is the greatest predictor of income, the average person who serves in the military will be above the median income during their life. Furthermore while it is sad that the upper quartile is underrepresented, to be only slightly off from the average means, that, as the numbers would bear out if you too want to wade through the mountains of charts, that the military and the reserves are actually a middle class establishment and not one of the poor.[96]

Then comes that cost issues of money. Don't you just love people who bring up how much money is being spent on a war? Besides how revolting it is that we can say we don't want to spend money on freeing other people—which is really saying we can actually put a price on someone's freedom, which I thought we fought a Civil War to end that mentality—it's actually unrealistic. A recent report by the Congressional Research Service and reported by the Associated Press[97] shows that the $648 billion spent in Iraq as of July 2008, is only about 1% of the country's GDP . . . which one should consider

> those who enlist, However, when one compares other factors that are still reported such as age, race, and education level between the 1999 and 2005 report (http://www.defenselink.mil/prhome/ poprep2005/summary/summary.html) one will find no statistically relevant change in these measurement, thus it would be foolish to assume that any relevant change in economic levels of the enlisted.

[96] One begins to see why Aristotle wanted a government made up of the middle class with the rich and poor excluded.

[97] http://www.foxnews.com/story/0,2933,391603,00.html

next to Vietnam at 2.3% of the GDP, the Korean War at 4.2%, and my favorite WWII at 35.8% of the GDP. Yes, $648 billion is a lot of money, but so far this war is fairly cheap in terms of both money and lives . . . Just imagine how cheap it would have been had we actually planned for the occupation as the future wars I'm suggesting will be. Also the liberals who want to complain about that $648 billion should look in the mirror first at their multi-trillion dollar entitlement programs before even complaining about the cost of spreading liberty.

Further, while no democracy in the world is beyond becoming unstable and degrading back into a civil war or a tyranny, if the rest of the world is democratic then there is external pressure to quickly return to a functional democracy because to be the only non-democratic nation in the world would be to be ostracized from the world politically and economically. No nation could be that suicidal (and if they were then I think that speaks to a world threat that needs to be contained). Economic necessity of being involved with other countries would almost immediately dictate turning back to democracy. Thus a policy of war would ensure a world where containment would be an effective solution.

Near world peace, and economic prosperity the like of which has only been imagined. But there's more . . . if I and Democratic Peace Theorists are correct then world stability will be apparent to everyone after only a few years of this kind of existence. After a decade or two, hopefully even less, it will become evident to every government that their standing militaries are rather meaningless. A world where everyone reasons with each other doesn't need even a tenth of the current military power. Now realistically it would come in the form of slow and across the board draw down of the numbers of arms and troops everywhere, but eventually you could realistically see a world where all you need is an Army reserves, a small Air Force, and maybe a smaller hybrid of the Navy and Coast Guard in existence. Isn't that the world we all want?

Doesn't that benefit outweigh any possible cost especially when those costs turn out to be pretty small by comparison.

A person who reaches that mark of five years without cancer has a new understanding of the value of life. Imagine what we will ascribe to the value of the world when we hit five years without tyranny.

Isn't it worth the temporary suffering?

Or have we given up on the value of life entirely?

Likelihood of Success

"Cowardice asks the question: is it safe? Expediency asks the question: is it political? Vanity asks the question: is it popular? But conscience asks the question: is it right? And there comes a time when one must take a position that is neither safe, nor political, nor popular— but one must take it simply because it is right." —Martin Luther King, Jr.

Now we come to the $64,000 question? Is what I have proposed here a realistic avenue to lasting world stability or is it just pie in the sky dreaming?

Republicans and Reincarnation

I see one of four possibilities for the future.

(1) We don't do what I've suggested and keep going in endless cycles of bloodshed and tyrannies popping up here, being taken down, and replaced by a tyranny somewhere else.
(2) We don't do what I've suggested, but world progression continues its slow march to world democracy on its own, and we reach the end game I've suggested without the massive foreign policy change.
(3) We do what I suggested, but find that the countries we go into slip out of democratic government as soon as we leave no matter how much help and infrastructure and time we give them. The end result of this is probably no worse than option 2.
(4) My plan actually does work and worst-case scenario has it maybe taking two whole generations for this plan to work.

Now, if you had asked me fifteen years ago which plan I thought was the best I would probably have gone with option number 2. I find nothing in option one to be realistic because it suggests that humanity is absolutely incapable of learning anything, an idea which history does not support . . . we may not have a great learning curve, but we do eventually learn. The world seemed to be on an inevitable course to worldwide democracy. Most of the world would have agreed with this. Academics like Francis Fukuyama were actually publishing essays and books with the title "The End of History" arguing that liberal democracy was going to eventually encompass the whole world and all political development after that would be minutia. But some annoying things happened, China unlike their Soviet parentage is proving to be annoyingly resilient in surviving as a tyranny, genocide is still going on throughout many parts of the world, and parts of the world are still latching onto the perversion of fascism . . . only this time they're coupling it with God making it more dangerous than ever. Now actually I still think option 2 would work—that eventually the world would adopt worldwide liberal democracy. I just think that if we continue with the uneven and incomplete support of liberty in the world I believe it will take generation upon generation upon generation for this to come to fruition; that millions, possibly billions will have had to die needlessly between then and now. It is the blood of millions I would rather not have on my hands.

Now let's say that we take option 3, we attempt my plan but it doesn't work. What is the worst that can happen? I have one word for it: Iraq. Granted I would argue that Iraq doesn't fit my plan because there was no actual planning of how to deal with rebuilding the country, and what was done after that was, at its best, can only be described as gross incompetence and negligence. However, if we're going to take that argument that this can never work, as option 3 presupposes, which I don't think is the case but we're going for the sake of argument here, then what is the worst that happened. We deposed a dictator and we familiarized a country with concepts of democracy which even if they aren't ready for them yet (as Germany wasn't ready in the 1920's) it sets the cultural groundwork for a future democracy. Some might argue that actions like Iraq are destabilizing to a region . . . because genocidal dictators harboring terrorist organizations and paying terrorists to blow up Israelis are such a stabilizing force. In terms of stability, at the absolute worst, for everything less stable now, there is something more stable and it comes out to a sum zero. So worst-case scenario, if my policy is instituted it will take just as long to reach worldwide democracy as in option 2, but it cannot possibly delay it.

But before we leave for a full analysis of option 4, let's deal with Iraq in a more full sense. Yes, we all knew I would get here eventually. I had to; to just ignore it would be morally and intellectually unforgivable on my part. But I first had to establish the philosophical ground on which to discuss it. Now I'm not one for what's called Monday morning quarterbacking, because the nature of war is chaotic and there is always some bad news even when you're winning that you can focus on. Still at this point it's fairly clear to see some of the broad strokes in favor and against the invasion.

In general, as I see it, here is what went right in Iraq:

1. We deposed a dictator with the intent of replacing him with a working democracy. This certainly is a major advantage over the 'it's not our problem' mentality of the previous century.
2. We won the war easily. Anyone who says we're still fighting a war is an idiot who has a limited understanding of the English language. What took so many years in Iraq was not a war, but being in the middle of an occupation. The war ended when the Iraqi Army was beaten, surrendered, and disbanded. Not to make this distinction is to show a level of intellectual shallowness that prevents any solution being attainable because you can't solve a problem until you actually understand the problem.

3. The military itself, as a whole (any group has a small portion idiots in it that the whole should not be blamed for), has performed beyond admirably and proven that in the end the free nations of the world have a near unstoppable military force.

Again, in general, here's what went wrong:

(1) The buildup to the war relied on an argument of weapons-of-mass-destruction and perceived threats and not of past acts of genocide and continuing tyranny. Further this buildup took the entirely wrong attitude to the UN and the other nations of the world.
(2) There was a complete and total lack of planning in how to rebuild the nation after we won the war.

What went right speaks for itself. What went wrong needs to be looked at to make sure that we never make the same kind of mistakes. So let's deal with the first mistake, how we went about the buildup. The first problem was that the Bush administration made the most ridiculous argument based on a perceived threat about Saddam's weapons of mass destruction. Let's ignore for the moment the point that every single intelligence agency in the world seemed to agree on this point. Whether it's true or not, it's a stupid argument. Even in the run up it had only two possible outcomes. Either they're not there and opponents of the war argue that the war was pointless, or they were there and opponents argue since he hadn't used them yet, he wasn't going to, thus the war was pointless. But a far more egregious problem is that this was a pragmatic argument. The inherent reason for this, and the reason why Bush has given neoconservatism such a terrible reputation, is that Bush was not a neoconservative. If you go back to the 2000 election, repeatedly Bush stated he didn't believe in nation building (a key neoconservative belief), but somehow after 9/11, daddy's isolationist policies didn't seem quite adequate. So he tried to latch onto the only philosophy that worked after that fateful day, which said you have to actually take on tyranny because if you don't it will spread: either directly by invading other countries or by funding terrorists that will go against its enemies (Saddam did both for those of you keeping score at home). So not really being a neoconservative he makes an argument based on pragmatics and not ethics and right . . . yet the neoconservatives take the black eye. An argument on ethics would have been untouchable because nobody was going to argue that Saddam was the good guy, that he hadn't butchered his people, that he hadn't committed genocide . . . because he had done all that and so much more. However, like all shortsighted people, it was not a question of 'what we should do' to Bush and his administration, but a question 'what can we do' that is in our best interest. Bush failed to provide a Just Cause for Iraq, even though one existed.

The second problem was how we dealt with the rest of the world. It was neither the "cowboy diplomacy"[98] that we were accused of, nor was it the building of a

---

[98] Which brings up a question. Why do people complain our action are like cowboys as if that's a bad thing. Here's the plot line for nearly every western: No one will stand up to the villain but the lone cowboy hero, who defeats the villain, sets everything right and either sticks around as sheriff or goes off into the sunset because he is no longer needed . . . what exactly is there to complain about in that?

coalition that Bush liked to tout. Either would have been better than the halfway monster that Bush administration created. It wasn't cowboy diplomacy because I remember the U.S. going to the UN, thus giving implicit authority to that corrupt organization, and asking for their permission. Further, we did, and still do, have allies involved in occupation. The problem is that Bush didn't seek to actually create a coalition, a lasting body that would stand against this kind of evil (probably again because of that completely shortsighted nature). Rather this was again just a pragmatic and temporary alliance that anyone could leave because they only came in for pragmatic reasons, not ethical ones, which would create lasting bonds.

Still, the biggest flaw in Iraq was the complete lack of planning for how to deal with the country once the army was put down. From maybe waiting until Afghanistan was more under wraps, to just disbanding the army and letting all those future terrorists go on their merry way without even a touch of vetting, to the apparent administration belief that the country would just rise up in a call for democracy (even though most of the rebels who wanted democracy had been betrayed by an earlier American policy and left to die at Hussein's hands), there was clearly a very disturbing lack of planning here. The coalition military did wonders in Iraq, but militaries are not designed to build democracies, that would be other people's jobs. There was a lack of oversight and forethought in most infrastructure rebuilding projects (although let's not forget that it's the nature of tyrannies to not build infrastructures for their populaces in the first place). And let's not forget that the country was rushed into a democracy to appease the world and critics, rather

Republicans and Reincarnation

than worrying about what is best for the country. Lots of possibilities, like breaking up the country into smaller countries, or taking more time to build everything up before handing political authority back to the Iraqis are all things that could have been considered, but these arguments are primarily academic now since we are far past the point of these being viable anymore. Unfortunately just leaving isn't an option either because all that does is continue the god-awful cycle that I described earlier in this chapter. Iraq is a mess, it didn't have to be, but it is; luckily, it could have easily been a much bigger mess had the military not been as effective as they are.

The thing to take away from this is that when and if we do this again, three things are needed. A cause based not on pragmatics but ethics. An alliance of nations held together by common cause to do what is right, not to simply protect themselves. And finally, lots of planning. Lots and lots of planning. Before you even fire the first shot there need to be piles of plans on how to rebuild everything in the country from the sewers and electricity grid to parliamentary procedure and several drafts of a constitution should already be written for the country to pick from and adjust rather than starting form scratch. I might even say a whole new cabinet position needs to be developed for this very purpose . . . and yet my hatred of bureaucracy makes me wary of such an idea.

Now if you did all of these things what would you have: Germany and Japan (you probably saw that answer coming as I've said it far too many times by now). But the point here is that the policy does work. As I pointed out with the example of Libya, dictators work a lot on fear for their position and if they think they might be next, they keep their noses clean. There is still genocide and blatant tyranny because the most the world's dictators are still convinced they can get away with (Mugabe's most recent "win" in Zimbabwe kind of proves this belief to be true). Revolutions do spark up when there is hope; the Cedar Revolution in 2005 in Lebanon which helped drive Syrian soldiers out of Lebanon[99] was certainly influenced by the hope for democracy caused by the invasion of Iraq; and one cannot forget the massive moves in the direction of democracy the world made in the wake of WWII (a coalition built not primarily on pragmatics but on what was ethical). Hope, liberty, and democracy go together in that the presence of any of them is like throwing gasoline on the fire that is the other two—increase one and you create a landslide of the others. History bears this out time and time again. It is only when something happens to impede one that the others come to a sudden halt. If we were to constantly and deliberately feed all three—it is likely, it is probable, it is logical, and it is supported by history, that all three would grow at an exponential rate.

I have no doubt that whether we work for it or not the world will eventually reach a state of complete democracy. However, it is a question of a path that would work but take billions of lives and untold amounts of suffering over a dozen generations. On the other hand, we can work to end tyranny, reduce the number to maybe not even a million dead and see the end result in only a generation or two. Recent history bears out that people can make the change to democracy quickly if given the hope to believe it is possible, thus making what I propose not only possible, but quite frankly very probable. Now no one can predict the future perfectly,

[99] Not that Lebanon is suddenly without problems, but it's a step in the right direction.

but what I propose is not impossible and the gains that it could provide are so overwhelming and better than the cycle of death proposed by the so-called pragmatists that I cannot see a logical and ethical argument against it that would stand up to scrutiny.

The Spiritual Side of Things

"Think thou also of thy duty and do not waver. There is no greater good for a warrior than to fight a righteous war. There is a war that opens the doors of heaven, Arjuna! Happy the warriors whose fate is to fight such war." Krishna to Arjuna, Bhagavad-Gita 2:31-32

A question you probably have been asking for some time now: why hasn't he mentioned anything about spiritual development or the New Age movement? And the reason is this: no war, no matter how just its cause, no matter how good its intention should ever even attempt to use a spiritual basis for its arguments. The argument for war must always and forever include only secular arguments, and then once the secular burden has been met, to see if it is in line with the spiritual beliefs that you hold. Any time God has been used in the run up to war, the results have never been pretty. I have used only three assumptions (1) that human life has value and is entitled to natural rights, (2) that people are ethically required to help one another against acts of violence (3) that liberty is an end in itself for government. These three assumptions can all be reached through pure secular-humanist reasoning, even though they very much agree with my spiritual beliefs. Now I am about to point out that New

Age philosophy offers no veto to the arguments I have just presented, and that these arguments further its principles of free will and spiritual development, ***but a case for a war can never, ever, EVER be predicated on spiritual beliefs***. There is too much faith involved there and not enough reason to ever justify the cost involved. Spiritual beliefs can be used to discredit the idea of a war, but they should never be used as justification. What I am about to present is not justification for my prior arguments; it is only showing that New Age beliefs do not contradict that argument.

The first reason that New Age philosophy does not contradict the idea of a Just War is the concept of the value of life New Age philosophy's focus on the quality of life over the quantity of it. Life's value is only truly used when it is used as a teaching tool for the soul, thus the suffering caused by tyranny and genocide offers little to any teaching and only a continuance of suffering. It allows those mired in fear and hate to stay mired in those negative emotions, giving them an external excuse not to see a way out it, and thus slowing any soul's progression. As such it is a faulty teaching tool that must be gotten rid of. Further, New Age philosophy's belief in reincarnation, that death is nothing but illusion in between life lessons, shows that much of the suffering of war becomes a moot point. Not that death is a good thing . . . but while I have already argued it is better for a thousand to die in a war to give a million the chance of liberty, rather than that million and one thousand living under tyranny, it becomes even more forgivable when those thousand didn't really die and those million are no longer under tyranny.

Another point is that, as New Age philosophy believes, this world is a teaching ground that mirrors both our soul and the next world in many ways, fighting tyranny is a good lesson in teaching people to fight their own darker sides. Why do you suppose the Bhagavad-Gita, Hinduism's highest spiritual text on dispelling the darker inclinations of the soul and reaching enlightenment, is told through the story of a great war against tyrants? The god Krishna's words in this epic poem are meant to have multiple levels because the same lesson is meant to be carried out on multiple levels of the soul. We cannot expect people to dispel their own fears in their soul if we allow the physical manifestation of those fears to walk around with impunity in this world. Krishna makes repeated points to his student Arjuna that he should not despair in killing his enemy for since they embrace force only, they are spiritually unenlightened and have no chance of putting aside their fears in this life, thus for all intents and purposes they are already dead, and there is little to no loss in killing them in war. New Age philosophy would not contest this evaluation of war as applied to a modern dictator and their thug armies (although, again, I would like to state that such a spiritual argument should never be used as initial justification to war). And without question, New Age philosophy supports the plan which causes the least amount of suffering over time, which would be the one that ends tyranny sooner rather than later.

However, some are going rightfully to point out that New Age philosophy supports peace and enlightenment. Yes it does. But what most miss is that New Age philosophy, and all of its roots through all other religions, are looking not at peace primarily as a means, but as an end. Krishna supported Anjura's war; Christ aided a Roman soldier and recommended his disciples carry weapons (not to mention whipping the money changers out of the temple is not exactly a peaceful way of resolving things); multiple New Age texts list the pagan goddesses Athena and Bridget (or more accurately the nearly forgotten spiritual figures that gave rise to the myths of these gods) as enlightened masters to call upon for guidance and these are goddesses of war. Another enlightened figure popular with New Agers is Hawaiian goddess Pele; just try taking a rock off Hawaii and we'll see how peaceful and loving the enlightened masters are[100]. Still another popular figure of New Agers is the Archangel Michael, who, although New Agers do not believe in the Devil or demons that need fighting, is always depicted with a sword. The fact is that since a good majority of religious figures had their violent side (Joan of Arc is a Saint with verifiable miracles to her name, and a staggeringly large body count as well) that I think it's justifiable to say that even the most enlightened see that sometimes peace as an end is more important than peace as a means. Yes, we would all love peace to be a means and an end, but we're just not there yet.

[100] For those that don't know, anyone who takes a rock off of Hawaii is plagued with misfortune and suffering that goes way beyond the definition of bad luck until they return the rock. This is proven by the fact that numerous rocks are mailed back to Hawaii every year by people suffering from Pele's curse. There are actually services that charge money to return the rocks. People pay these services and they make money . . . that suggests to me Pele can be enough of a bitch to justify paying money to have a rock returned to an island. See http://www.snopes.com/luck/pele.asp

Republicans and Reincarnation

Finally, there comes the argument that doesn't fighting a war, for most people, ruin their spiritual development; that making them kill other people is pushing them further down the karmic ladder. This is a preposterous argument because no person can truly know what lessons another must learn in that life. I'm sure that many have come to this life needing to learn lessons about helping and protecting others; and many of them can learn these lessons putting their own safety on the line to bring liberty to others. Some may have the karma of needing to be a warrior in that life, the only relevant distinction is are they a warrior who is fighting to bring liberty and end long term suffering, or are they in opposition to that. What I have proposed only ends suffering long term, and thus even being a soldier can lead to spiritual enlightenment and growth.

As such, the secular argument I have set forth is not in any way in contradiction to the New Age reverence for the quality of life, the encouragement of free will, or its nature for long-term thinking.

I have lived too long in a world that does not realize that liberty is the first and most important of all political virtues. Without liberty nothing else matters. People say they believe in liberty, that they wish to defend their liberties; they wish to see liberty spread throughout the world. This is what they say, I see little to no action to back this up. I see a world filled with tyranny, with slavery, both literal slavery and the slavery of many countries' citizens to their respective governments. I see the very nature of what makes us human, what makes us superior to all other forms of life, free will, discarded by numerous civilizations the world over. And I do not see the necessary step being taken to destroy this disgraceful state of existence. We have, within our grasp, not only the ability to combat this evil but the real possibility to end it.

Chapter 9

THE CRIMINAL INJUSTICE SYSTEM: FORGIVENESS DOESN'T MEAN YOU DON'T HAVE TO PAY

"First thing we do, let's kill all the lawyers."—William Shakespeare, King Henry VI, Part II, Act IV, scene ii[101]

From this point on, the fact is that we're primarily going to be dealing with minutia in this book. The large points—people must be free (economically, politically, spiritually) and that freedom must be protected by government—has already been addressed in the two largest ways that federal government deals with people, these being capitalism and actively opposing tyranny have been dealt with. Yet somehow, government, in all its

---

[101] Okay, now before anyone takes me to task over this quote, yes I know that in context the quote is meant to mean that lawyers as defenders of the law are, in actuality, a defense against tyranny, and that those trying to establish a tyranny need to kill all the lawyers to do this. My day job is as an English teacher and you don't need to tell me this. However, while I will admit that we do need lawyers, hell I'll even go as far to say we need the ACLU in all their insanity, any sane person will admit that many lawyers nowadays have forgotten their duty to defend the justice through the law and would rather now subvert it through the law. And while the ACLU has repeatedly defended the indefensible, every just system needs a devil's advocate to keep the rest of us honest . . . just maybe not as many of them are needed.

myriad forms and levels, deals with more than just these two points. I'm am going to cover three more, not to say that I couldn't have chapter after chapter after chapter about every little aspect and every single department, bureau, agency, and policy that every level of government (Federal, State, County, City) covers. Further, I won't be covering anything close to a comprehensive look at every aspect of the topics I'm covering. Let's be honest here, you would never have picked up a book that thick and I would have had to spend so much time writing it that I would likely reach enlightenment before the book hit the publisher. Therefore, we're going to narrow it down to three topics, and not every aspect of those topics, that are near and dear to everyone's heart and I trust you can extrapolate the general principals that are to be applied to all government from there. Those three areas are the Criminal Justice System, Environmental Policy, and the Education System. Now onto what we laughably call a Justice system.

Now, I could go on endlessly[102] on how one of the most central problems with the criminal justice system is that the so called "Canon of Ethics" that Bar Associations across the nation are supposed to follow are disturbingly lacking in... oh, what's the word... Ethics. There's zealous representation of a client which is what it's supposed to be, which morally would be ensuring a guilty client got

---

[102] No really I could get at least 3 books out on how much I loathe defense attorneys. If I had to spend an afternoon with an IRS agent or a defense attorney I would rather spend it with the IRS agent.

no more than they deserved with a healthy dose of mercy and that clients an attorney believes to be innocent, work is done to get them off—and then there's what it really is, at least morally, aiding and abetting in the commission of a crime. A human being, no matter how lacking in common sense, who has made it through four years of undergrad college, and another four in law school, passing the bar, and making through an internship, cannot seriously be believed when they say some of these people are innocent. Sadly however, this rant must end because the bar association is a semi-private organization (depending on the state) that polices it's own and isn't exactly in the purview of what government should be legislating.

So what can the government legislate? Well a lot of things, but when it does it usually lacks that sort of long term planning that I told you before that both conservatives and New Agers like so much. So often in the criminal justice system, as with anything politicians get their hands on, only short term fixes and popular policies are put into place, and not long term solutions that work to eradicate the problem instead of fixes that only please the people temporarily. Any long-term solution needs first to look at the root causes of a problem and try to solve those before it begins to work on the effects of that problem. As doctors are fond of pointing out, you treat the disease not the symptoms when you can.

So what are the causes of crime? I see two main causes. The first major cause that makes people break the law is need. Economic need, be it real or merely perceived is a very real cause of crime I will admit, no matter how un-conservative it sounds of me. Jean Valjean wouldn't rob a house and subsequently spend twenty years in prison if he had a job and money to buy bread for his family in the first place. You may think that this sounds very liberal of me to say, but please consider that I have previously said that liberal policies like income redistribution and heavy government control and spending are what cause economic problems in the first place. You follow conservative policies in the economic field and you will see economic prosperity and thus lower crime.

However, this doesn't solve all crime. There are a vast majority of poor people who don't commit crime, and lots of rich people who do. And this leads to another major problem—probably the problem that comes in before we should consider the issue of needs. Now in terms of reality few people commit crimes because they're dying of starvation at that very moment, so what is real root of most crime? Bonus points to anyone who just said fear. It is often not the actual need, but the fear of a need that causes people to react in such a way that it violates the rights of other people. Stealing, as they perceive it, frees them from that need. Violence offers them power, in their own mind at least, and thus they perceive it as a way to control their fears and the world around them. And while the economic prosperity and personal liberty offered by most conservative policies can offer a path to reduce these fears, it is often more an issue of character and ethics for the individual person. There are people who, no matter how bad things get, no matter how desperate they are, no matter how much they stand to lose, will not violate the rights of other people. Also, there are people who will, and when the chips are down, we call these people criminals. Moreover, while we can hope for the best and try to build a system that provides the fewest opportunities for these hardships, there will always be people with these ethical flaws until all of humanity moves several steps up the ladder. So as this is a personal issue of character and spiritual growth, there is no way for simple government legislation to deal with the root of the problem. If we can't treat the disease, we have no choice but to treat the symptoms.

Imprisonment: How, when, and why to lock them up

The first most obvious way we treat the symptom is the prison system. We put criminals away. This is a good thing. There are just some people who shouldn't be out on the streets (Child molester, rapists, repeat murders and employees of the IRS, for instance). Unfortunately, there is a really psychotic thing that happens when you hear people debate how long people, especially politicians, should be locked up; they debate on whether criminals should be locked up to punish them or to reform them. I find this a foolish argument because the correct answer is they should be locked up for as long as they are threat to society. The criminal justice system is not about the point of locking criminals up—it's about protecting the rest of us who didn't break a law. Protection must always be first and foremost in our minds when society locks away criminals.

Which leads to the obvious questions of what kind of prison terms are appropriate for which crimes. Well first off, rape, child molestation, and first-degree murder are clearly crimes where we have to lock people up for their entire lives. I don't really care if you think you can reform a child molester or not, the fact is that even if this or that child molester can be reformed (which is something I have my doubts about being able to do in the course of a single life) the fact of the matter is that the simple risk they pose outweighs any possibility of keeping a reformed human being locked up (and if they truly were reformed, then they would agree with me because they more than anyone should hate people like themselves and know what kind of danger they are to the innocent). So while we may abide by the idea of it is better to let ten[103] guilty men go free than one innocent man be sent to jail, once convicted I would rather a thousand reformed child molesters stay in prison than for one more child to be abused. The same applies to rapists. The possible suffering they could cause is not worth the gain of giving someone who has been reformed back their freedom. If they're truly reformed they would feel guilt for what they would have done, and that guilt would make them understand the need to keep them locked up. Anyone who is crying for their freedom because they have been reformed probably hasn't been reformed so much as they want more easy prey.

I include first degree murder[104] in here because someone who can have so little respect for the value of life as to plan, not just flip out and react, but to plan to a murder requires such a callous nature that I fear for

---

[103] Defense lawyers should take note that it says 10 guilty men to 1 innocent, not as they seem to think everyone goes free and we simply empty out the prisons.

[104] As always, reason dictates I am going to have exceptions. For instance a battered wife who takes time to plan the murder of her husband, that's not morally questionable, that's the perfectly justifiable defense of "he had it coming." A defense I whole-heartedly support.

the safety of those around such a person. Even if, unlike rapist and pedophiles, murderers don't make their victims suffer for years on end (in both cases the families of the victims are forever suffering) such people are not safe to be around the general populace.

Another group of people who should be locked away for the stay of their natural lives are people who violate "three-strikes" laws. I'm a big supporter of these kinds of laws, and wholeheartedly believe all states should have them. These are laws that say if a criminal commits three separate felony crimes at three separate times then, clearly, there is something very wrong with their learning curve. One way or another they don't seem to get the idea that society will not tolerate violations of the law, and since they show no such ability to learn from their mistakes they do present a very real danger to people around them and thus should be locked for extended periods of time if not for the rest of their natural lives. This again isn't done to simply and cruelly punish, it is done to protect innocent people from the acts of people who are clearly out to hurt those around them. Now we can hope the solitude of imprisonment will help them overcome whatever problems they have to the point that in their next life it will not be an issue, but in the final analysis, the freedom of a person who repeatedly acts to hurt others and violate their rights is a threat that needs to be contained. They are people who clearly first and foremost resort to violence and force and thus cannot be fully trusted in society based on reason before force.

Now what about those criminals we need to lock up for a period of time, more to make a point to those who haven't committed crimes yet with the not so subtle "you really don't want to do that," penalties behind them, whom we are not going to keep behind bars for all eternity, but who need to be locked up for some period of time because they do present some kind of threat to the public. Should we try to punish them or reform them? Both. Let me deal with reform first. The fact of the matter is that if these are the kind of people we are going to be letting back into society then it would be beyond foolish not to try to reform them. If the goal is protection of the innocent, then a reformed criminal is certainly far safer an individual than one who only has their criminal tendencies to fall back on. Education and vocational training should be a big part of prison life. I'm also willing to grant that criminals, probably more than most people, could be in use of a good psychologist, so if we're spending money on counseling before sending them back to civilian life, I'm actually not going to begrudge that money since it will probably lower the chances of my getting robbed, mugged, or killed. So reform should be a big part of life in prison because, the simple fact is, that it is merely long-term protection for the rest of us.

However, punishment should also be a big part here. The simple problem is that in all actuality our legal system doesn't punish nearly enough. Here I don't just mean the fact that TV's, gyms, cigarettes, and conjugal visits are too common in prisons. I'm talking more in the sentencing aspect of the criminal justice system. Too often in sentencing we allow first, second, third offenses to be plea-bargained down to slaps on the wrist of community service or parole or time served. Anyone who has ever taken basic psychology, or has ever been involved in raising or teaching children, knows that all this does is teach someone that there are no consequences to their actions. By the time we actually do send someone to prison, they've already had the conditioned idea that their actions will not result in stiff consequences burned into their minds. The legal system needs to stop thinking that people made a mistake and deserve a second chance, and rather need to provide a stiff example up front to discourage future acts of illegal behavior. I would go as far as to say that any first offense be it felony or misdemeanor needs to be punished by jail time, no questions, no exceptions. If only a week in a jail for a first offense, it will encourage people to not want to ever go back before they have developed the hard to change habits that get them into the position of having to go to jail in the first place. This is especially true of juvenile[105] cases. If all juvenile cases were punished with a mandatory minimum of two weeks in jail, I would actually bet large sums of money you would see not only a noticeable, but a drastic drop in the overall crime rate within only a few years.

On the flip side, we need to start identifying people who are not safe to return to society and keeping them in prison even if they have served their time. The main way I suggest doing this is by, and some lawyer out there can figure out the legalese on this, making being a member of a gang, especially a prison gang, must be made into a felony (I would actually prefer federal crime). This would have the advantage of keeping people who clearly have little

---

[105] Especially graffiti. Severe monetary (at least a $1000 per incident) and jail (starting with a minimum of a month) punishments need to start being put into effect for this crime. Although the "broken-windows" theory of dealing with criminal activity may not solve all crime it certainly has never been shown to have anything close to a negative effect. Nor could scaring adolescents away from crime long before they get into anything major have any major negative effects.

respect for law or concepts such as right and wrong, not to mention IQ's not higher than single digits, away from the rest of us who aren't human only in the genetic sense, since this is a group that poses a fairly large danger to civilized life. I really don't care what tearjerker story you pull out about this or that reformed gang member. For every single story you pull out there are about a million incidents of drug selling or using, assault, rape, murder, and a whole host of other various depravities. Somehow the occasional reform doesn't seem to balance the scales enough in my mind to warrant a knee-jerk desire to give this sorry excuse for human life a second chance right away.

All in all, the guiding light here, as with everything, needs to be the reduction of fear for the most people and the opening of possibilities for the most people. The somewhat harsher punishment I'm suggesting may decrease the opportunities for a few, but it is a few who weren't exactly taking advantage of whatever opportunities they had in the first place. Further, by being much more severe on first offenses we more clearly encourage people to look at the opportunities they have around them. And needless to say that even if this wouldn't reduce criminal natures, which I believe to be beyond unlikely, it would at least reduce crime and thus fear in the general populace. There's really no down side here.

The Death Penalty

Now don't try to get ahead of me here, because I may shock you with what I'm about to say. The death penalty needs to be abolished. I don't care what facts or stats you

Republicans and Reincarnation

can throw out to me on how effective it is at reducing crime or protecting people. In the short run, I don't doubt your numbers or your conclusions; I don't disagree with them. However, I have read from several New Age sources a similar sentiment to the same following statement from medium James Van Praagh (I'd put it my own words but they fail to have the weight of a spiritual medium which is kind of required in this case):

When a person is violently taken out of the physical body before the predetermined, natural time for the soul to leave, there are spiritual consequences. As in suicide, the magnetic tides of the soul must stay within the earthly atmosphere until its natural time to leave. When a spirit of an individual is forced out of the body by capital punishment, the personality of the criminal remains exactly the same as it was prior to execution. When it reaches the other side, it is usually scared and angry because more than likely it is not highly evolved and is ignorant of spiritual laws. In most cases, such a soul roams endlessly throughout the lower astral world with other like-minded souls. Because these tormented souls carry a mind-set of anger and hatred, they often seek revenge for their untimely deaths. They search the earth for weak-minded humans whom they can mentally influence to kill or hurt others. Sounds like a movie doesn't it? But it is very true.[106]

I know that does sound a little unusual. But if it is true . . . well then if we're making decisions based on the long run outcomes, not merely on short-term gains, then I don't think I have to waste anymore of your time trying to convince you. If you believe, the argument is

---

[106] Van Praagh, James. *Talking to Heaven*. Signet, New York, NY, p. 183-184

self-evident. If you don't, nothing I can say will change your mind, because the death penalty does seem actually to reduce crime, but again if this is correct then in the long run it's actually going to spur on more crime and suffering.

The War on Drugs

Now you might be thinking that as a believer in absolute free will I'm going to take the attitude that if you want to shove poison into your system and completely ruin your life, hey free will means you have the right to absolutely destroy your life. And I'll admit that there have been times in my life that I have felt this way. However, while you might have the right through free will to destroy your own life, it does not translate into any legal right to sell morons the tools through which they can destroy their lives. Nor should you be given a free pass for being an idiot, putting something into your body that makes you lose control of yourself and then be given a free pass when you hurt others. Thus, I propose four major changes to the way drugs are treated by our criminal justice system.

The first, and probably least shocking, is that any crime committed under the influence of any narcotic should be treated in much the same way that we treat crimes committed with the use of a gun—we should raise the time spent in jail drastically. This would probably scare most drugs addicts to make sure their habits are kept out of sight (for the most part this is already true) and the people who aren't bright enough to be scared by this, have such a slow learning curve that it is probably much safer for society to keep them away from the rest of us.

The second thing we need to do is decriminalize possession of narcotics in small quantities. Granted I want to reduce drug use, but throwing people into prison for having a small amount of marijuana or cocaine is only going to introduce them to criminal life in prison and ruin their opportunities in life as they now have a felony on their record. This will also help reduce many of our prison population problems.

The third and slightly more drastic charge is that selling drugs (which, let's be honest here, is usually a charge we're going to be put on members of gangs and organized crime) should be raised for the upper level and mid level dealers from a sentence of a few years to one of a few decades. I think the simple logic of one kilo of drugs equals one decade in prison works out fine for me. This will not always be easy to prosecute, but hopefully it will offer another hindrance to the selling of drugs.

However, my fourth and final argument, which I realize is not going to be the most realpolitik thing I have ever suggested, but it will work in the long run (and you know how I love long term solutions) is the most drastic. If we're going to fight a war on drugs, then let's make it a real war and not just one of words. I have a hard time believing that between the CIA, FBI, NSA, and DEA we don't know most of the worlds drug fields, drug lords, and drug suppliers. And I have a hard time believing that the Special Forces divisions of the US military (heck, I'm sure we could invite all of NATO to join us) don't have enough explosives and snipers to make short work of these people. Ever see *Clear and Present Danger*? I'm only suggesting that unlike that novel/movie, we're upfront with the world about what we're doing. I'm sure some countries will raise a public fuss about the US military killing their citizens, but will they really be upset about drug lords being taken out . . . only if they were on the take. There may be a lot of public wrist slapping and some public *mea culpas* of all the countries involved, but I doubt anyone is going to end trade treaties or go to war over the killing of drug dealers. I also seem to remember that the US military was in prime position to go in and burn down the Afghanistan poppy fields—will this turn some of the locals against us? Maybe, but I'm willing to stay in Afghanistan longer if it means having to take the time to kill everyone in the drug business there.

These policies will do several things. It will reduce the supply, reduce the efficiency of the trade itself, and when drugs do get to the idiots who use them they won't be so in your face about it. At that point, I really don't care. If you want to commit slow suicide in the convenience of your home, that's your business.

Illegal Immigration

I had a hard time deciding whether or not to put this particular topic in the chapter on social issues or in with law enforcement. I finally decided to go with law enforcement mainly because the chapter was looking awfully short, and because border patrol is a law enforcement duty.

Again, I think you're going to think that it's the free will issue that is going to make me say there shouldn't necessarily be borders around the world—that the world should be open to everyone to cross any border to find the best job they can, wherever and whenever they can. And yes, I will say that that is my long-term goal—however, we're not there yet. Now I see four main sources of border control issues in the United States.

The first is legal immigration. I have absolutely no problem with legal immigration and actually believe it should be much, much easier to get into this country legally. Now the tradeoff is, I believe, that if we're going to loosen the rules on getting into the country we need to tighten the rules on staying and getting citizenship, not because I have anything against most immigrants—the fact is that most immigrants are more American, and have a better understanding of what this country stands for, than their native born counterparts—but I also live in the real world and know that right now terrorism is a bit of a problem, and thus the healthy paranoid in me just wants to be a little more a cautious about keeping an eye on who we're letting in. However, for the most part I say let more people in.

The next three types of immigration are all illegal immigration, and I'm going to break this into three sections: illegal immigrants from Westernized countries, illegal immigrants from third world Asia and Africa, Europe, and illegal immigration from Latin America.

For the most part illegal immigrants from Westernized countries are not the biggest problem. Their coming here doesn't particularly harm this country or their country very much. As such, I propose mainly fines and deportation. It's more of annoyance than a severe problem. The only caveat I have is that if they prove to have a criminal record anywhere or if they commit a crime while in our borders, well then I believe they should be locked away for a very, very long time . . . and then deported.[107]

The second type of illegal immigration is from the third world. More often than not, this is due to the fact that to stay in their own country is pretty close to a death sentence, and asylum is not being granted fast enough by the State Department to cover all of these people coming in. For the most part I have great sympathy for these people. Often the country from which they are coming from is so corrupt, tyrannical and backwards (China comes to mind) that they have no way of changing their country and the only way to avoid suffering is to leave. As I said I'm sympathetic, and they have as good an excuse as anyone, but there does need to be some kind of punishments (I'm thinking fines and really long waits to become US citizens[108]) for subverting the laws.

Finally the problem that most people think about when they think of illegal immigration: Illegal Immigration from Latin America. From the above you might assume that I have great sympathy for this group. I do; life in Central and South America is certainly anything but a trip to Disneyland for a good portion of the population. Further, you probably have surmised that since my goal is always to reduce suffering, the suffering caused by deporting this group of people who are often simply seeking a better life, is uncalled for and should be stopped. However, you're probably also thinking of the economic costs from border patrol, identify theft,

---

[107] Unless they're a drug dealer, then we should just deport them, and, as suggested by the previous section, they then become a military sniper's problem.

[108] And they do have to eventually become US citizens or we are sending them back.

influx of criminal activity, and social services is simply too much of a burden for the American people to have to deal with. All these are valid points. However, they are all irrelevant because they mostly take only a short-term look at the problem.

The long-term view needs to look for a way that both the countries of Latin America and the United States can benefit. Now with the refugees from most third world nations, there presently is no way of fixing those countries' problem right now. North Korea is not going to be fixed whether one freedom fighter stays or leaves, the problems are just too deep. However, most of Latin America's problems while large, are not insurmountable. For the sake of argument, I'm simply going to use Mexico as my preferred example for the rest of this section. What are Mexico's biggest problems? Corruption, lack of economic opportunity, crime. Most of Mexico's largest crime problems (i.e. the drug cartels) have already been dealt with in the immediately previous section. As for lack of economic opportunity, I'm sure a good portion of international corporations would love to invest in Mexico for labor cheaper than US workers, but more than your current average Mexican salary if it weren't for all that government interference and corruption. So that leaves corruption. Now unfortunately this problem will not ever be solved as the Mexican citizens most driven to find a better life have the option of seeking a better life in the US by coming in illegally.

The current system of allowing illegal immigration in America takes some of Mexico's most driven people and relegates them to pseudo-slave class in America. Yes, I am saying that if you are arguing to let illegal aliens stay you are arguing for a slave class. Make no mistake I'm calling you a racist. Sadly, for those of you opposed to closing the borders, we got rid of the Confederacy and what it stood for about a hundred and fifty years ago. If the borders were secured and closed, then let's not look at the immediate effects to the US or Mexican economy, because those become irrelevant in the long run. In the long run, with nowhere to go but to fix their own country, with not imposing a constant brain and labor drain on Mexico, the populace of the country would be forced to solve its problem, forced to become a more just, more efficient, and probably a more capitalistic country. The end result being two countries with economic and political prosperity, instead of one leaching off the other for its slave class. Are lettuce prices going to go up somewhat? Yeah, but cheap lettuce is a bad argument for the perpetuation of a slave class. Is there going to be emotional suffering in the initial stages of deporting this large population of people who are reasonably trying to seek a better life? Yes. But the suffering of a few million people now with the result of the entire population of the country being prosperous and successful for generations to come somehow does not balance out the suffering imposed on the same populace by perpetually keeping them at the lowest rung of the population economically—by letting them be in the US while we let them suffer in poverty. Long term the only just answer is to close the borders and help Mexico solve its problems.

Now once the borders are closed and secure, I'm not saying there cannot be any kind of worker program, but such a program must be predicated on either short-term work only (say you can only come over for three years and not bring family, thus keeping your long term allegiance to Mexico and working to see Mexico improve itself) or must be predicated on becoming American citizens (this way you could bring family over). This lack of loyalty to either country that the current system perpetuates is destructive to both nations in the long run, because the people involved feel no need to work for the betterment of either society, and thus leads to the decay of both.

Civil Liberties

Patriot Act! Patriot Act! Patriot Act! I hear it screamed by every single liberal I get into an argument with as if this is the end all be all of arguments and I've suddenly lost the argument once they said it.

So before we get onto my points of what rights some people may have overestimated, let's go over what rights you have. You have the right for the government essentially to leave you alone if you are not doing anything to harm anyone. You have a right to privacy as long as you don't make things public. You have the right for no one to know about your private life without you letting them, unless it's the government and they have a warrant from a judge. As a U.S. citizen you have the right to know what you are being charged with, the right to see a judge quickly for arraignment, and the right to defend yourself . . . usually (I'll get to those exceptions in a moment). These and so many other things are your natural rights as a human being. But you can lose all those rights, don't forget that. The theory of natural rights states that you can lose some or all of your rights if you have violated the rights of others. Further, it states that we give up some of those rights for the protection of ourselves and others. So let's keep in

Cris A. Pace

mind in the following discussion that none of those rights are absolute under the right circumstances—we may wish to create a government that violates or infringes on the fewest of your rights as possible, but we aren't willing to risk anarchy, chaos and destruction to do it.

That said, let's dispense with a lot of the Patriot Act hatred right away. Was the Patriot Act passed with too few checks and restrictions? Yes. Was it passed by a Congress and President that were acting off fear and not reason? Yes. Should parts of it be rewritten or simply discarded? Yes. But here's the thing, courts have already struck down a lot of those provisions. With the ACLU out there as a necessary, albeit sometimes very annoying (and sometimes insane), check against government abuse, I'm sure some more parts of the Patriot Act will be overturned. In 50 years, the Patriot Act will not so much be taught as a violation of citizen's rights as it is a clear example of the system of Checks and Balances working as they should. One or two branches of the government go too far in a moment of panic; the other branch slaps some sense back into them.

So now that we've established hysteria might not be called for over violations of your civil rights, let's actually define what the government has the right to know, the right to do, and when and where they can do these things. Regrettably, this section is going to be a little vague, mainly because there are simply too many variables and contingencies to account for to lay down clear hard and fast rules (Why do you think so much of the Constitution is rather vague? I mean what exactly does "probable cause" mean? Because the Founders knew that there was too much grey to account for in rules, too many unforeseen possibilities to delineate specifics, and that reasonable definitions and boundaries can only be applied on a case-by-case basis by the authorities at the time[109]).

Let's start off with all the basic stuff about you. Records, files, credit card information, phone call records . . . all that stuff that other people already know (as in the people you pay your bills to) but the government doesn't have immediate access to. The government has a right to that so long as they can get a warrant from a judge. The tried and true levels of "probable cause" should be in place. Also, the government should be allowed some leeway to immediate searches if there is the threat of an immediate crime being committed, so long as all such searches go before judicial review and stiff penalties are imposed if the review feels they did not have probable cause. If they look at my bank records with a reasonable suspicion that I was planning a terrorist act within the next 48 hours, they should wait and get a judge to sign off first, if however, I had just talked to a terrorist on the phone (I have no idea why I would, but let's say I dialed a wrong number) and they were sure that said person was planning to blow something up in the immediate future, then I think it's better for everyone that they look first and get the review later, rather than have to track down a judge get a signature, look and find out that I'm a rather boring individual. If they looked and didn't have reason to, according to the review, a three-strikes and you're fired system should keep the federal authorities from looking in too many places without needing to (and the strike goes against everyone on whatever investigation looked at my information). The other times will probably be

---

[109] One may however argue they overestimated the mental prowess and common sense of the authorities who came after them

honest mistakes. Honestly, these people have more things to worry about right now than how much money I'm spending at Safeway or my rather obscene college loans, I doubt they're going to look unless they felt there was some pressing need.

Should I be informed before, during, or after they look? If it's a mild to zero threat and they're just dotting the i's and crossing the t's in an investigation, then probably before. If there is a reasonable suspicions I'm involved in something that could harm other people, but the check finds nothing, I should be informed afterwards. If they find something, I shouldn't be informed until I'm being arraigned on charges. Anyone who claims that the government should inform every one of the searches they are conducting, is, quite frankly, out of their mind. Yes, in most simple everyday crimes, sure inform the people before they conduct the search. Most crimes only involve a single person. But when dealing with things like organized crime and terrorist organizations, we're talking about a network that involves dozens to possibly hundreds of people. If you tipped off one the rest will go to ground that would, in the end, put more people in danger, the very thing the law is supposed to prevent. Everything needs to go up for judicial review either before, in the case of mild to severe crimes, and within 24 hours after in the case of the most extreme dangers, but there are times and circumstances where going to get a warrant is not logically called for. These cases are few and far between (unless you're a character on *24* in which case you're likely to have at least 20 of these pop up on any given day, but they do exist in real life too, just a little more spaced out) and there should be a slight amount of wiggle room written into the law for federal

Republicans and Reincarnation

authorities to use when the need is great. Conversely, punishments need to be stiffer than slaps on the wrist for authorities that overstep the limits of common sense either in terms of fines, firing, or real jail time. Further the documents of every investigation should be released publicly (probably with a copy FedEx'ed to the ACLU) so an element of outside scrutiny can further be introduced into the system as yet another check on abuse. [110]

Torture

Then comes that unpleasant issue of torture. Now obviously physical torture should be outlawed without question. The reason for this is two-fold, both equally valid. First, it's a sick and perverted practice that degrades the torturer more than the tortured. Equally important, but more pragmatic, is the fact that from every single report I've read or discussion from experts I've heard is

[110] On a side note, I, and every other human being go dropping dead skin cells, hairs, and sweat all around every day. I personally cannot maintain any illusion that my DNA code is somehow a secret from those who would want to find it. As such, I don't see why the government (and only the criminal investigative side of the government with no right or permission to share it with any other agency be it governmental or private) shouldn't be allowed to take DNA samples like they do fingerprints, taking a sample from just about every person brought into booking or who comes in for any kind background check. I can only image the number of crimes this could be easily solved if this were the case.

that physical torture doesn't yield reliable information. When a person is actually suffering physical pain, most will tell you anything you want to hear, or what they think you want to hear, just to get it to stop, if only for a moment. Thus, any information gathered from this method becomes doubtful and thus the results that we wished to get, that is, actionable intelligence, are never fully attainable.

However, mental tortures (sleep deprivation, sensory deprivation or overexposure, water-boarding) which don't actually physically harm the victim and leave no chance of physical pain or death (unless there is a preexisting medical condition, but given the type of person we would be using this on, I'm not going to lose sleep over the occasional heart attack) is reasonably acceptable to use under any form of logical reasoning. Both in the fact that no lasting or sadistic[111] pain is induced, thus not degrading us and in the fact that information retrieved through these means, when used by professional interrogators, are reliable and accurate.

Also the fear of torture can be very motivating factor, as such I would say the government and military should not only not discourage, but maybe even subtly encourage, Hollywood to portray the U.S. in film and TV as more than willing to torture terrorists and such.

---

[111] I want to make clear here that I am only advocating this in cases of the need for intelligence from captured terrorists or enemy soldiers. If it is done for any other reason than to get information that will save lives in the long run, like say Abu Garaib prison, it is sadistic—and all the guilty parties should then spend the rest of their lives in a dark hole in Leavenworth.

Overall Criminal Justice System Changes

Overall the criminal justice system should be reformed specifically with the protection of the public first, the protection of individual rights of the innocent a close second, and reforming criminals coming third . . . As opposed to nitpicky attention to legal technicalities and what is politically popular first, reforming criminals through methods that don't always work; second, and public safety somewhere down there.

Chapter 10

THE SKY ISN'T FALLING ... BUT IT COULD BE A LOT PRETTIER
PROTECTING THE ENVIRONMENT FROM THE ENVIRONMENTALISTS

Now to say that taking care of the Earth and the environment is a big thing for most New Agers is a bit of understatement. I'm not going to contest that belief in any way, shape or form. It is absolutely correct to want to take care of the planet, animals and just the general environment. However there is an effective way of doing it, and then there is what we're doing right now (which isn't even close to effective).

The Sky is Not Falling

First off, before we get all worked up about this, this will not be a chapter about global warming. Every year I see new record low being reached all over the world. And let us not forget that the end of the Ice Age, the Medieval Warming Period (circa 1000 CE), the Little Ice Age (circa 1600 CE) and the ending of the Little Ice Age (circa 1800 CE) were all major changes to the average temperature of the planet and mankind had nothing to with those. Let us also not forget that the explosion of

Krakatoa island pushed more particulate matter into the atmosphere in the late 1800's than industry put up in the entire 1900's and it didn't seem to cause any irrevocable and disastrous temperature changes in the environment. Therefore, while I won't deny that climate change does occur, I am not anywhere near arrogant enough to see mankind as the sole and most egregious cause. So there will be no rampant hysteria in this chapter screaming that the sky is falling, as if we were Chicken Little or exceedingly boring Vice Presidents with PowerPoint slide shows and blatantly incorrect facts.

However keeping the environment clean is a good thing. I don't particularly like how the air in Phoenix, where I currently live, seems to, sometimes, have texture to it. I've never been a fan of having to buy purified water, even though I do because I otherwise have to deal with looking at sediment at the bottom of the glass (and that's more than just a Phoenix problem). I would like not to have too many carcinogens thrown my way in what I eat. But again, let's not get carried away. Phoenix is surrounded by dirt on all sides and is in a valley, even without cars I would have some grit in the air occasionally, smog doesn't make it better, but it is not the end of the world. Water from the tap tastes bad just about everywhere, doesn't mean it's toxic. And at the rate that scientific studies are declaring things carcinogens, I expect basic water, oxygen and food of any kind to be declared as cancer causing within the next ten years.

Still, hysteria aside there are verifiable reasons why we have the Environmental Protection Agency. The problem with this agency is not that it doesn't deserve to exist (like, say, the Department of Agriculture or the current form of the Department of Education) but rather that since its inception it has had no real power given to it to stop pollution, and what power it has been given has been massively abused.

Further, while pollution by corporations is a terrible and disgusting problem, it is not the biggest problem out there. The lack of resources for the coming generations is a far graver problem, and while some have acknowledged the problem, I haven't really seen anyone doing anything justifiable about it.

The EPA: Replacing an Army of Bureaucrats with Pen Knives with a Few Guy with Machetes

The inherent problem with the EPA isn't that it already does things which are the responsibility of the Departments of Agriculture and Interior, it isn't that it's a bunch of bureaucrats and few scientists, what scientists it does have prefer to act like Chicken Little instead of actually looking at real data, that when it does do something it often cares more about some tiny fish surviving than actual people surviving... which don't get me wrong, are all problems.... but the main problem is that, like so many governmental actions, it has no understanding of human nature.

One of the primary functions of the EPA is to enforce environmental policy. You pollute the EPA will swoop in and fine you. There is one big problem with this. Environmental Policy is treated more like a civil lawsuit than a criminal act. It assumes that people will either do the right things, and that when they don't a simple fine will be enough. Let's look at human nature and see how this is wrong. Most of the time people do choose the right thing, but a lot of the time they don't, that's why we have the government in the first place. Second, yes in terms of individuals, fines work well as deterrent to most crimes because most people see it as their own personal money, for corporations money is seen in terms of cost of business only. Third, businesses don't fear fines if it's cheaper than the cost of disposing of something properly.

So here is my suggestion, change environmental law to require two things. First all fines should be listed not as a dollar figure, but as a percentage of the offending company's gross income (as to be determined by IRS accountants... even the devil has his purposes sometimes) for every violation. You charge three companies with a 15% of their gross income fine for dumping chemicals improperly, no company in America will dare risk that again after those first three fines to show that we're serious. It would take thousands of the current fines to make a dent like that; the current fines project all the fear of a nerdy bureaucrat penknife. 10-20% of your bottom line, that inspires a level of fear equivalent to seeing a professional wrestler with a machete in his hand standing before you. Second and more importantly jail time needs to be imposed for everyone from the guy who dumped the pollution out of the truck to the CEO of the company. American's propensity for whistleblowers and deal-making during prosecution should help to convince executives to keep their hands clean, after all a criminal trial is a far higher cost to your bottom line than the current cost of having to pay your PR department extra bonuses for coming up with lines like "Do people care, people do" to make up for the fact that you've dumped lots of oil on the Alaskan shoreline.

A Better Environment Through Technology

Now a very common line being repeated in the political campaigns is the desire to invest in and support new technologies that will get us away from burning oil in our cars to burning corn/hydrogen/yet undiscovered miracle chemical or simply having electricity in our cars. They suggest tax incentives to companies spending money on research. Because once again that is an effective use of money and clear understanding of human nature . . . oh wait, it's not.

Let's look at this situation: I'm going to pay you (because that's what a tax cut is to a corporation) to do research into something. You don't have to actually come up with anything that will really cause you to shift away from your current money making device. (And keep in mind the nature of the internal combustion engine ensures that that it will eventually fall apart and require you to buy a new car, so the current system has a built in obsolescence . . . versus an electric car which doesn't have a million tiny explosions going off every day thus less wear and tear on the machinery itself thus in the long run less need to buy a new car). Just do research, don't come up with anything, just do research, and we'll pay you. However if you actually do come up with something that works, it will hurt your bottom line, and we'll stop paying you because we don't need you to do anymore research.

Who here thinks those tax breaks for research are going to work?

There is no incentive there to create a working, efficient and cheap electric car. And if there is no incentive, no company is going to do it. Right, wrong or indifferent, greed is a natural part of being human. When coupled with a long-term perspective, greed can and often is a good thing. The problem is another habit of human nature is to only think in the short term. People don't realize that their business is a dying one and it would be better to get on the ground floor of a new one, rather than staying with what they know, trying to wring every last dollar out of it before it dies. People resist change if they have no incentive to do so.

Instead of tax breaks for research, or this or that minor incremental change in emissions, how about we go for broke. Stop all other tax breaks. And then make a single blanket offer: The first company that designs an engine with no (or at least almost insignificant) emissions that can run for 350 to 400 miles at 65 miles per hour before having to be refilled gets fifty years of absolutely no corporate taxes. To get the zero tax offer they will have to give up full rights to patent rather agreeing to take a nominal fee for every engine built off their concept by all their competitors ($1000 per engine sounds fair, but I haven't worked out the numbers, I'm sure a professional economist could come up with a more realistic number, but the number is unimportant at this point). After the engine has been patented, it will be illegal to build or sell any cars with a traditional internal combustion engine (yeah that will cost a lot up front, but the fact that we won't need oil anymore will more than pay for itself). If an individual comes up with the design and not a company, then that person never has to pay taxes again, ever—no sales tax, no income tax, no property taxes, no taxes on their phone or electricity bill—and they get to pick 50 of their closest friends who also get the no tax deal (and they still have to get paid for every engine built off their design). If you don't think every company and inventor in the country is going to jump on this like hyenas on a wounded gazelle you're crazy. If you made an offer like this I would say you would have your miracle engine within only a few years . . . because while necessity may be the mother of all invention, having bills to pay is one of those great necessities in life, and offering a way out of all those bills, a truly powerful motivator.

Competitors not wanting to pay that fee will come up with their own designs and own ways of designing a zero emission engine, and soon you would have a plethora of designs all efficient in their own way.

Or we could try what we've been doing for the last few decades. Because that's worked so well.

Actually Weighing Individual Costs and Benefits

Here is one question everybody forgets to ask. If we have electric cars, where are we going to get the electricity to power them? That's right you can't just pull electricity from the air (well actually you can, but I haven't seen anyone invent any kind of engine that can actually harness static electricity at any level I would call efficient). Electricity still has to be generated somewhere. But where? Coal plants? Gives us all the smog we were trying to get rid of by going to electric cars, and coal is a limited resource so I'd rather have it around to make more steel than to simply burn. Hydroelectric dams? Kills fish and drastically changes the ecosystem. Solar Power, not actually as efficient as Hollywood likes to make it sound. Wind power? Not terribly efficient given the amount of land it takes, and I've heard the complaint it kills birds (although I find the research on airborne wind turbines quite promising). Nuclear power? Radioactive waste. I could go on . . .

My point here is not to dissuade the use of these fuel sources (well, actually, I'm not big on coal and dams) but to point out that every fuel source has a trade off. Many on the wacko environmental fringe will argue against any and all forms of producing energy because of this or that cost or waste product. They don't realize unless you accept at least one of these methods of producing electricity, society is going to sink back into the 15th century. Now while that may be the dream of every fringe nut job ecoterrorist and most Islamofacists, I think the rest of us, even those of us who would consider ourselves to be environmentalists, would like to keep the lights in our house running. So until someone figures out how to make cold fusion work and power the world on a pound of waste from the local city dump what we should be looking for is the form of energy production that creates the most energy, for the cheapest overhead, with the least impact on the environment.

Believe it or not, that would be nuclear power. The main costs are building the plant, which pays for itself quickly, security, and the main harm to the environment is the nuclear waste. Now I will grant you if a huge earthquake and tsunami hit a plant that is both old and not carrying enough coolant that can be a problem (but store lots of back up coolant, replace old reactors, and maybe not build them on active fault lines and it becomes less of a problem). And I'll grant that improperly stored nuclear waste can create huge problems. However, when stored in a room lined with thick walls of dense metal, and when placed far away from heavily populated areas, the storage of these materials poses no threat to the environment or the public. France, quite intelligently, relies on nuclear power as their primary source of power, and I have yet to hear about any reactor leaks, or genetic mutations[112] popping up in France. I haven't even read of anyone claiming France has higher cancer rates. Just think how many barren areas where no intelligent life exists in the U.S. there could be to store nuclear waste (e.g. the Salt Flats, Death Valley, IRS buildings).

An irrational Chicken Little fear of nuclear energy keeps us from having this cheap and clean form of energy, and any one or any government claiming to care about the environment would be clamoring and demanding this, and every country sane enough to be trusted with fissionable materials, should switch over to nuclear energy.

Meanwhile let me deal with an effective but highly environmentally dangerous form of producing power: Hydroelectric dams. While they do wonders at producing electricity, they also do irrevocable damage to whatever ecological system they are put into. They kill wildlife populations, and drastically and usually harmfully damage the landscape. Unless there is a serious threat to human life, the policy of the U.S. (and quite frankly every government on Earth) should be to never again build another dam. However, unlike the radical fringes of the

---

[112] Like developing spines.

environmental movement I would say that while existing dams have caused great damage, the damage is done and quite frankly can't be fixed. The fact is that all the dams in the Pacific Northwest, which have done a handy job of driving certain species of salmon to extinction, have already done their destruction, and even if you tore them all down, the fish are, in all likelihood, still going to be extinct in a few decades. At this point, the benefits do not outweigh the costs.

This leads us to another major point of how environmental policy needs to change. Natural resources to humans are usually more important than natural resources to animals. Thus if it's the choice of thousands of farmers being without water and thus going bankrupt and ruining the surrounding economies, versus hurting some tiny fish that exists in only a small place of the earth, was never in high numbers, and now risks extinction . . . well, my bias is for the humans. Environmentalists, like so many of their liberal brethren, are a little shaky on history. They need to go back and read what gave us the overabundance of species of wildlife on this earth. To review briefly, about five mass extinctions over the history of the planet have driven to extinction about 99% of all species that ever existed (all without the help of humans). This is partly due to a process called survival of the fittest. Perhaps some species are found in only one small part of the world in small numbers because they're not fit to live anywhere else, and if anything were to change in the environment (which happens a lot in the history of the world, again, without the help of humans) they would die off anyway. Furthermore, let's not look at all interference of human beings as being bad. (Little known fact the introduction of oil pipelines in Alaska has actually increased the caribou populations . . . apparently the heat generated by the rushing oil encourages the caribou to mate with greater frequency, usually right under the pipeline, and thus has increased their previously dwindling numbers.) History tells us that nature is going to kill most of these species off anyway, now we shouldn't actively try to help in achieving that end, but nor should we psychotically and irrationally defend every single species that is not equipped to adapt to changes in its surroundings (unless they're really cute, like Giant Pandas). The fact is that the ecosystem and most species are not as fragile as some environmentalist like to imply in their propaganda. Keep in mind through the entire four billion year history of life on Earth is a history of struggle against other species and the environment; it is a system not meant to save everyone and if it had been designed not to force a survival of the fittest response, multicelluar organisms would probably have never developed, let alone crawled out the ocean, developed lungs, brains, and cable TV (okay maybe that last one isn't our finest moment in evolution). The only time anyone even suggested all the species will get to be saved is the fairy tale called Noah's Ark[113].

While we should try and save as many species as possible, never should that come at the explicit cost of human civilization.

---

[113] Isn't it ironic that many liberals, while all too willing to ridicule and insult Christians for an irrational beliefs in the Book of Genesis, will cling to the same irrational beliefs behind it, and while they may demand, correctly, that only evolution should be taught in public school science classes, aren't actually willing to let its most basic premises work their way out in real life.

Limited Resources

There are about six and a half billion people on Earth. 6,500,000,000! It doesn't take a degree in Economics or Environmental Policy, or even a reading of Jared Diamond's *Collapse*, to realize that there might not be enough food, water, oil and other such resources just lying around to bring everyone up to a first world standard of living.[114] And while capitalism is the only system that can create wealth out of work and ingenuity (unlike every other system which just moves wealth that already exists around) it again doesn't take a Mathematics major to see that it isn't creating wealth fast enough to let everyone join in the fun next week. Now those of you familiar with economic theory, or had a really good history teacher, may have the name Malthus running through your heads. Who? Thomas Malthus was an early 19th century political economist who said that because population grows faster than increases in food production every so often you will have more people than you have food for, and the only way that society corrects itself is through war, famine and disease. A little dark, I know. Further, the major growth of the economy during the Industrial Revolutions of the 19th and 20th centuries has generally shown Malthus's predictions were more pessimistic than

[114] That should be the eventual goal after all. By first world standard of living, I'm not saying that everyone needs to drive a SUV, have a large house, and massive amounts of disposable income.

reality tends to operate. While the math of his projections may have been too pessimistic, the underlying argument was not. Simply look at sub-Saharan Africa, a continent rich with resources, yet filled with famine, and tell me that population doesn't grow faster than food production. Remember what your gas bill was 20 years ago before a billion people in China started using as much oil as the rest of the industrialized world does, and compare that old bill to what it is now, and tell me that population growth hasn't made the cost of basic resources exceed tolerable levels of inflation. So maybe there really are too many people on the planet and its current level of infrastructure.

Now is there any way to solve this? War, famine, and disease. Not pleasant options . . . not to mention actually causing any of these for the purpose of lowering population is called genocide. So those are clearly out. And short of the bird flu hitting all on its own natural self, while that might do the trick, this problem isn't just going to fix itself. Killing people is obviously out of the question, and just hoping it will go away is as stupid as the previous option is unethical and revolting. The only option I can see is to slow the population growth in the world.

Now how to we do that?

You know all that money we're spending on food, medicine, and abstinence programs in the third world. They're not working. While it's good news that first world nations are not reproducing like rabbits, it's not exactly comforting that the third world is more than making up for the slowing growth of industrialized nations. So we have nothing to lose at this point, if we are hell bent on sending aid to the third world, then we should probably start sending condoms and birth control pills—lots of them. That might seem a little cold, but the fact is, at present, there are not enough resources to give everyone the life which every human being is entitled to an opportunity for, and as is there is no way to ethically reduce the current population (someday technology will allow 6.5 billion to live a first world standard of living, but not today), our only hope is to worldwide slow and hopefully reverse the growth of population.[115] The fact is that if the current growth rates continue we will see Malthus's war, famine, and disease on an epic scale. It is more cruel not to try to do something to at least delay, if not prevent this from happening.

The National Parks System and the waste of a Department of the Interior

So many things the government does could be merely leased over to private industry and private corporations, albeit with strict oversight, and done far more effectively than the government does them. The National Parks system will serve as an excellent example of this.

A teacher of mine, a good person but not the brightest of all the stars in sky, once asked me when I claimed that businesses can do just about anything better than government: "Would you want to sell the Grand Canyon to some corporation and have them put a giant dome over it?" As if that settled the argument. He then said, "Would you really want to have to pay to get into

[115] I'll discuss this concept further in the chapters on education and the future of foreign aid and world government.

Yosemite." I really wasn't trying to provoke an argument at the time (and I needed the grade) so I decided not to challenge his obvious hatred of private business (besides it wasn't a government class so there was little relevance to the conversation). However, these two points, (which I've sadly since that fateful conversation heard repeated by many people[116]) are sadly ridiculous. If we were to sign over the national park to private management, it would not ruin nature, but make it more effective.

As to putting up a dome over this or that natural wonder . . . why would any business do such a thing as it would be at prohibitive cost (and businesses don't like to do things that cost that much money) with no possibility for profit. Further, as opposed to now where when I visit a National Park and I'm usually accosted by trash everywhere, business would have a profit based incentive not only to not mess with the skyline, but to keep the place clean, because where as current park rangers and employees get paid regardless, businesses need to encourage people to come to the parks. Further, as I said regulation and oversight does need to occur, and I seriously doubt any such regulation would allow for destroying the park itself. Business would also be more cautious and concerned with the tending of national parks—after all, if they burn down no one is going to come and pay the admission fee. Thus, we would likely not have to watch the Southwest burn down every other summer.

The other complaint is that we shouldn't have to pay an admission fee to go see the Redwood Forest, or the

---

[116] Honestly, I would not be brining up something this ludicrous if it wasn't for the fact that I must have heard this, I'm not kidding, at least a dozen times in the past decade or so.

Republicans and Reincarnation

Grand Canyon, or Mount Rushmore. This disregards that your taxes are already paying that admission fee you currently have to pay, plus the admission fee to all those other national parks that you didn't go and see. I'd rather just be charged for what I'm using (above what the Park Service is already charging for next to nothing). Further, as again companies like to make a profit, perhaps their maps and information boards won't all look like they were last updated in the Roosevelt[117] presidency. Maybe the information will be more interesting, more frequent (like in places you actually have a question) and more convenient. Because they also want you in a good mood when you hit the gift shops (which hopefully will include a much better selection of items, like things you might actually want to buy. Think about it, any private organization's gift shops are always much nicer than the national parks one[118]).

Or we could continue with the inefficient method of poor service, trash-ridden trails, and not making a profit because the system is overstaffed with government employees.

---

[117] And I don't mean Franklin.

[118] And as a personal complaint of an Arizonan, maybe not everything in the Arizona national parks will be covered in pictures of Kokopeli. I like Kokopeli, but I, nor anyone needs a hundred and fifty things with him on it.

Chapter 11

EDUCATING OUR CHILDREN INTO THE IDIOTS OF TOMORROW
THE PROBLEMS OF MODERN AMERICAN EDUCATION AND THE SOCIETY AROUND IT

"Without education, we are in a horrible and deadly danger of taking educated people seriously."—G.K. Chesterton

I could probably write a book on this subject. I know I could, because numerous people have already done so and have barely begun to scratch the surface. Some are rather thick at that. And many of them have some very good ideas. So I am not going to go over every single aspect of the educational system that is a problem (otherwise known as just about every aspect of the education system), but rather focus on a few broad swaths here . . . besides if I get going to long on this one I might never stop.[119]

Where to start? How about where education actually begins, and I don't mean kindergarten.

---

[119] Actually I would have to stop, since I tend to write this book in short sections as a break from the mountain of papers I have to grade.

Republicans and Reincarnation

Having Children

So many of the problems I see in students, arguably began in the first years of their life. I'm not going to say that teachers don't have great power to irrevocably misdirect (and often do) the lives of their students, but as often as teachers are to blame, parents are just as often to blame. It is a much-repeated joke[120] among teachers about parent teacher conferences that the only parents that show up are the parents we didn't need to talk to, since the parents that show up are the ones who have kids passing. Or we get parents who have what I call, "Not my Little Angel" syndrome.

"Your child is failing"
        "Not my little angel."
"Your child cheated on his test."
        "Not my little angel."
"Your child attempted to burn down the school and we have video of it."
        "Not my little angel."
"Your child grabbed a girl by the hair, shoved her face to his crotch, and said 'I might as well rape you now, and get it over with."
        "Boys will be boys."[121]

---

[120] It's a joke because the only two reactions to this situation are to laugh or to cry. Most of the time we choose to laugh only to maintain our sanity.

[121] I did not make this one up! The situation and the response actually happened. I wish I was making this up, (I also wish

Or my personal favorite, the parent, who despite my calling home throughout the semester, giving weekly progress reports, posting those reports in class and on the internet, giving the student a copy of it to take home, sending home midterm grades, offered to stay after school every day to tutor them (which they never show up for), etcetera, etcetera . . . comes in the day before the end of the semester screaming: "WHY IS MY CHILD FAILING!!!!" To which one of these days I'm going to lose it and respond: "Because your child is an idiot, and I've just become convinced it's a genetic condition."

So, while I will admit that I and my fellow teachers get to take a great deal of the blame for why America's youth are profoundly lacking in so many respects, please be willing to admit that we're not always the only ones at fault.

Now honestly, I realize, that if you're reading a non-fiction book on politics and religion in what is most likely your free time, I may be preaching to the choir just a little. While we've all run into educated morons, I will say that there is a mild correlation between the lacking education level of a parent and the amount of egregious problems we have regarding their children. I also realize that my status as a bachelor at the time of this writing gives me very little standing for giving advice to parents. But bear with me, I'm not going to get too detailed or preachy. Just some general observations that I can make from the New Age/Conservative philosophy standpoint.

First off, have less children. I know I covered this in the last chapter, but it deserves repeating. And it deserves

---

they had just put the boy down like the rabid animal he was) but sadly that is not the case.

Republicans and Reincarnation

repeating not only for the fact that there are too many people on Earth, but because at a personal level having lots of children isn't all that helpful.

First off, let's start off with the blatantly obvious reason why you shouldn't have lots of children: They cost money. Lots of money. The average child is going to cost you $350,000[122]. Three Hundred Fifty Thousand Dollars. Or depending on your income level about five to ten years of work. Now granted you can scrimp and save and have hand me down clothes but the fact of the matter is that that bill is not going to be that much smaller. College (and you all should be demanding that your child go to college, but if you're going to demand it, then you should shoulder part of the responsibility of paying for it) alone could very well bankrupt you if you have more than one child.

But economic realities are not the only reason that you should keep your procreation down to singles, there are psychological benefits as well. Now many people foolishly believe that having lots of children is psychologically healthy for a child, and that only children grow up anti-social and unable to make strong connections to other human beings. This belief continues despite the rather startling lack of psychological evidence for this. Here's the trick to make sure your only child knows how to make connections with other humans—get them connections with other humans. It so simple isn't it. Play dates, parties, and school functions. You'll find it

---

[122] That's a rough average of what I got off of about 10 sources. That's also in 2007 dollars so by the time they're twenty and in their Junior year in college, inflation will likely be more in actual dollar amount.

amazing how social all children are when they have the opportunity to be social.

But let's talk about the more important reason not to have lots of children. Modern research has shown that while people with children are happier than people without children (did it really take a psychological study to prove that?), people's relative happiness decreases with the more children they have. Children take nearly 100% time and effort. Children take 100% of the love you have to offer. Last time I checked 100% divided by 2 is not 100%. At some level you know this, and at some level you know every moment spent with one child is a moment not spent with the other one, and you will always feel a little guilty over that undesirable decision. Now does that mean every parent who has more than one child is less happy. No. I'm sure there are exceptions, there always are. I'm just saying that you shouldn't necessarily consider yourself an exception (because most people aren't).

Also don't think that it's for your child's happiness, not yours, that you're giving them siblings. Trust me, lots of people are not thrilled with their siblings. As long as your child has friends, they'll survive not having siblings.

Obviously, parents should be instilling the principles of responsibility and character (yes you are responsible for your actions), critical thinking, and empathy for others, always to strive for the best because they are capable of anything they set out to do . . . among those other basic lessons you're supposed to teach your child from day one. But enough about parenting for the moment, let's move onto formal education.

Public Education

"If you meet the Buddha on the road, kill him."—Buddhist Proverb

Now before I get onto some of the main issues of what education should and shouldn't be, I should make very clear what education can't do. It is actually a very large area of ground.

Now some very foolish people I have known have spoken of teaching as if it is the end-all be-all of fixes for all of society. I've known teachers who think the same thing . . ."if only the middle school teachers had done their jobs we could teach them how to be great human beings" which I'm sure the middle school teachers are saying "If only the elementary school teachers had done their job, we could teach them to be wonderful young adults" . . . and I'm almost absolutely certain the elementary, middle, and high school teachers are all saying "If only the parents had done their job . . ." And ironically, the parents are probably saying the same thing about the teachers. Notice who isn't getting the blame? Little Johnny and Sally themselves. Because either nature or nurture (from parents or teachers) are at fault.

Now in a vacuum that might be a valid argument. (However, this book doesn't exist in a vacuum. You picked up the book because it had "Reincarnation" in the title, and the phrase "New Age" in the subtitle. Don't lie, you did. Even you conservatives out there, it's part of the reason. You know I'm right. So with reincarnation and

New Age values in play, it creates a completely different landscape.)

Yes, parents and teachers are very, very important. They have the ability to expose a child to new ideas and thought. Kind of. Don't forget that the soul of that child, the person who they really are, chooses its parents (and by some extension its genetics), its background, social class, and such all for a karmic reason, every event in their life is so that they can learn for themselves or that they can teach others through their example. If we go from the most basic New Age premises:

- God did not create a meaningless world[123]
- God is in everything I see because God is in my mind[124]
- I have invented the world I see[125]

When we consider these, along with every other principle I have previously mentioned, we become forced to admit that (A.) There is a purpose to being here and (B.) that the universe will provide us with everything that we need to accomplish that purpose; that the universe will provide every lesson that we are ready and willing to learn; that even the concept that the universe will not or cannot provide a person with a lesson that they can use is simply preposterous . . . because God did not create a meaningless world, and as illusionary as this world is, it is not meaningless—it is a place to learn, and as a place to learn it will provide us with the lessons we need. Any denial of this is a contradiction because it suggests that

---

[123] A Course in Miracles: Workbook for students p. 23
[124] Ibid p 47
[125] Ibid p 49

Republicans and Reincarnation

perfection cannot be found in this world, which is the entire purpose of this world. We may not understand how this or that is meant to teach us the truth and put away our fears, but every situation is meant to teach, and every lesson everyone is meant to learn is provided to them if they're willing to listen.

Why am I ranting about this?

Because, in the end, and trust me on this, you can't teach anyone anything they don't want to learn. You can fill their heads with facts (and maybe they might even remember them until graduation), but you can't teach them the truth. Truth is a very elusive thing even when it's not being debated, because it can only be discovered by a person on their own. It can't be that they haven't been exposed to the truth, God is already a part of everyone's mind and soul, and thus it is impossible to not, at some level, know the truth. Thus, you cannot be taught what you already know. This is the meaning of the above quote about killing the Buddha. Teachers, or parents, can't teach you anything you don't already know, and if you place all your faith in a teacher, or the Buddha, as being able to teach you the truth, then you've missed the point completely. For someone really seeking the truth, a teacher is a distraction from the real search, a distraction that must be ignored or eliminated (kill the Buddha) on your journey through life.

The fact that society has not progressed is not necessarily education's fault. At least in the modern world, it isn't as if all the knowledge of the world isn't available in libraries and the internet for anyone who wants to search for them. It isn't as if the deeper more important lessons of life aren't right in front of all of our faces every single day. People don't make stupid decisions because they haven't been taught correctly or because they haven't been exposed to the truth. The universe is desperately trying to show every person the truth every moment of existence with all the subtlety of an Ayn Rand speech; people make stupid decisions because the ego by nature is a stupid, irrationally selfish, illogical thing and people throughout history have too often chosen to listen to their egos and not that aspect of god within them.

Now does this mean that we shouldn't teach anyone because as I just claimed the universe will provide? Let me respond with, "Are you part of the universe?" The answer is obviously yes. How about "Are you part of God?" Again, for a New Ager, the answer is yes. And since the goal of God, and the point of the universe to bring people back to truth, I guess that means that yes, in as much as your life is to live in such a way that you learn all the lessons existence has to teach you, it is through teaching those lessons, through being an example to others, through embracing those higher, more God-like aspects of your being, that you are in tune with yourself. So don't come back to me with any of that fatalistic "If you say the universe will provide, and everything will unfold as it should, then I don't need to do anything" ridiculousness. It's merely another trap of the ego, and you should have none of it.

"When the student is ready, the teacher will appear."—Buddhist proverb

So, now that we all do agree we should teach people, (even though it may be to no avail to this or that individual student), what should we teach?

One of the major problems is that modern education in the world says we should shove all this college prep information into teenager's heads whether they want it or not. Ignoring questions of effectiveness, efficiency, and whether or not this will lead to happiness in their lives (which trust me these questions need to be asked at some point, just not here, because I don't have the time) there is a bigger issue, and that is the fact that this system completely ignores the concept of free will.

Several rather naïve conservatives I know argue that all the problems in this country stem from education and if we only were to teach correct ideas and get rid of all the touchy feely liberal tripe the country would improve within a generation. Now, I'll admit that the modern public education system is a joke. As a high school English teacher I am constantly beyond infuriated that I get students (mostly juniors and seniors) who come to my class feeling completely entitled to their beliefs and feelings even when they can't offer even the most basic justification for those beliefs, believing they have a right to a high grade despite the level of their work, despite how late they turn it in, despite the fact that they can barely read, don't have a clue what a semi-colon is, and have absolutely no understanding of cultural literacy. (And my math department counterparts are equally infuriated about having to teach juniors and seniors how to multiply, divide, and use fractions). You might think I'm exaggerating, but I'm not—I am not even close to exaggerating. I don't know what Middle School or Elementary School teachers think of High School teachers, but I can assure you that competent[126] High School teachers would willingly savagely beat our lower grade predecessors who clearly failed to do their jobs. However, a deeper problem exists.

For the sake of argument, let's say we were able to completely and effectively revamp the entire system. Under this system no child would leave elementary school without being able to read at a sixth grade level or higher, write complete sentences, know grammar rules, add, subtract, multiply, divide, use fractions; no child would leave Middle school without reading at a 9th grade level or higher, writing five paragraph essays, doing basic research and citation, know Algebra, and have a decent survey of the Science and Social Sciences; and not leave High School without knowing all the equivalent level skills of English, Math, History, Science, and the Arts. Under this system we would encourage self esteem, not through rewarding every half-intelligible sentence with praise worthy of a Poet Laureate, but encourage them to seek to do better because through doing a good job (and I do mean having high standards as to what a good

---

[126] I want to make it clear that I by no means am implying that most high school teachers are competent. Most aren't. I personally had 19 different teachers in high school, looking back I'd say about 11 of them were completely unqualified to teach. If my memory is accurate the stats get worse when I think back to Middle and Elementary school. Further, while I would say I am currently very fortunate to work at a school of mostly competent, maybe not exceptional but competent, fellow teachers whom I respect, of the hundreds of fellow teachers I have met since entering the profession I can say that the emotions I most often feel for most teachers is disdain, disgust, and contempt for them and the bad reputation they give the small portion of us who actually do teach.

Republicans and Reincarnation

job is)—that will give them high self esteem. Under this system, critical thinking skills will be taught and tested for . . . We wouldn't teach students that the Pilgrims and Indian got along—they didn't. We wouldn't teach that Lincoln freed the slaves or that the Civil War was fought over slavery—both are incorrect. We wouldn't teach a lot of things we tend to teach elementary school children because we assume that they're just not ready to understand, so we'll give them a dumbed down fairytale. No, the problem with dumbed down fairy tales is that people believe them.

Under a system like this . . . people would still be idiots. We've kind of already established this—you can't teach someone who doesn't want to learn.

You can teach responsibility, that does not mean someone will be responsible. You could teach every moral and value you think is correct. You can teach why other philosophies are wrong, detailing the flaws in the logic. You can teach a lot of things, it doesn't mean a person is going to learn it. This is because the modern American education system takes the old adage that "when the student is ready, the teacher will appear" and turns it upside-down and inside-out and puts students in the same classes and same system whether they are ready to learn or not, and whether they need to learn it or not.

Now I'm not even going to come close to saying that school should be teaching anything spiritual in class (although we should stop being idiots and change it back to "Christmas Break" and not "Winter Break"[127]). But there are simple changes that can be made to help people

---

[127] Anyone who has a problem with the modern ideal of Christmas of "peace on earth, goodwill to men" and charity and giving, is a person so depressed, so dark and so anti-social that they need to

at different levels of spiritual growth, even without making it blatantly spiritual.

The modern system: Dump It

"You know there is a problem with the education system when you realize that out of the 3 R's only one begins with an R."—Dennis Miller

Where to start? Obviously with Preschool, Kindergarten, and Elementary School.

Now, as far as I can tell here are the problems with these levels of education: self-esteem, actual learning, and social promotion.

Self-Esteem. It's an important thing that children believe they are capable of anything (which they are). It's important they are rewarded when they do something right. It's important that they be encouraged at every opportunity. This however does not mean that they should be congratulated for not being able to read at a first grade level when they're in the fifth grade (of course I'll get to that little problem in a minute).

Now I may be speaking from a certain level of distain held by high school teachers for our earlier level counterparts, but is it just me that most elementary school teachers seem more concerned with a child's emotions than the fact that the child actually learns anything. I don't mean to be insulting, but the fact that every year I have to go over the eight parts of speech, and my math counterparts have to teach a few students how

---

be ignored if not locked up. Yes all you atheists out there, I'm talking about you.

Republicans and Reincarnation

to multiply, it means someone somewhere isn't exactly doing their job. Is this every elementary school and every elementary school teacher? No. I remember having some great ones. However, I also remember some completely incompetent ones.

So how do we correct for this? Well, we actually teach them. If they're actually learning the basics then I don't care how much fun and self-esteem building they do. If they're actually learning something, they should feel good about themselves.

How do we make sure they're actually teaching? Well there was this idea called "No Child Left Behind." It actually sounded like an interesting idea when it was first proposed. Testing to make sure students are actually learning. Here's the problem, or at least one of the many problems, with that truly dysfunctional bill. Every single state was allowed to make their own test. No real standards were in place so a state could write whatever they wanted to, and when it proved too difficult for the kids to pass, did we punish the teachers for not teaching the students? No, every state then watered down their test to the level that a mentally retarded chimpanzee stood a decent chance of passing. Even then, when a child completely bombed the test, they weren't held back until they actually learned something. I think the flaws here are beyond obvious, and the solutions are probably equally obvious, but I'll go through them for those of you who are too stupid figure this out on your own (by that I mean Congressmen, Senators, State Legislators, Boards of Educations, employees of the Department of Education, and members of the teacher's union).

Solution Part One: The Federal government needs to set down some actual standards that every state needs to meet. "Student will be able to accurately identify all eight parts of speech in context by the end of the second grade." "Student will be able to correctly multiply double digit numbers without the aid of a calculator by the end of the fourth grade." "Student will be able to write simple, complex, compound, and compound complex sentences." I think for elementary school that we don't need to worry about anything more than reading, writing, and mathematics.

If these standards are not set by the federal government and not set in such a way that private interest groups are kept out of the decision making process they will be weakened to such a level to be utterly meaningless by individual states or by special interests (like the teacher's unions who would love to keep standards their members are held to as low as possible). Now any state is free to go above and beyond these standards, but a minimum level needs to be set for the entire country.

Solution Part Two: The Federal government needs to come up with a test for all of these standards. This test needs to be created by an independent agency that has nothing to do with the teacher's union (otherwise known as the bane of American Education). The same test needs to be administered in every school in the nation. There needs to be a test for every single grade level. Yes, I will be the first to admit that a standardized test cannot test everything, especially at the higher levels of critical thought and reasoning. But guess what, essentially everything we want an elementary school student to know in terms of formal education can be tested on a multiple choice and written exam.

Solution Part Three: No student gets to go onto the next grade level unless they have passed with C on the test. Will a lot more students get held back initially? Probably, but better they get held back in grade level than always trying to play catch-up to their peers, always feeling stupid, always failing, and then actually having real self-esteem problems. They shouldn't be able to leave 5th grade without being able to read at a 5th grade level, write a full paragraph using complex sentences with commas and everything, and maybe even add, subtract, multiply, divide and know how to use fractions. I know it's a grand and strange concept to expect this of a child . . . oh wait, it's not, it's actually a bare minimum standard of which every child who is not mentally handicapped is more than capable of achieving. It might take a small percentage an extra year to make it, but better they learn it than simply being shoved into the next level so far behind it will keep them in a tailspin that will lead to their complete failure.

Solution Part Four: Any teacher who cannot consistently get 70% of their class to pass every year should be fired. Now some years there will be a class that falls below that standard. Believe me, some years you just get a class of students who are simply incapable of learning. Every so often you get that class. So one bad year a decade is probably forgivable, but any teacher that can't get most of their students to pass year after year, that's not the student's fault that's the teachers. Fire them.

Solution Part Five: To fire inept teachers, the teacher's unions will need to be disbanded. Now some teachers claim they need teacher's unions to protect them. This is ironically usually the same teachers who don't understand why they aren't being treated as the professionals they think of themselves as—they don't quite understand that professionals in the work force don't have unions.

Cris A. Pace

Teachers unions have an incredible ability to protect teachers who are so inept it isn't even funny[128]. In fact the only people teacher's unions actually aren't big into defending is teachers who actually do their jobs, because they have a tendency of making all union teachers look incompetent (which they are). Hint to parents: if most of the teachers at school belong to a teacher's union, don't send your child there, unless you want your child to learn nothing.

Solution Part Six: Charter schools. Charter schools offer competition to the public school system, which has for decades institutionalized complacency, low-standards, feel-good education, and mediocrity. Charter schools at their best solve these problems through personalized and previously untried methods. Now sometimes these don't work, and sometimes the charter school is worse than the public school. However, if the previous five points are put into place, then it will become more than clear which schools are performing and which ones are not. Charter schools that don't work will quickly fall away if they do not have students passing the standardized tests. The advantage to this is that Charter schools that out perform their public school counterparts will grow, which will usually do two things. It will take some pressure in terms of classroom size (which is a big issue in teaching, trust me a class of 25 is twice as easy to teach as is a class of 35 . . . it's even more effective with 15-20), which

---

[128] I've seen a teacher who actually hallucinated seeing Smurfs, again I'm not making this up, on a daily basis, protected by the teacher's union. The woman was beyond certifiably insane, but the union protected her to the point where the school didn't fire her per se, as much as it bought her out, because the union made it next to impossible to fire her.

will make instruction in the public school more effective. Secondly, competition always causes people to try harder to succeed, and with the test being regulated all the way off in Washington D.C. there is no other way to succeed than to actually teach students.

Middle School and Junior High

Now with most of the solutions of I've just addressed being continued into middle and high school, that will cut down on a good many problems and issues in modern American Education. However, with middle school I need to address three additional issues.

The first is that in addition to the basic grade level appropriate reading, writing, mathematics standards (students shouldn't be promoted without being at grade level reading, being able to write a 5 paragraph essay and a basic research paper, able to do first year Algebra by 8th grade, and basic geometry by 9th grade) history and science standards need to be added. Middle school should provide a general survey of all of world history, American history, Civics and Geography for the social sciences; a survey of the main braches of science (Biology, Chemistry, Physics, Astronomy, Geology, etcetera). A survey and nothing more. They should know Newton's laws; they should know the order of Persian, Peloponnesian, Punic, and Roman Civil Wars. They should know how a cell divides and what the Renaissance was. At this level they don't need to know what happened in 1066 or the difference between mitosis and meiosis. A survey of the basics is all that is required at this level.

Cris A. Pace

However, at this level a second standard needs to be put into the reading standards of American education and continued throughout high school. Too often, you'll find that students have no common basis of reference to draw from; in education circles we call this cultural literacy. Cultural literacy standards are the set of references that, for better or worse, Middle America expects you to know if you grew up in America. (You'd be surprised how few students actually know these things). No one outside of English teacher gatherings expects you know all the works of Shakespeare, but if you met a person who didn't know "To be or not to be"[129] or had never had heard of "Romeo and Juliet" you'd think they'd lived their life in a cave. Now ideally the standards of history and science courses provide the basic cultural literacy of these fields, but literature is a far more difficult field. Not just because there is so much out there, but also because English teachers often teach whatever they want irrespective of whether it's relevant to the student's education.[130] And I'm even hesitant to say this because I do enjoy having the liberty to choose what I want to teach in my class; however, it gets equally infuriating not to be able to reference a work of literature because some of the students have read it and some haven't. Therefore, what I suggest is that in addition to the other standards

---

[129] And I'm not talking about the intricate, multiple Shakespearian interpretations of the Hamlet's soliloquy, I'm talking about someone who literally didn't recognize that line "To be or not to be" as a line from some famous work.

[130] I had a teacher in high school who thought it better to teach a bunch of useless existentialist works for almost a whole year than actually teach more than a classic or two. Thank god I enjoy reading on my own or I might never have learned that literature actually included decent works.

that one book (maybe two) be added to every grade from 6th grade on. For instance, every 9th grader should read *To Kill a Mockingbird* and *Romeo and Juliet* or every 11th grader should read *The Scarlet Letter*.[131] This would give a common basis to every American child's education and make for greater understanding of their culture and even aid in communication with others. This would still allow teachers to teach a great deal of their personal choices, but some baseline could be established for the entire culture.

The second change that needs to occur regards the change that in recent decades America has gone from a Junior High of 7th-9th grade to a Middle School of 6th-8th grade. I'm not sure why. Anyone who has ever dealt with 9th graders knows that they are nowhere near mature enough to handle high school, and throwing them into high school isn't going to make them more mature, it more than anything induces a kind of post-traumatic stress syndrome in them all year long, making teaching them anything next to impossible not to mention

[131] Here would be my suggested list:

6th Mythology by Edith Hamilton or some comparable work about Classical Mythology

7th The Adventures of Tom Sawyer by Mark Twain

8th: Flowers for Algernon by Daniel Keyes and the works of O. Henry

9th: To Kill A Mockingbird by Harper Lee and Romeo and Juliet by William Shakespeare

10th Of Mice and Men by John Steinbeck and the Diary of Anne Frank

11th The Scarlet Letter by Nathaniel Hawthorne and The Glass Menagerie by Tennessee Williams

12th One of Shakespeare's four great tragedies (Hamlet, Othello, King Lear, or Macbeth) and Frankenstein by Mary Shelly

their presence tends to be mildly disturbing to the upperclassmen classes, especially elective classes which freshmen inevitably get thrown into. This change is also necessary for the third change that I'm going to suggest.

Education in many parts of Europe and Asia has one advantage over American education. They allow for the fact that not everyone needs the same level of education. We may hold to the egalitarian ideal here in America that "everyone is created equal" but no one is foolish enough, at least I hope no one is foolish enough, to believe that an injunction about equality before the law and equality in the value as a human being, means that every one has equal talents, abilities and skills. Some people are not going to college. It's a fact, even if college was free and open to everyone, not every student has the mental acumen to make it through a four-year undergraduate degree. It's just a fact of existence and nothing to be ashamed of. But it does no one any favors to shove everyone into the same kind of high school experience.

Many other countries in the world have realized, quite rationally, that sending everyone through the same educational system may not be the brightest idea. In America we've, to a degree, realized this too, through our use of Honors, Advanced Placement, and International Baccalaureate courses for higher end students. However the problem is that these upper end classes are often open only to students in socioeconomics areas of affluence and wealth—thus many highly intelligent students in inner cities are repeatedly denied even the opportunity to shine (yeah that's egalitarian of us). What I propose is taking our system of offering higher and lower end education and make it an aspect of the system, not just a perk offered by some districts. As with many other countries, I propose a three-part system. An upper end track based on the Honors/

Republicans and Reincarnation

AP/IB model for the upper third of students; a middle track designed on the current average level of education with the goal of getting students into community college at the very least, and from there if they can choose to further their education if they want to; and finally a vocational track of schools for the lowest portion of students. Now how do we determine who goes where? The fairest way I can think of is at the end of the 9th grade year a four-part system comprised of teacher recommendations, test scores, parental wishes, and student wishes is put into place. If all four areas agree little Johnny should be going to the vocational track, then vocational he goes. If however the scores and the teachers say middle level and the Johnny and parents want the upper end he goes to the upper end school. If anyone of these four areas says a higher level, then it is highest level we go with (unless with what I hope will be the rare case of teachers and scores saying vocational and the parents demanding the highest because they're suffering from "Not my little angel syndrome" in which case the middle level should probably be recommended). Unlike some other countries however, each and every student's case will constantly be up for review and anyone who wants to move up a level should be allowed to, it should be made more difficult to go to a lower level unless it is absolutely in the student's best interest.

Why do we need to do this? Well, we all accepted that different souls need different lessons, and then it becomes even more obvious that different people need different lessons (you don't even need to be a New Ager to admit that one). Some people need Calculus, and in depth study of primary sources in American History, and the ability to figure out the acceleration of an object shot into the air, and know all the muscles in a dissected cat, and understand how Iago is a reflection of the darker side of Othello.

Some people only need to know how to do algebra and geometry, know enough biology and chemistry to be able to watch *An Inconvenient Truth* and know bunk when they see it, or sit on a jury and have enough biology to know when O.J's DNA shows up at a crime scene that it means beyond the shadow of even unreasonable doubt that he's guilty as sin; they only need enough reading skills to listen to a politician's speech and realize that while they're talking about grand esoteric ideas that they've actually said or proposed nothing; some only need enough history to know that the last two-thousand years of history cannot be easily reduced to a class struggle, nor can the American Revolution be simplified into a bunch of rich white guys trying to hold onto their wealth. And in between these two extremes there is the middle ground of the country.

Now ideally I would love to see 80% of students in the highest end, 15% in the middle ground and 5% needing only the remedial level kind of school. I realize that at the present that might be a bit of a far-fetched dream. Nonetheless, it should be something we should strive for. However, this should be a goal that should be enforced through rewards and punishments to schools that can and cannot get their students up to these levels.

High School

But how will we set up this grand change in education. First of all, it needs to be federal law that every school district (charter and private schools excepted) have all three of these levels offered at the high school level. No exceptions in the public school sector. I don't care if it's in the middle of Alaska or inner city L.A. Every district must provide three separate tracts of high school education. For the more rural communities this may require drastically increasing the size of the school district to make three tract systems economical. I'm willing to put up and pay a few extra tax dollars to pay for bussing if it means American education will finally provide the education every student deserves and needs (and, really, how often do I say I'm willing to pay more in taxes?).

However, especially with upper end education, competent teachers become an absolute necessity. But how do we get competent teachers, because trust me the current system of training teachers is not working. And this is not only a high school problem. The current system is to require teachers to go through some sort of college teacher training program which stresses psychological and sociological theories of learning, how to prepare a lesson plan, and theories among other things. Since "No Child Left Behind" along with this comes a lot of hoopla over certification, which basically means a teacher, has to pay to sit around another year of classes that teach them methods of how to teach children. Now most people who aren't in the education field hear "certification" and think it means that teachers teaching math have a degree in Mathematics or a related field . . . sadly this is not the case, certification has more to do with lots of touchy feely classes on how to deal with students and make them all feel special. These teaching methods required by "certification" primarily, at least in my experience, vary between the so blatantly obvious any teacher who doesn't just know them intrinsically is an idiot, to touchy feely "let's play a game" worthless tripe. I have probably sat through over two hundred hours of teacher training either in college and/or since becoming a teacher; maybe twenty hours of that was worth anything. (The joke of teacher in-service training goes as follows: Those who can, do. Those who can't, teach. Those who can't teach, teach teachers). Here's the problem: good teachers, like artists, aren't made; they're born. Either someone has the gift to teach or they don't. It's that simple—and no amount of in-service training is going to correct that problem. So the next time you hear about a call for teacher certification, slap the politician or pundit calling for it. It's worthless. Requiring a B.A. in the subject being taught, a minor in education, and a student teaching stint is all that is required. Anything after that is flash and show without substance, without benefit, and probably with a large price tag for both the teacher and the taxpayer.

So if you can't train good teachers where do you get them from? As remiss as I am to suggest the following, it is the only way I can see out of our current problem: Pay teachers a lot more. Now some may claim that teachers make too much as it is. For your average incompetent teacher that is oh so true. In this country, most teachers are paid on what's called a salary schedule. The more years you work, you get an automatic pay raise, the more education you have you get an automatic pay raise. Doesn't matter if you're competent or not, doesn't matter if you actually can teach or not. Work for twenty years, get your Ph.D.[132] while you teach and make $90,000 a

---

[132] Which I have a real problem with, as any teacher who has enough time to get their Ph.D., is probably not spending enough time working on his or her class. Besides having a Masters or Ph.D. doesn't make you a more qualified teacher by a long shot. I'm sure we've all met people who have advanced degrees and are complete idiots. (Ever noticed how often its

year for nine months a year work. Now, if you're doing your job as a teacher nine months a year is fine, because it can be a beyond taxing and stressful experience that can require three months of vacation just to decompress fully or you will have a nervous breakdown . . . but sadly too many teachers don't take their job seriously enough to justify that need. So again, how do we change this?

First, we need to look at the reason why people take a job. People take jobs for three reasons. The first is because it is a calling, they do it because it is natural to them as breathing, to not do this job is to let a part of themselves die, and these people will do it whether they get paid a lot or not. These are your great teachers. They're not nearly paid enough. Just below the level of calling are people who are out to make a successful career; they wish to succeed in a profession and be recognized at least monetarily, they may not have the divine passion that those following a calling have, but they will always perform at the highest levels because they know that's the only way to be recognized and get the paycheck they wish to earn. Not many of these people become teachers, even though they would make good and competent teachers. Why? Because they're not about to spend 4 years in college just to make 30K out of college and another 4 years of higher education and thirty years in a job just to make another 30K to 50K. They know in the private sector if they distinguish themselves they will earn far more out of

---

these incompetent fools who always resort to the argument, "Well I've got two Masters degrees" as proof of their intelligence or will belligerently yell at you "you don't know anything about teaching, I've got a Masters in Curriculum Design" when they're trying to tell you things that basic common sense and scientific research have both disproved.)

the door, make raises far faster, and probably deal with fewer stresses.[133] And finally, you have people who are just interested in getting paid. The quality of their own work has no value to these people; they will simply do the bare minimum of what is required not to get fired and nothing else. Professions like teaching, jobs at the DMV and being a member of Congress appeal to these people.

Therefore, the only way to make teaching more tempting to that second group out for their pocketbook is to raise the salaries of teachers. Further, the system must be changed from years of service and education level to something more along the lines of years of service and quality of teaching. A new system that not only takes education but quality of teaching, ability to perform inside the classroom and outside, student performance on standardized tests (averaged over years to allow for the occasional bad year), parental and student reviews,

---

[133] Before you roll your eyes at how stressful teaching is, keep in mind that teaching, done properly is an 80 hour a week job, that requires not only teaching, but hours upon hours of grading; attending, coaching, or supervising for your students; becoming emotionally invested in your students successes and failure. It's like having two jobs plus the emotional drain of parenting 30 to 120 children . . . plus all the usual stresses of your own personal life. Oh, and to top it all off, once you've given your heart and soul into helping this or that child to succeed as much as any devoted parent, unlike the parent, you never hear from them again, never get to revel in their future glories that you helped in a small way to achieve . . . not to mention in modern America where so few children wish to succeed you have the heartbreak of failure after failure you tried but couldn't prevent. Say a lot of things about teachers and teaching, but don't ever tell me it isn't a stressful profession when done properly.

Republicans and Reincarnation

taking on extra responsibilities and so on must be instituted. These reviews must then be standardized into something along the lines of a ranking system that one can, but not necessarily will move up over the years, and that one can as easily be demoted should performance decline. If a teacher does not climb at a certain rate by a certain number of years they are to be fired, and a teacher's performance, which continually declines over a certain period, is again to be fired. This second change if instituted properly will help keep the first group of inept teachers to a bare minimum.

Will this cost more? I hope so. I hope it means we will get more great teachers who earn more. Where are we going to get the money to pay for it? Well short of selling the organs of IRS agents to the highest bidder, which is a plan I'm not actually opposed to, I suggest we start taking funds from welfare programs to pay for this. The more effective our education system becomes the less we will need to pay for welfare programs. I'd rather invest in the future of not having people on the dole, than pay for the lazy and inept. The other way to help pay more money to teachers is something that has been suggested before, yet still never put into practice. Teachers shouldn't have to pay taxes. At all. For what we're entrusting teachers to do, for how basic education is for a well run society, the easiest way to pay teacher more money is to just exempt them from all income, social security, Medicare, sales, and all other forms of taxes.[134] It's an easy way to give a

---

[134] It goes without saying that if we put this into place, then police, firefighters and military personnel should also be exempted from taxes, as they are just as necessary to the proper functioning of a society. IRS employees and elected officials should be paying triple what everyone else is.

raise, and I doubt that that much of the government's income is based on them for its proper functioning.

If you did all this, then more people out for a successful career would consider teachering and few buffoons would be allowed to stay.

A Final Word on Parenting and Education

"You may give them your love but not your thoughts, For they have their own thoughts. You may house their bodies but not their souls, For their souls dwell in the house of to-morrow, which you cannot visit, not even in your dreams. You may strive to be like them, but seek not to make them like you. For life goes not backward nor tarries with yesterday. You are the bows from which your children as living arrows are sent forth."—Kahlil Gibran, The Prophet: On Children

A soul cannot be taught anything it does not wish to learn, but it cannot learn anything it is not taught either. So the student, parents and teachers are all responsible for the development of an individual person. Parents need to focus on teaching their children to think, to ask questions, to be curious, to expose themselves to as many ideas as possible and be critical of all of them, and to strive to push themselves further than anything their parents can dream for them, and to be responsible for their own actions. Teachers need to be entrusted with teaching the same lessons, albeit through more specific subjects.

Chapter 12

RELIGIOUS WACKOS, FLAMING HOMOSEXUALS, PEOPLE WHO ONLY SPEAK ENGLISH, AND SO MANY OTHER THINGS THAT PEOPLE GET WAY TO WORKED UP ABOUT.

The Tricky Policies of Social Issues

I have been both dreading and looking forward to this chapter. Mainly because it's those touchy subjects that people get irrationally over-excited about. Most of the problems in this chapter are the things that get bantered around over and over again as the great issues that tend to define an election: Gay Marriage, The Separation of Church and State, Abortion. All of them central issues that people (on both sides) use to make decisions on whom they are going to vote for. All of them issues that aren't worth the time of day for any rational person. These are the issues of bluster and haberdashery, pomp and circumstance, bull and . . . well you get the idea . . . and absolutely no substance or importance whatsoever.

While actual problems exist (the economy, foreign policy, etcetera.) the American public would rather debate some of the following issues. It's almost like the Roman Senate spending years debating what honors to bestow upon Caesar while the barbarians are at the gates. We all know how well that one ended. But onto the insane obsessions of America.

Gay Marriage

Get a life! Both sides of this issue! Really, I couldn't honestly care less about this. To you religious people out there who think marriage is only between a man and a woman I would suggest you go back and look at Ancient Rome and Greece where as much of our practices on marriage come from as they do from the Hebrews.

And to you on the other side, really, does your life only revolve around what the government sanctions. What do you care what some idiots think. If you love each other, why does a piece of paper matter?

So both sides are idiots (but we knew that already, and get prepared for this being a common theme in this chapter).

So here is my solution, it is intended to please no one, but it will solve all the problems.

The government will only, only, only recognize civil unions between any two human beings. All wording in all states will be changed to say civil union. The word marriage will be completely stricken from the legal code and the entire system of government. Marriage will be a religious institution, and as such, the government won't touch it. Now if you're a man and a woman who get a priest, pastor, rabbi, or imam to marry you, and want to call it a marriage, fine. If you're two men or two women who can find someone from the above list to marry you and want to call it a marriage, fine again. In fact, call it whatever you like no matter who marries you. It's just that the government won't call it marriage. You may say that if you're a gay couple then individuals won't recognize your marriage because it's not sanctioned by the government, but really, those close-minded people weren't going to do that whether the government called it a marriage or not, so get over it.

There, nobody got what they wanted but all objections are settled. Everyone' equal, and no church is forced to do anything they don't want.

The Separation of Church and State

Okay, before we get going into this too far, the Constitution does not say there is a separation of church and state. The actual words are "Congress shall make no law abridging the freedom of religion." The words "separation of Church and State" come from a letter written by Thomas Jefferson (note that it was the same Jefferson who made reference to God when he said, "all men are endowed by their Creator with certain unalienable rights"). The original intent was that government shouldn't tell religion how to run things and no single religion should have sway over the government. That being said, while we can certainly admit a Judeo-Christian preference to our Founding Fathers, it is just a bit tacky to shove only that religion into people's faces.

For instance, let's look at the Ten Commandments. Now some claim that the Ten Commandments are the source of our modern legal system. Let's run over this list here. Thou shalt have no other god (1). Thou shalt make no graven images (2). Thou shalt not take the lord's name in vain (3). Thou shalt keep the Sabbath holy (4). Thou shalt honor thy mother and father (5). Thou shalt not steal (6) Thou shalt not murder (7). Thou shalt not commit false witness (8). Thou shalt not commit adultery (9). Thou shalt not covet (10). Okay I'll grant you that this country has a distinctly Judeo-Christian background . . . . but, come on, can anyone seriously say that the 10 Commandments are the basis for our legal system? Last I checked, only murder and stealing are against the law all the time, and false witness is only illegal when under oath or signing a legal document. Okay, if you're going to be technical, adultery is also a crime, a class 3 misdemeanor in Arizona where I live, but honestly, when was the last time someone was actually prosecuted on a charge of adultery. What is that? Two and half, maybe two and three quarters, out of ten? I'm not going to actually go look, but I'd wager money that you could probably find more similarities to the modern legal code and the Code of Hammurabi. No doubt, the Mosaic Law is one of the cornerstones for our system of laws, but it is not the most important by a long shot. Thus, displays like the one in the Supreme Court that also show the 12 tables of Roman Law, and the signing of the Magna Carter in addition to the Ten Commandments are fine. Still, to just display the Ten Commandments in front of a court is not just egregiously tacky it's unbelievably ignorant. However, while I would say they shouldn't be put up, there is equally no reason to declare a Holy War over some ignorant judge putting them up, it is one of the pillars of our legal system, and just accept it. Although I would consider voting any judge so ignorant to find that as the only basis for our legal system out of office. And if the symbol of the Ten Commandments or a cross has been up for ages, there is no justifiable reason to take it down.

As for other things like Christmas displays in front of city halls, does it really hurt anyone? I'm not a Christian by any stretch of the imagination, but I love Christmas. I know followers of Judaism, Buddhism, Baha'i and atheists who love Christmas, and I've seen members of Islam on TV also praise the holiday. By now, in America, it's lost a lot of the religious trappings and has become (at its best) simply a time to think of others and be more charitable. Who could hate that? Only Ebenezer Scrooge and his modern ilk (otherwise known as the ACLU). Guess what guys? Just because you live miserable, sad and pathetic lives, doesn't mean we have to as well. If it harms no one then don't worry about it. There isn't even a plausible slippery slope argument available here that this will cause the government to be more biased against other religions. What's the worst that would happen? People will actually be nicer to each other. Well thank god we have the ACLU to protect us from that. Get over yourselves, it harms no one, it makes some people happy, it's not worth fighting over.

So let's agree to this. No shoving new instances of this or that religion in people faces above and beyond what everyone has always done, and the nut-jobs on the other side will shut up and stop trying to destroy every reference to even the concept of religion. The simple fact of the matter is that both extreme sides of this argument are crazy and annoying, and when you engage them they only get more so; I suggest we all stop taking these cases simply ignore the religious/atheist psychos until they go away.

Abortion

Ah! The issue this country is far, far, far too concerned with. The issue that people vote on as if the opposition winning will mean the end of all civilization as we know it. "You're voting for Bush! But he'll appoint judges that will overturn Roe v. Wade!"[135] Not foreign policy, not tax policy, not environmental reform, or health care, or civil liberties. Almost inevitably, in this country, the partisan argument over candidates first and foremost goes for how this or that candidate stands on abortion. Why? It is a policy that one way or another effects a relatively small number of people. I don't get it?

Now before we go any further I feel that I must set down what must logically be the New Age and Conservative position on this subject. Keep abortions legal but don't let the government pay for a single one. Now let me explain how I justify such a stance. If you are a New Ager then you believe in reincarnation. Further, you believe that every act and choice is a learning experience for the person involved and that sometimes one person needs to make one choice that is right for them, while the exact opposite choice is correct for another person in the

---

[135] Swear to God, that's word for word the first argument I heard from the head of a Democratic organization. Variations have been heard from others, far too many others. It is almost always the first knee-jerk reaction almost any Democrat has against any Republican candidate. And the reverse is true for most Republicans. It's pathetic.

Republicans and Reincarnation

same situation with different lessons to learn. Thus, one woman may need to learn to take more responsibility, and thus the correct choice is to keep the child. Another may need to learn that life must first and foremost be lived for yourself, and thus the correct choice should be to abort the fetus. Some people make the correct choice for themselves, some do not. It makes remarkably little difference to the fetus. Every soul going into a fetus knows what it is getting into. Those going into women considering abortion know, going in, that they may be aborted; they hold no ill will if that is what the mother chooses. They just get reborn in the next available child that fits their karmic needs. Since you can't know what the correct choice for the woman considering an abortion might be, you can't legally deny them the choice.

Now I know many Christians will attack this position—that from their rather dark inclination to believe in a God that only gives you one shot, is rather logical position from their premises. I can only say that the New Age argument, which relies on a belief in reincarnation and thus not denying a soul the opportunity for a life, has none of the contradictions of the usual Democratic Party stance on this issue.[136]

I should not have to explain, at this point, why I don't think the government shouldn't pay for abortions. I don't think the government should pay for anything.

However, whatever my stance on this, this is not the most pressing issue facing America today. In the face of the much greater issues facing our civilization and anyone who votes on this issue first and foremost, or even brings this issue up, as a reason why they will or will not vote for a candidate is an idiot. Actually let me

---

[136] See the beginning of Chapter 1.

go a step further from this point forward anyone who even brings this issue up in political discourse, I don't care what side they're taking, is too incompetent to be allowed to vote. There are about a million or so issues, programs, and choices that involve the government that are more important, and anyone who doesn't realize this simple and rather obvious truth is a fool.

Yes, we would all like fewer abortions, but until humanity as a whole grows up to be able to control their sexual urges we are going to have unwanted pregnancies—and as long as that occurs some women will choose (some correctly, some incorrectly) to not keep the fetus. Just deal with this fact one way or another, and let's move onto some slightly more important issues.

Language

"English only" you've heard the words before. How you've heard them presented is probably a different story. You may have heard that English Only is an attempt to preserve our culture from outside influence. Anyone making that argument clearly doesn't realize what a bastard language English really is: A Germanic grammar system with a Celtic/Germanic/French/Latin/Greek vocabulary, peppered with idioms and vocabulary from nearly every culture English speakers come in contact with. There's a reason English has more words than any other language—we've stolen all the other languages' words.

The next claim goes that forcing people to learn English is racist. An equally perplexing argument, as

Republicans and Reincarnation

Americans tend to want the white immigrants to learn the language about as strenuously as they want the nonwhite immigrants to learn it, and are fairly accepting of just about anyone they can actually communicate with no matter what shade of light is refracting off their skin. So a claim of racism is just as foolish.

However, let's remember our bias toward long-term solutions that work for the most people. Now mix that with a simple knowledge of history and sociology that tells us that no single aspect of culture brings people together as much as a common language, and nothing can drive them apart faster than an inability to communicate, and it becomes very obvious that a single language must prevail in any nation if it is to survive. Obviously, English remains the *franca lingua* of American (and the world) and should remain so.

Now how is this a government issue? Well first off, two things should be done to actually encourage everyone to start speaking and communicating in the same language. The first is that the government (at all levels) should cease printing documents in any language other than English.[137]

The second and probably more important one needs to be that the FCC needs to stop issuing licenses to non-English speaking TV and radio stations. Some petty people are going to call me a racist for that statement, but it is anything but. Foreign language media encourages

---

[137] Obvious exceptions are for anything dealing with nonpermanent travelers within the country, such as customs information, and any preliminary information on how to become a citizen should be printed in native languages; the test for citizenship however needs to be in English as all things that come after citizenship, like voting ballots.

people not to have to learn English, which only deepens the feelings of not being a part of the overall society, which if anything actually fuels, at best, a sense of us vs. them, at its worst it fuels racism on both sides. Handicapping immigrants by not encouraging them to learn the language of the masses, by keeping them apart and thinking of themselves as apart, now that's real racism. America has an incredibly long tradition of taking in the cultures of every immigrant culture that comes to its shores, so long as that group adopts America as their home, their country and their language. I see no reason to believe that would stop if we continue to encourage incoming immigrants to actually become part of the American culture, but that will only occur if they learn the language.

Political Correctness

Racism, sexism, homophobia. Yes all these things still exist. The 2008 elections kind of prove all three. Don't believe me do you? You're thinking that we elected a black man, how can you say that it shows racism. Well I knew people who said they were voting for him because he was black, and just so you don't think I only associate with stupid people, I heard similar sentiments of people being interviewed on the news. I hate to tell you this people but caring whether someone is white, black or what-have-you is racism. People are people, and should only be judged on their merits. Voting for a man because he's black, falls just a little short of "I have a dream that one day my children will be judged not by the color of their skin, but by the content of their character." This country still has some serious racism problems. Here's my advice: stop caring. Really. Only when we stop caring if you will be called a racist for critiquing someone who belongs to a minority (which is very much a racist attitude) will racism really vanish. Don't care at all what color someone is, don't care from what country their ancestors came from, and don't care what injustices were done against their ancestors. It's all racism, soft racism, but as long as you care, it will continue.

A friend of mine replies when I tell him that he shouldn't care that his ancestors came from this or that country that, "If you don't know where you've come from, then you don't know where your going." Seemingly wise, but incorrectly used if attributed to your ethnic heritage. The world is too small and interconnected in the modern world to say that one and only one country's history shaped you. World history has shaped everyone in the modern world, and yes, a person should know history to learn from it and not repeat the mistakes of other people, whether you were related to them or not. I have Irish, English, French and German, does that mean I should want to go to all those countries to see where my people came from . . . no . . . now I do want to go see them because they're beautiful places, but I also want to see Japan, Scotland, Egypt, and Greece . . . not mention I was in Italy, from which I don't believe I have any ancestors, before I was in Ireland or England. Your ancestors are not you, and the idea that they are needs to end, because it is soft racism.

Sexism is also still a big issue in this country. From the absolutely deplorable treatment of the two main women running for political office in 2008 to the disgustingly prevalent machismo attitudes of many in this country.

The hatred of homosexuals is also still too prevalent in this country. Just look at the fact that many states in America voted to define marriage as only "between a man and a woman" despite the fact that the courts hadn't legalized gay marriage in their state.[138]

I could give more examples of sexism (in reality it's more like misogynic tendencies in this country) and homophobia but really, do we doubt this?

So what do we do? Well as individuals, I suggest calling out every instance of overt racism, sexism, homophobia, and if nothing else shame these people into silence before they can spread their filth.

However what should the government do? Actually, relatively little. One must keep in mind that these beliefs are personal beliefs, and if we are to be a free society, people have to be legally allowed to believe anything they want, no matter how wrong or disgusting. Please feel free to scream, ostracize, and even punch these people all you want (although you're probably not going to convince them of the error of their ways through violence, and it won't exactly do your own karma a great deal of help either, but I'll understand if you choose to take that route). Still the government has tried to get involved (or people argue it should get involved) in three main ways.

The first is through education. This is the most dangerous, even though the intentions are likely the most

---

[138] I am not saying that California doing that was right either, but it was the foreseeable extension of one side pushing a cultural issue too far too fast onto a group that wasn't ready to accept such a change. However the dash to define marriage as such when no such direct assault has been made on personal beliefs, no matter how unjustified, cannot be described as anything but homophobia.

laudable (road to hell and all that). While tolerance and issues of justice, equality, and right and wrong are more than appropriate discussion topics for a high school history or English classroom, do we really need to be pushing this stuff in elementary school. Yes, racial tolerance should be brought up, because for better or worse small children can understand this concept, they can see it. However, issues of the equality of homosexuality don't exactly belong in the curriculum of kindergarten; children that young can barely understand that concept. For better or worse bringing up this subject to a child before they can understand it will result only in the child seeing the unfortunate hate that this topic brings up in too many adults today, and a prejudice that may have been ignored or forgotten will be instilled again in children. Yes if a child makes a bigoted remark it should be dealt with by a teacher, but institutionalized and curriculum forced equality, even for the best intentions, smacks just a little too much of indoctrination and brainwashing. At that level it's too difficult to teach the complexities of right and wrong in society to children, better to focus on responsibility, self-respect and common courtesy at that level, which if learned, will expand into tolerance when they grow up.

The next issue again of government instituted political correctness is the current obsession with having this history month and that history month. At this point, do you really think that anyone is a racist because they don't know this or that racial group has contributed to the advancement of civilization? I will agree all racist/sexist/homophobic people are deeply ignorant. But it isn't the kind of ignorance that can be corrected with a "Did you know the contributions of (fill in minority)?" public service announcement. Going hand in hand with this is higher education's obsession with multiculturalism. If anything selecting to honor this or that group at a certain time of the year is racist in and of itself. If it was worthy of honor it was worthy of honor at any point in the year. If you just pull out minorities to honor in a history class it makes the contributions of a Booker T. Washington, Dubois, Evers, or King seem trivial and only picked out because it's that month. If you focus on works of literature only because of the ethnicity, it implies that the works of a Lao Tzu, Sun Tzu, Li Po, or Tu Fu are selected only because of where they were born not because they are exceptional literature. And then the other problem with so called multiculturalism is that it really only focuses on one culture, the modern one, with literature, history, and so one selected only from about the last century or so. Rather than simply have this minorities month but instead teach history and literature in terms of true importance and literary greatness would actually reveal the whole cross section of civilization if taught properly, but without the soft racism of and "here's the Latino who was important during this point in time."

A final issue of political correctness that sometime gets bantered about is the idea reparations. I don't know of any serious rational human being of any ethnic background to ever advocate for such a ridiculous concept, but it seems to be a popular topic with Liberal Arts College students (who can often go on to be politicians), and TV pundits—so while I think, I hope, no one is seriously advocating this, I'll just kill it right here before some pundit throws it back at me. The argument of reparations is another aspect of racism in this country that argues because my ancestors were slaves, you who may or may not be the descendant of slave owners should pay me for their suffering. Again, it makes this bizarre connection to

Republicans and Reincarnation

the idea that a shared ethnicity has anything to do with an individual. However, for sake of argument let's say you get to sue one ethnicity for crimes committed against another in a century gone by. How far back does this go? Can I sue every one of English decent because of what they did to my Irish ancestors? Can I sue Germany for what they did to my French ancestors? Can I and every other person of European, Middle Eastern, and North African ancestry sue Italy for centuries of oppression under the Roman Empire? I mean if one is valid, then so is the other. But, you say, the descendants of slaves are still oppressed in this country because of the scars left by racism left their descendants at a disadvantage. More likely, people of all races are less than striving to improve themselves, and thus most people stay merely in the class to which they were born in[139]. However, there are more than enough rich, successful, and powerful people of all races in this country to more than prove it is not an institutional racism that prevents people from succeeding.

Freedom of the Press

The Fairness Doctrine, you may of have heard of it. It's a current belief that for every opinion offered on radio or television opinion shows, then that news provider has to offer equal time to the opposition to voice their opinion. Let's just ignore what may or may not be motivating

---

[139] If you actually do large studies of any social group you'll find that the majority of most people's descendants tend to climb down the social ladder slowly but surely, so if you're starting at the bottom . . .

Cris A. Pace

the passage of this doctrine, and let's look at not only its unconstitutional and unethical premises and how it demonstrates in a clear and simple way everything that's wrong with the government's opinion of itself.

"Congress shall make no law abridging the Freedom of the Press." When you take out the other clauses involving other rights, that is exactly what it says. Pretty clear isn't it. Congress can't stop the press from printing (or saying) anything they darn well please. Yeah the "clear and present danger" limit applies here too, but other than that I fail to see the little footnote that says, "except when Congress really thinks the people aren't getting the whole story (or more accurately the story that the party in power wants you to get); then its okay." To be honest you'd have to be heavily medicated or just plain dumb to think forcing media to say things they may not want to is in any way shape or form Constitutional.

But more to the point this displays the typical, and quite incorrect, contempt government has for the people it governs. Ignoring the obvious fallacy of believing there are only two side to any topic, this proposed legislation reveals that most in government think people are not smart enough to go find information for themselves and have to be presented with their choice right there or they wouldn't know to go look for alternative ideas. I'll grant that I will never be arguing that the masses are a particularly bright and thoughtful bunch, who can think critically about information presented to them . . . but compared to the way any government system works, the masses are all members of MENSA. I don't know which is more frightening, that 465 of the most isolated, petty, greedy and corrupt people in the nation (i.e. Congress) think they know what people should be hearing better than those people themselves, or the fact that the public keeps reelecting most of them. I do know however, that if you give Congress the power to say what can be broadcast on the news, the system will never change. General rule anytime the government acts based on the idea it's smarter than the average person, nothing but harm can result.

Health Care

"American businesses often can't afford to hire as many employees as they would like because of rising health-insurance costs; employees often can't afford to quit to chase their better-mousetrap dreams because they can't risk going without coverage. Add to this the system's moral failings: about twenty-two thousand people die in this country annually because they lack health insurance. That is more than the number of Americans who are murdered in a year."—Steven Coll, The New Yorker

"Everyone has a right to health care!" I hear screamed from politician after politician, and they continue to vote my tax dollars to pay for providing health care. Really? Because I thought rights are things you would have with or without the government being there. Natural rights come from this thought experiment called the state of nature. In the state of nature, think of being stranded on an island like Robinson Crusoe, you have your life, you have liberty, to have a right to whatever property you work for, you have the right to pursue happiness, you even have the right to friendship (if only in form of talking to a volleyball), but do you have the right to health care? Well you have the right to maintain your own health, which no one in America is currently being denied. However, in every thought experiment I've ever had, I failed to imagine Dr. Greg House and his ducklings wandering through the forests of the state of nature just looking for people to diagnose and treat.

Outside of the thought experiment, rights are things people have always had a right to no matter what the circumstances, even when they are being denied those rights. By the current line of argument that people have a right to health care, then people back in Rome had a right to modern health care methods, even before they were discovered. I fail to see how this is possible.

Further this implies that people have the right to the time and energy of another human being, that doctors, nurses, and even the makers of drugs and medical supplies are morally obligated to provided their services or products whether they are paid or not (keep in mind if you admit they deserve payment then you deny it is a right). But to then claim that health care is a right makes doctors, nurse, etcetera, nothing but slaves to everyone else in society. Hardly in line with more basic rights like liberty, now is it?

Still, whether or not people have a right to health care (all you can really say is that no one should be denied health care if they can pay for it, which only socialized medical care does), there is the issue that it costs a lot. However, before we can deal with how to lower the costs, let's deal with why it costs a lot.

Why does medical care cost a lot? I'm sure you could guess what I'm going to say—the government. The government who with every passing year has taken more and more of an active nature in the control, regulation, and general havoc of the medical system. The same government, which prevents insurance companies from crossing state lines, because that would actually result in more effective competition and drive prices down. Why? Because they listen to ridiculous statements like the one quoted above. "More people died because lack of medical insurance than are killed by homicide." I'd love to see how the methodology of that little statement was reached. The leading cause of death in this country is heart disease, which (1) is more often than not more a cause of your bad lifestyle than a lack of medical care—really, would a doctor telling you to stop eating nothing but fast food have done it—and (2) no hospital can refuse medical treatment for any emergency, so it wasn't like you show up with a heart attack and are turned away. I can only assume they mean by that statement that lots of people without health insurance died of cancer, implying if they had medical insurance they would have caught it early and have lived, which makes a fascinating assumption that catching cancer means you'll live; I'll grant it improves your chances, but cancer is not the dreaded disease it is because everyone lives.

More importantly complaining that people are dying because of having no health insurance is doing something they try and teach doctors to never do—it's treating a symptom and not the disease. Lack of health care is a symptom of poverty, poverty and lack of economic advancement, which I have already repeatedly laid at the feet of government interference. Thus if we got out of the economy, far fewer people would be reduced to welfare and poverty, thus far fewer would lack medical insurance.

But that's not the only way the government screws up medical care. Let's look at a few other ways. Medicaid and Medicare. Welfare for medicine. But it's helping the old and the poor get medical care, you say. How is it helping them? First, it's paying for medical supplies. But as anyone who has studied any economic system knows that two things occur when the government starts paying for something. First, if there are government plans to pay for something, there are more cases of fraud in that industry, because the government is full of idiots who don't catch fraud cases until it's too late to actually catch someone, thus making it a very attractive target to those looking for a good con. Who pays for the activities of fraud? Well, either doctors will raise their prices to compensate for the fraud or the government will just have to raise more money to pay for it. Either way you get to pay for it in the end. The second way government interference affects the cost of medicine is that, again anyone who has studied any system of economics knows this, when the government subsidies anything, the prices raise to account for that subsidy. If a drug costs $10 and the government decides to subsidize $8 of that drug, it's amazing how all of a sudden the drugs from some companies will actually cost $17 dollars. Is that overly greedy on the drug company's part, yeah . . . but right, wrong, or indifferent it's what happens. And with every increase in subsidy, the price goes higher still. So the government steps in and says they can only charge so much for this drug or that drug, or that they can only hold the patent for so many years, well then two things happen from there those same drug companies will then keep releasing new name brand drugs which are only slightly different from the last version, but that they still can hold the patent to (and they will spend lots of money and kickbacks to HMO's and doctors to push those drugs) which help to keep those drug prices high, or the drug companies spend less on research for drugs that will not yield them lots of money (cancer-drugs, cholesterol-drugs, antibiotics) and go for drugs that will yield money (erectile dysfunction, birth-control, allergy drugs) because the government doesn't regulate and subsidize those as much as those other drugs because they're more of a convenience not a medical necessity.

Think about this, do you think drugs cost less in Mexico because they have such great medical policies from the government, no it's because they have no medical care from the government. And why do they have cheaper drugs in Canada, because they're charging so much in taxes to pay for their socialized medicine (so you're still paying, and the medical care is so great in Canada, that don't forget that anyone with money in Canada crosses the border and has medical treatment done in the U.S.) Socialized medicine also creates incredibly long lines for everything, because if you're not paying for it, you'll go see a doctor for every pain, scrape and fever, rather than just toughing it out, which makes it impossible for people with real problem to get into see their doctor (go look up stories on British dentistry and how many citizens of the U.K. are not just pulling their own teeth because they can't get into see a dentist to see how well socialized medicine is working . . . god alone knows what they're doing when they can't get into see the cardiologist.) The other problem that results from the fact that everyone goes to the doctor over everything in socialized medicine is that doctors will prescribe drugs at the drop of a hat these days, especially antibiotics, which has the fascinating evolutionary result of creating drug resistant bacteria and viruses (TB, staph, and the flu are all already becoming super-bugs which are even resistant to third generation antibiotics and antivirals . . . pandemics are naturally occurring events, I'll admit, but socialized medicine is probably not helping to make their eventual effects better).

However, amongst all of this, everyone needs to remember a single fact that a lot of people don't want to face: Every single person who is now alive on this planet will one day die. Every one of us. Our souls may be immortal, but our bodies are not. And it is very important to learn to put this rather infantile fear of death away. Just think, the average life expectancy in the U.S. continues to rise every year. This is certainly not an indicator of worsening medical care or more unreachable medical care. Rather it is merely the fear of a lack of medical care caused by anecdotal exceptions to the superior medical care received in the U.S., hyped by the media, and thus playing on everyone's fear that they will come down with a terrible disease in their life. The rate of cancer is about 1 in a 1,000 in the general populace. Granted I have a better chance of getting cancer than winning the lottery, but at the same time I have better odds in any casino in the world than I do of getting cancer. Yet, despite the mild improbability of it, people are absolutely horrified by the idea of it. And it is that fear that drives the call for socialized medicine—not a real lack of it.

Chapter 13
IN A PERFECT WORLD THE UN BUILDING IS DEMOLISHED ONE WORLD GOVERNMENT THAT WORKS

"Unless some effective world supergovernment for the purpose of preventing war can be set up . . . the prospects for peace and human progress are dark. . . . If . . . it is found possible to build a world organization of irresistible force and inviolable authority for the purpose of securing peace, there are no limits to the blessings which all men enjoy and share."—Winston Churchill

What a wonderful and noble idea, a one-world government. Liberty, peace, security, the right to determine your own life for everyone. It is what we should be moving toward. It's just that the United Nations has absolutely nothing to do with this world, which I truly do believe, will come about some day. Why not the U.N. you ask? Let's look at some of its clearly inferior points.

First off the U.N. is simply too inefficient in its organization to do anything of value. Committee after committee after committee, each with overlapping standards and objectives, each with no real authority to act. The U.S. government was designed by the founding fathers to be inefficient in its checks and balances system so that the government wouldn't be too active—however, the U.S. Constitution was created to counter the Articles of Confederation which were too inefficient to run a country as large as America (and it was only 13 states back then)—and sadly the United Nations makes the Articles of Confederation look like the model of efficiency. Just take one of the U.N.'s most important functions (or at least what one its functions was supposed to be) keeping world peace. This function is theoretically the main purview of the U.N.'s Security Council. The Security Council's membership is made up of a body of representatives from different nations; the exact make up rotates with the years, and five countries with permanent seats on the Council (The United States, Great Britain, France, Russia, and China). Each one of these permanent members can veto any resolution passed by the council. That's right five different nations have veto power. Even in the theoretical realm, this is a bit beyond simple checks and balances. Essentially giving any nation that sits on the council carte blanche to do whatever they want without having to worry about the U.N. But beyond the theoretical realm, which two countries have consistently been the poster children for human rights abuses, tyranny, and all around evil in the world since the end of World War II? That would be Russia and China. Giving these two countries seats on the Security Council would be like letting a serial killer be the judge and sit on the jury of their own trial. The rest of the councils and committees at the U.N. are equally screwed up.

Honestly, if you had described the kind of inefficiency, corruption, and downright evil perpetrated at the U.N. to someone in the 1940's, they would have said that the kind of government you described was just the kind of thing the U.N. was meant to stop.

Why Reform is Not an Option

Some would argue that all that is needed is merely a reform at the U.N. However, reform will not work for several reasons.

The first is that the corruption and inefficiency has lasted for too long. If the U.N. were still only a few years old, reform might be possible and warranted, but it's existed for over half a century. The image of corruption and incompetence is too entrenched into the image of the U.N. with not a single good deed or example of proper working to counter balance that image. It would take literally centuries of nothing but perfect behavior to out live that image (just ask any German if the past acts of your ancestor are easy to shake off no matter how exemplary you current behavior is).

The next point would be how do you reform an organization where the main reasons you need to reform (i.e. all the countries perpetrating human rights abuses, tyranny, and so on) are already in the organization and will fight tooth and nail any change that is not in their favor. Further still, we, the forces of democracy and Liberalism, are outnumbered three to one in population and 20 to 36 in simple votes against the tyrannies of the world[140]. I somehow don't see the villains voting to reform themselves out of existence . . . do you? Thus, any reform that is accomplished will be superficial only.

---

[140] See Chapter 8 for where I get these numbers from.

Finally and most importantly, there are just times when renovating a building would simply take too much time, money, and effort. Every single aspect of the U.N. is plagued with efficiency and corruption. Like a house with dry rot, termites, mold, and a poor foundation, it's just easier, less costly, and more efficient to tear the old house down and build a new one in its place rather than renovate it at an unjustifiable cost.

So we must put something else in its place. The United States and its allies must withdraw and form a new organization that will do what these previous failures have abysmally failed to do: make the world safe for liberty. So what do we put its place?

An Alliance of Principles

"History is now choosing the founders of the World Federation. Any person who can be among that number and fails to do so has lost the noblest opportunity of a lifetime."—Carl Van Doren

Before we create a coalition or league or whatever you want to call it we have to find out what the problems with the previous systems of world government were that allowed them to fail.

The League of Nations had two main flaws, it stood for nothing, and it had no power to back up its proposals.

The first problem, the fact that the League stood for nothing, the U.N. attempted to solve with its Universal Declaration of Human Rights—a preposterous document which tried to model life on earth after some Utopian fantasy rather than legitimate rights that actually every human is actually entitled to. We have gone from standing for nothing to standing for the wrong things.

Let's take a look at some of the problems of this insane document to see where and what changes we have to make to whatever replaces it.

First off, the preamble of the document simply lacks any of the emotional kick that Jefferson so beautifully put in the original Declaration. However let's get onto the real meat of the document.

Article 1. All human beings are born free and equal in dignity and rights. They are endowed with reason and conscience and should act towards one another in a spirit of brotherhood.

It doesn't bode well for an organization when its very first article is laced with stupidity and ignorance. Okay the first sentence is absolutely correct at least in theory (I don't think children born in Darfur are being granted the same freedom and dignity I have, but they do still have a natural right to it). However, the second sentence is already going too far for a government organization; it's telling people that they have to be nice to each other. Yes, that is the ethical way to act, but government's only function is to prevent violence against people, not to force brotherhood on them. Any attempt to do so is a basic violation of the freedom spoken of in the first sentence. As long as you don't actually harm anyone, you have a right to be a jerk, it won't help you in your quest for happiness in this world or the next, but you have free will to do it. The U.N. fails to believe in your god-given free will.

Articles 2-18 are pretty clear straightforward Classical Liberal rights of liberty, property, due process of law. Although Article 12's "No one shall be subjected to arbitrary interference with his privacy, family, home or correspondence, nor to attacks upon his honor and reputation. Everyone has the right to the protection of the law against such interference or attacks" I have to assume only applies to governments because I have under my freedom of speech the right to impugn the honor or reputation of anyone so long as what I'm saying is true. Just watch: O.J. Simpson is a psychopathic murderer. Jimmy Carter's actions during and after his presidency are effectively treasonous. Also Article 19, "Everyone has the right to freedom of opinion and expression; this right includes freedom to hold opinions without interference and to seek, receive and impart information and ideas through any media and regardless of frontiers" forgets to make clear you have a right to express your opinion through any media you choose, that does not mean the Media industry actually has to publish your opinions. You have no right to a microphone or audience.

Article 20 states that:

(1) Everyone has the right to freedom of peaceful assembly and association.
(2) No one may be compelled to belong to an association.

Someone should probably inform unions of the second part of this article, as currently people are forced to join unions whether they want to or not.

Article 22. Everyone, as a member of society, has the right to social security and is entitled to realization, through national effort and international co-operation and in accordance with the organization and resources of each State, of the economic, social and cultural rights indispensable for his dignity and the free development of his personality.

Huh? If I ever figure out what that means, I'm probably going to be very upset at how it's giving rights that you don't naturally have . . . but wording and syntax remain too confusing for me.

Then you've got to love this little bit of socialism:

Article 23

(1) Everyone has the right to work, to free choice of employment, to just and favourable conditions of work and to protection against unemployment.
(2) Everyone, without any discrimination, has the right to equal pay for equal work.
(3) Everyone who works has the right to just and favourable remuneration ensuring for himself and his family an existence worthy of human dignity, and supplemented, if necessary, by other means of social protection.
(4) Everyone has the right to form and to join trade unions for the protection of his interests.

So according to part 1 then someone, probably the government, has to provide you with a job regardless of you competence, work ethic, or ability to get anything done. I don't recall anyone ever having a freedom from unemployment, because that basically means you can never be fired no matter how substandard your work. Part 3 is really fun because it basically says that you have a right to enough money to live off of, whether you work for it or not. Somehow I don't think the state of nature was ever thought of to exist like that. Articles 24-27 continue under the same socialist delusion that fails to make the distinction between the right to earn something, which you do have, and simply the right to something, which you don't have. Because to say you have to right to any physical thing for free (with maybe the exception of air) is to say you have a right to the work of another person without having to pay for it, in other words making that person your slave (a violation of Articles 3 and 4 I might add).

Articles 28-30 are standard boilerplate.

So according to the U.N. by now we have no free will, the right to an audience for anything you say, the right to lie around on your ass and get paid. I think I'm beginning to see some of the problems with the U.N. Clearly, when setting about with the new form of world government, all the socialist excrement should be removed and maybe some more protection of free will and liberty clearly put in.

So here is my suggested edited version (that anyone is free to use, hey I stole most of it anyway):

Preamble:

Whereas all human beings are endowed with certain unalienable rights,

Whereas the purpose of human existence is the attainment of personal happiness through whatever means seem most likely to ensure said happiness,

Republicans and Reincarnation

Whereas governments are instated among men to secure these rights so that the personal quest for happiness will not be hindered by the infringement of others on their rights,

And whereas are these rights are unalienable all have a right and duty to oppose any infringement of these rights wherever they may be found,

We the signers of this declaration avow not only to uphold the rights enumerated here, but to defend them whether our interests are directly affected or not. Among the rights that all human beings are entitled to are:

Article 1.

All human beings are created free and equal in dignity and rights. They are endowed with reason, conscience, and free will, and a responsibility to use them.

Article 2.

Everyone is entitled to all the rights and freedoms set forth in this Declaration, without distinction of any kind, such as race, color, sex, language, religion, political or other opinion, national or social origin, property, birth or other status. Furthermore, no distinction shall be made on the basis of the political, jurisdictional or international status of the country or territory to which a person belongs, whether it be independent, trust, non-self-governing or under any other limitation of sovereignty.

Article 3.

Everyone has the right to life, liberty and freedom from violence by others.

Article 4.

No one shall be held in slavery or servitude; slavery and the slave trade shall be prohibited in all their forms.

Article 5.

No one shall be subjected to torture or to cruel, inhuman or degrading treatment or punishment.

Article 6.

Everyone has the right to recognition everywhere as a person before the law.

Article 7.

All are equal before the law and are entitled without any discrimination to equal protection of the law. All are entitled to equal protection against any discrimination in violation of this Declaration and against any incitement to such discrimination.

Article 8.

Everyone has the right to an effective remedy by the competent national tribunals for acts violating the fundamental rights granted him by the constitution or by law.

Article 9.

No one shall be subjected to arbitrary arrest, detention or exile.

Article 10.

Everyone is entitled in full equality to a fair and public hearing by an independent and impartial tribunal, in the determination of his rights and obligations and of any criminal charge against him.

Article 11.

(1) Everyone charged with a penal offence has the right to be presumed innocent until proved guilty according to law in a public trial at which he has had all the guarantees necessary for his defense. (2) No one shall be held guilty of any penal offence on account of any act or omission which did not constitute a penal offence, under national or international law, at the time when it was committed. Nor shall a heavier penalty be imposed than the one that was applicable at the time the penal offence was committed.

Article 12.

No one shall be subjected to arbitrary interference with his privacy, family, home or correspondence, or to false attacks upon his honor and reputation by their government. Everyone has the right to the protection of the law against such interference or attacks.

Article 13.

(1) Everyone has the right to freedom of movement and residence within the borders of each state. (2) Everyone has the right to leave any country, including his own, and to return to his country.

Article 14.

(1) Everyone has the right to seek and to enjoy in other countries asylum from persecution. (2) This right may not be invoked in the case of prosecutions genuinely arising from non-political crimes or from acts contrary to the purposes and principles of this document.

Article 15.

(1) Men and women of full age, without any limitation due to race, nationality or religion, have the right to marry[141] and to found a family. They are entitled to equal rights as to marriage, during marriage and at its dissolution. (2) Marriage shall be entered into only with the free and full consent of the intending spouses.

Article 16.

Everyone has the right to earn and own property and to earn profit alone as well as in association with others. (2) No one shall be arbitrarily deprived of his property or profit.

---

[141] Or as I suggested in the previous chapter we should change this wording to civil unions.

Article 17.

Everyone has the right to freedom of thought, conscience and religion; this right includes freedom to change his religion or belief, and freedom, either alone or in community with others and in public or private, to manifest his religion or belief in teaching, practice, worship and observance.

Article 18.

Everyone has the right to freedom of opinion and expression; this right includes freedom to hold opinions without interference and to seek, receive and impart information and ideas through any media and regardless of frontiers that is available to them. Access to media shall never be denied by government interference.

Article 19.

(1) Everyone has the right to freedom of peaceful assembly and association. (2) No one may be compelled to belong to an association.

Article 20.

(1) Everyone has the right to take part in the government of his country, directly or through freely chosen representatives. (2) Everyone has the right of equal access to public service in his country. (3) The will of the people shall be the basis of the authority of government; this will shall be expressed in periodic and genuine elections which

shall be by universal and equal suffrage and shall be held by secret vote or by equivalent free voting procedures.

Article 21

All of these rights are conditional on one point. Anyone who actively and intentionally with malice aforethought attempts to violate the rights of the innocent forfeits their right to appeal to these rights. They must be stopped through the most just and humane means that are practical.

Or something like that. Nothing more than this is called for. Start with these simple principles. Free thought. Free action. Free commerce. Government is only to defend us against the infringements of others, not to provide our own happiness.

A League of Relevance

I am a citizen, not of Athens, nor of Greece, but of the world.—Socrates

A second problem that cropped up from the League of Nations (and the U.N.) is that there is no way to enforce mandates. With both organizations, member nations can choose to not participate in any action taken by the organization. It shouldn't take a genius to figure out that nothing will ever get done this way. So like it or not the next government must be set up on principal to compel its members to act. Just as any state in America that refused to follow a just and constitutional federal law

Republicans and Reincarnation

would be considered in rebellion and subject to legal and economic recourse, so must all the members of such an alliance that needs to replace the U.N.

This requires two things. First, not every country in the world can be allowed to join this league. One of the things that has made the U.N. so unbelievably irrelevant is that anyone can join, no matter how disgusting their country's government is—North Korea is a member of the U.N., a fact made only more disgusting by the fact that such sovereign and independent nations such as Taiwan and Tibet are not allowed to be members, because that would annoy the butchers from Beijing. No really, they'll let a genocidal lunatic like Kim Jung Il in the building, but not the Dalai Lama.

So to say that this league lives up to its standards only those countries that live up to those standards can be allowed in (look at that list of free nations in Chapter 8). Now a second tier of limited membership should be offered to countries that are still not there yet but are well on their way (France and Israel, for example, may have their economic problems, but they are in the end on the good guys side and that should be recognized).

The next most important thing is that more than dealing with countries outside of the league, the league must police itself, constantly keeping an eye on its own members and imposing sanctions or whatever force is necessary to ensure that the rights that are meant to be upheld by this league are being upheld.

Some might complain that this could be used against America. Yes, it could, but if the only other countries in the league are the free nations of the world, then their censure would be a valid point.

On a similar note, I have had the argument from those on the more conservative side of things that the U.S. should always be in charge, number one, and never second best in anything. And to suggest that a government should go ahead of Washington D.C.[142], as this league would have to be, is un-American, not patriotic, and just wrong. Unfortunately, this is not only too isolationist a view to be functional in a world where everyone is moving up the karmic ladder, but it's simply not pragmatic. In a world that has embraced democratic republican and capitalistic values, in other words Classical Liberalism, it would be impossible for the United States to be on top all the time. It would be like one state of the US to always out-perform the other 49 at all times in history (which I don't think can ever be said of any state). We'll go up, we'll go down in power, in economic success, in influence around the world, and up again. It's the capitalistic system. This is a fact for all things except one.

In one way, the United States will always be the center of the world. As an ideal. Just as the ideals of Athenian democracy (for all of it's flaws) now rules much of the world, and will likely continue to spread even though Athens itself is no longer the center of the world; just as Roman republican values of law and infrastructure continue to essentially be a guiding light despite a rather well publicized fall of the Roman Empire; just as while the sun now sets daily on the British Empire, Britain still has left a permanent and wonderful mark on the world through the genius of British common law—so shall the United State forever be in charge. The ideals that formed the U.S. in an ungodly hot Philadelphia room in the

---

[142] As if they're doing such a bang up job.

summer of 1776 and were then refined over the course of the next two hundred years are not likely to die from the world. That is the only part of America that must be preserved at all costs. Whether the United States of America itself is top dog is unimportant, so long as the idea of it remains in charge the world over. Because it is that part that makes America great, not the economic power or the military might, those are only effects of that great idea, and as long as the idea remains powerful so shall America live forever.

Now, with this organization in place there will be a combined force that will stand against those governments and situations that are opposed to the principles on which it was founded. I suggest that this be done through two ways; military might (a policy that has already been discussed in Chapter 8) and through focused foreign aid.

Foreign Aid That Works

The United States government literally gives out billions of dollars each year to countries around the world. Military funding, medical funding, infrastructure work. If you thought we gave a lot out in personal or corporate welfare, just take a look at what we give out to foreign nations. And today most of the industrialized world gives out aid to developing nations. However, there are two problems with this money being given out.

The first is that we tend to just give away cash to countries. This may sound nice, because we all like to get large amounts of cash handed to us personally, but that doesn't quite work with governments. The United States is one of the least corrupt governments on Earth, and good lord is that truly a horrific statement . . . the governments that receive aid are doubtfully more honest than we are so, in practice, very little money actually reaches where its supposed to be. Money sent for infrastructure goes to build mansions. Money for defense repairs goes for genocide. Money for medical supplies goes to buy guns. And it doesn't do too much better if we just send the actual things like food or medicine as those more often than not get diverted by corrupt politicians toward the black market to line their own Swiss and Caribbean bank accounts.

Still, that's not the only problem with giving foreign aid; the other problem is that just about every country that needs aid gets aid. That's a problem? Yes, it's a problem, because of the amount that we're wiling to spend is split between everyone and what is given out is not enough to solve anyone's problems.

Now I'll be the first to admit that welfare of any kind is not usually the best policy however, the intent of foreign aid is more like government sponsored education, which gives people the tools to take control of their own lives, versus a simple dole check that encourages being a couch potato. Most foreign aid is meant to help with infrastructure, defense to protect from civil unrest, and to combat major medical epidemics all of which can be crippling to even the most industrious populations. However, no country ever gets enough money to actually combat these problems. Even if the money isn't stolen by the locals' levels of bureaucracy, it simply won't put a dent in the problems at hand.

Republicans and Reincarnation

Moreover, this is where the efforts of a new world body can help to end the fruitlessness and inefficiency that permeates the current system. The first thing that needs to be done is that all foreign aid needs to not be distributed by and through the league itself. This way it will not be thirty plans that may not be working together, and worse may work against each other through doubling up some aspects while not covering others (not to mention the fact multiple different programs offer more opportunity to skim and embezzle by shifting funds all over the place).

The next change that must be made is that spreading money all over the place has to be stopped. Yes, it may seem heartless and cruel to say that some countries deserve aid and others don't, but that is not the intent. If aid was concentrated on one or two countries in an area, such as Sub-Saharan African, rather than sending aid to every country it would allow that country to develop a fully functioning infrastructure (roads, water, electricity, medical care to stem epidemics, standardized education) at a first world standard. Coupled with incentives to encourage businesses to invest in those countries for development it would allow for a fully functioning economy at a first world level. So instead of a group of countries just hobbling along you get a successful nation. And the long-term effects get better! As the economy grows to first world level it will need to import not only resources, but workers from the surrounding countries which has the twofold benefit of bringing more people into the first world standard of living, but also reduces the strain on their own countries. Further with yet another free nation brought into the league, that's one more country to contribute aid thus furthering aid for the next country in line; one more country that will not be producing citizens whose dissatisfaction with scraping out an existence can lead them to turn to violence and terrorism, thus the world is safer; one more country not likely to wage war on its neighbors. Prosperity is infectious, as that country grows it will bolster the surrounding area—business expansion alone will cause the need for infrastructure to be expanded (which will be paid for by private businesses not foreign nations).

My suggestion would be for one developing nation on each continent to be selected at a time. The nations need to already be on the track to having a Classically Liberal democracy (giving this kind of aid to N. Korea would be pointless) and agree to become a full member of the league, and be bound by that agreement.

A final provision, is that while all the actual work should be done by the inhabitants of the country (otherwise there will be no investment in it after the initial construction), every single piece of clerical and administrative work must be done by a branch specifically created to deal with the creation of such infrastructure (something like Halliburton meets the Peace Corps, but not unethical or inefficient).

Just as the previously discussed policy on destroying tyranny will eliminate the negative barrier to freedom, this policy will allow more positive avenues of opportunity to use that liberty to form. When used together, they offer everyone a chance to achieve their full potential as a human being.

Combined, these policies will not create a world government that is the oppressive new world order isolationists fear like five year olds fear the monster under their bed, but rather the next step in the evolution of the world.

Chapter 14
WHY WE DON'T LIVE IN A PERFECT WORLD ...

... Aside from the obvious reasons ...

"We live as though the world were what it should be—to show it what it can be."—David Boreanaz as Angel in Angel

In the end, however—no matter how much I ramble on about the government, about what it can and cannot do, what it should or should not do—everything comes down to an individual decision made by all of us, made every single moment of our lives. Now we may or may not have the power to affect the government or policies as large as the government, but that is really irrelevant. No matter how bad the government is, no matter how restrictive, how oppressive, how tyrannical the laws and the corrupt officials, your life is still completely your responsibility. Your happiness or lack thereof is only the fault of you and you alone. It may be easier or harder to get there depending on the surrounding environment, but in the modern world, happiness is available to anyone who wants to work for it.

However the natural inclination to be happy is not just to be happy, but also to spread that happiness; we can't give others happiness, that's up to them. But it doesn't stop us from trying. And there is no better place to do that then here and now. When we're happy, we feel as if we have to change the world to see how wonderful it is, it can be. But this desire to change things for the better has not always been the norm.

Every culture in history has expressed the necessity to accept the world as it is. European monarchies and tyrannies, even the democracies of the ancient world, abhorred change and sought the status quo. Almost every major change was actually an attempt to return to the old way which society had evolved out of. This seldom worked, but it was the nature of the world. Eastern cultures saw even less change than European ones. For each culture there is a reason. For Western cultures, there was a heavy belief that this world is corrupt and one must just accept it and one will be rewarded in the next life. In Eastern cultures, there was the belief that the world was an illusion and that to escape it one must turn inward and solve the problems there. Neither culture stressed changing the actual world. Except for one. America. Americans have never, as a people accepted things the way they are. Sure they just wanted to keep the rights guaranteed them by the British Constitution, but they chose probably the most radical way of doing it. They intended a government that was actually prevented from doing things instead of an active government with power, a clear change from the rest of the world. America is the only country to ever fight to liberate another race, we are the only country to initiate the liberation of an entire country as a direct action, not merely a side effect of returning an attack on our people (although Britain does equally deserve recognition as one of the only countries to initiate the use of military force to end genocide). We are essentially the only people who do not accept the world as it is.

Republicans and Reincarnation

Yes, the world is an illusion, but it is an illusion that is a reflection of the errors in your own mind and soul. One cannot be solved without solving the other. New Agers hold that life on this plane of existence is an illusion. It's a game. In some ways no different from Monopoly and chess. Monopoly and chess are based on certain rules, ideas, and premises from the "real" world, and reflect it in certain ways, but you could hardly say you live your life and Monopoly or chess by the same rules. In the same way, this world is a game to the next. This one is based on rules from that one, to teach us those rules, but it is not that world, and the rules for existing in each are quite different.

But if it's only a game, why should we care about this world and not just focus on the next? Don't we all hate the person who gets halfway through a game and stops paying attention—the person who walks away when they start losing Monopoly or just gets bored by chess? The game of this world, the point of making it a better place, not just for ourselves but for everyone is politics. It can be a revolting game, reflecting the rather horrific nature of fear. However, it can still be used to make the world a better place—by reducing the barriers to free will, but not by giving people prosperity—only by allowing the chance.

The principles of this book cannot be taken in part. While the specifics of any section maybe slightly adjusted to fit this or that specific situation, liberty, capitalism, and all the rest have to go together, or not at all. For better or worse, of the two political parties out there, the Republican Party is the closest to these ideals. Now I know that the party platform is not going to be changed overnight, but we need to push it as far and as fast as is possible. The recent horrific defeat of the Republican Party in the 2008 elections and its resurgence in 2010 offers a unique opportunity to provide the party with a new, more correct, direction to be pushed in. It will by no means be an easier transition without trials, but it will be one that is worth it, not only because in the long run it will create a world where you personally can move up the spiritual ladder with more ease, but that all will have the opportunity (they may not take it, but that's up to them).

It's not just an idealistic dream, but a practical and achievable reality, but it will require everyone pushing at once on all these issues in the proper direction.

SUGGESTED READING

As promised, a suggested reading list, I will be listing the books in order of most recommended to mild suggestions. Each of these authors tend to have other works that likely are of equal value, but unless I think that selections are either of equal importance or of such varying topics that two titles are required I have tried to keep the list to one title per author. Also I am mildly sure that the authors I list for New Age beliefs probably do not agree with my politics on 100% of things, and I'm sure it's vice versa with the political writers—disagreement is good, find what you agree with because the reasoning makes sense, leave the rest. I have also included a short list of fiction titles designed to illustrate some of the philosophical points made in this book.

Chapter 1: Basics of Philosophy

<u>Aristotle for Everybody</u>
By Mortimer Adler

While philosophy always might seem to be a bit daunting of a task to undertake, it is the basis for all politics and ethics. I recommend starting with Adler's works because while his style is a little dry at times, it is a good and scholarly introduction to Aristotelian philosophy, which is in my mind the only proper foundation for philosophical thought.

Cris A. Pace

<u>Nicomachean Ethics</u> and <u>Politics</u>
by *Aristotle*

If you're only going to read two works of Aristotle's, it would be *Ethics* and *Politics* that you should probably read. *Ethics* and its lessons are still relevant and applicable to modern life, especially if you want to know how to live a happy life. *Politics* is a bit more theoretical as it's talking primarily about Ancient Greek city-states, but it does work as a wonderful background for further political discussion. Both of these works are not reader friendly; do not expect to just blow through them without taking lots of breaks, lots of personal notes, and maybe looking up a lot while reading for clarification. What survives of Aristotle's writing, while great on ideas, is a bit thin on style. Sorry, but you should read them.

<u>A History of Knowledge</u>
<u>b</u>y *Charles Van Doren*

I am recommending this one mainly for the fact that any understanding of politics cannot exist in any pragmatic way outside of an understanding of history. Van Doren's work offers a good overview of world history from beginning to present without being just a simple listing of dates. I would also recommend for ease of reading and depth of history, Susan Wise Bauer's series on the history of the world, *The History of the Ancient World* and *The History of the Medieval World,* being the only volumes published at this time.

Chapter 2: New Age Beliefs

A Return to Love: Reflections on the Principles of *A Course in Miracles*
by Marianne Williams

A wonderful introduction to *A Course in Miracles,* from an equally wonderfully writer. Most will recognize the beautiful quote from Chapter 7, "Our deepest fear is not that we are inadequate. Our deepest fear is that we are powerful beyond measure." The rest of the book is as insightful, although not as often quoted.

A Course in Miracles

This volume is as close as I can find to a corner stone to most beliefs of New Age beliefs . . . I might even go as far as to call it a New Age bible, but that might be going a bit far. Again, it's not a weekend read, but rather something that should be read in short bursts and meditated on in the space between.

Life After Death and How to Know God
by Deepak Chopra

A good look at how to understand and apply many of these New Age principals to one's life in a more practical way than *A Course in Miracles*. Chopra also has several wonderful books on health and attracting abundance in one's life.

Cris A. Pace

Tao Te Ching
and
The Bhagavad-Gita:

Translation and Commentaries by Paramahansa Yogananda

I actually would recommend that everyone should read the *Bible*, the *Tao Te Ching*, the *Bhagavad-Gita*, the teachings of Buddha, and all holy books. There is truth in all of them. However, I find Westerners are least familiar with these two works. I would recommend finding multiple translations of the *Tao* as it is written in poetic form, and translating poetry can always be very difficult. I recommend this version of the *Bhagavad-Gita* because it not only provides an excellent translation, it also gives a very in-depth analysis of each and every line (although if you want a straight translation go with the Penguin Classics version translated by Juan Mascaro, I've found it the most readable for a simple introduction to the work).

Divine Guidance
by *Doreen Virtue*

I find Virtue's (yes that's her real name) to be both very inspirational and helpful in putting my beliefs into practice. Many of her works, including this one, deal with the rather practical aspect of improving commutation and understanding with the higher planes of existence and its inhabitants (Angels, Ascended Masters, ect.).

<u>Don't Kiss them Goodbye</u>
<u>b</u>y *Allison Dubois*

<u>Talking to Heaven</u>
<u>b</u>y *James Van Praagh*

Both of these works deal with what happens on the other side of death and communication for those who passed over. As this is often the introduction to New Age beliefs for many people, I thought it best to include two of the more well spoken mediums (not disparage or endorse others).

<u>Evidence of the Afterlife</u>
<u>b</u>y *Jeffry Long, MD with Paul Perry*

<u>The Tao of Physics</u>
<u>b</u>y Fritjof Capra

Chapter 3: Conservative Beliefs

<u>The Conservative Mind</u>
<u>b</u>y *Russel Kirk*

A good historical look at the history of Conservative Thought in theory and in practice. Fair warning though, you may just want to chuck it after the first few chapters.

<u>The Virtue of Selfishness</u>
<u>b</u>y *Ayn Rand*

There are some serious flaws in her logic at times, but overall Rand makes a very convincing case for rational self-interest, a line of reasoning that is not found enough nowadays in modern culture which seems to only vacillate between the two extremes of altruism and hedonism.

Novus Ordo Seclorum
by Forrest McDonald

An excellent look at the thought process behind the formation of the U.S. Constitution. This in an invaluable resource if you've ever gotten into an argument with someone who foolishly argues the Founding Fathers just wanted to create a government to benefit the rich and only the rich.

Parliament of Whores
by P.J. O'Rourke

Probably one of the most readable authors on this list, O'Rourke provides keen insight into the working of the U.S. government in between his biting wit.

Democracy in America
by Alexis de Tocqueville

Probably one of the least readable authors on this list, but Tocqueville's analysis of 1800's American society is still frighteningly accurate and relevant. A must for anyone who wants to understand America . . . no matter how difficult it is to make it through the book.

Chapter 5 through 7 Economics

<u>New Ideas from Dead Philosophers</u>
<u>b</u>y *Todd G. Buchholz*

<u>Eat the Rich</u>
<u>b</u>y *P.J. O'Rourke*

<u>Basic Economics</u>
<u>b</u>y *Thomas Sowell*

<u>Economic Facts and Fallacies</u>
By Thomas Sowell

<u>Capitalism and Freedom</u>
<u>b</u>y *Milton Freedman*

<u>The Road to Serfdom</u>
<u>b</u>y *F.A. Hayek*

<u>The World is Flat</u>
<u>b</u>y *Thomas L. Friedman*

I'm not going to go over each of these titles because I basically picked them as a selection of what I consider as a necessary course in modern economic theory and practice. I would probably read them in the order I have listed, but it really makes little difference.

In Defense of Globalization
by *Jagdish Bhagwati*

A little more specific in its focus than the above titles, but as globalization, and its ties to interventionist ideals, is so important to the ideas of this book, I would recommend you check this one out.

On The Wealth of Nations
by *P.J. O'Rourke*

Now honestly, I would say some day if you have the time, you should actually read Adam Smith's *On The Wealth Of Nations*, however it's really dry Enlightenment reading, and P.J. does a superb job condensing the ideas of Smith into a far more svelte and clever edition.

Chapter 8 and 13 Foreign Policy

Peace Kills
by *P.J. O'Rourk*

The U.N. Exposed
by *Eric Shawn*

On the whole there are few books that are relevant to foreign policy, as so few of them actually deal with theory and so many of them deal with current issues, which half the time are a little out of date by the time they hit the shelves. Op-eds of conservative journals and newspapers are probably a little more useful here. These, however, are a few of the exceptions to finding a good grasp of the current situation around the world.

Chapter 10: The Environment

Collapse
by Jared Diamond

I personally believe that Diamond slightly overestimates the impact of environment in leading to the destruction of society to the exclusion of all other causes, but I am not foolish enough to state that it isn't a large factor. As such it is an important read to realize that while environmentalists can often be annoying Chicken Littles, there is a strain of reasoning behind their nonsensical hysterics.

The Skeptical Environmentalist
by Bjorn Lomborg

Countering those annoying environmentalists who like to believe hype and headlines over real scientific facts and data, this book, while very detailed and certainly not a beach pleasure read, is very useful at beginning to understanding what is and isn't a real environmental concern.

Education

The Worm in the Apple
by Peter Brimelow

The Closing of the American Mind
by Allan Bloom

<u>The Well-Educated Mind</u>
by Susan Wise Bauer

<u>The Power of Self-Esteem</u>
by Nathaniel Braden

<u>Waiting for Superman</u>
by Karl Weber editor

I would recommend this as a good place to start with looking into education issues more or less each one shows that people cannot rely on public education to teach their children or themselves.

Social Issues

<u>The Death of Right and Wrong</u>
by Tammy Bruce

<u>How to Talk to A Liberal (if you must)</u>
by Ann Coulter

Again, these are topics that have an annoying way of changing all too quickly, but these two offer a broad view of the current situation with wit and depth.

Fiction

<u>Atlas Shrugged</u>
by Ayn Rand

As I said before, not everything Rand has to say is correct, but she presents a great starting place and raises the questions that you should be asking yourself. Even its daunting 1,000 pages should not be a turn off . . . most people I know can't put the book down after they get past the first 300 pages.

The Robe
by Lloyd C. Douglas

Along with Douglas' other famous work, *The Magnificent Obsession,* these two works do an excellent job at showing how rational self-interest requires a strong strain of charity to others, not out of some misplaced sense of duty, but because it does bring happiness to the person performing the acts of charity. If you're the kind of person who likes to watch movies that go along with books, understand that I'm not fully convinced the writers of the movie ever read the book, because, aside from a few names and plots points, they have next to nothing to do with one another.

The Sword of Truth Series
by Terry Goodkind

On a whole an excellent fantasy series designed to illustrate philosophical principles while telling a compelling story. Starting with the novel *Wizard's First Rule*, of particular interest to the idea discussed in *Republicans and Reincarnation* are book six in the series *Faith of the Fallen* which details the superiority of capitalism, both morally and practically, over any government run system, and book eight *Naked Empire* which deals with the arguments in favor of a war to liberate.

The Celestine Prophecy
by James Renfield

The Celestine series as a whole provides a wonderful overview of the basic principles of the New Age movement. Plot and characterization are sacrificed to get the theme across, but it's still a good read. The movie is also fairly enjoyable, although a bit more cursory in terms of depth of the ideas.

What Dreams May Come
by Richard Matheson

A good look at what happens to us when we die and cross over. Although fiction, it is well researched and probably very accurate. The movie while visually stunning, is less reliable as a source.

Lost Horizon
by James Hilton

A classic novel that shows what society might be like if the principals similar to the New Age movement were to be put into place. The movie is also very faithful to the book, although director Frank Capra decided to add a rather naïve speech near the beginning endorsing absolute pacifism.

That should keep you busy, albeit well-read, for a few years.

Made in the USA
Lexington, KY
21 September 2015